Atoms, Bombs
&
Eskimo
Kisses

Atoms, Bombs

Eskimo
Kisses

A Memoir of Father and Son

Claudio G. Segrè

VIKING

VIKING
Published by the Penguin Group
Penguin Books USA Inc., 375 Hudson Street,
New York, New York 10014, U.S.A.
Penguin Books Ltd, 27 Wrights Lane, London W8 5TZ, England
Penguin Books Australia Ltd, Ringwood, Victoria, Australia
Penguin Books Canada Ltd, 10 Alcorn Avenue,
Toronto, Ontario, Canada M4V 3B2
Penguin Books (N.Z.) Ltd, 182–190 Wairau Road,
Auckland 10, New Zealand

Penguin Books Ltd, Registered Offices:
Harmondsworth, Middlesex, England

First published in 1995 by Viking Penguin,
a division of Penguin Books USA Inc.

1 3 5 7 9 10 8 6 4 2

Photograph credits
In photo section, pages 1 and 5 (top): Courtesy of Los Alamos Historical Museum
Photo Archives; 12 (below), 13, and 14 (below): Reportagebild; 14 (top):
Pressens bild. All other photographs from the author's collection.

LIBRARY OF CONGRESS CATALOGING-IN-PUBLICATION DATA
Segrè, Claudio G.
Atoms, bombs and Eskimo kisses : a memoir of father and son /
by Claudio G. Segrè.
p. cm.
ISBN 0-670-86307-6
1. Segrè, Claudio G. 2. Historians—United States—Biography. 3. Historians—
Italy—Biography. 4. Fathers and sons. 5. Segrè, Emilio. 6. Physicists—
United States—Biography. 7. Atomic bomb—New Mexico—Los
Alamos—History. 8. Manhattan Project (U.S.)
I. Title.
DG465.7.S43A3 1995
530'.092—dc20
[B]   95-7629

This book is printed on acid-free paper.
∞

Printed in the United States of America
Set in Janson
Designed by Francesca Belanger

For my family, friends and fans
who wanted to know
what it was like

CONTENTS

PREFACE

"The worst misfortune that can happen to an ordinary man is to have an extraordinary father." So quipped the late-nineteenth-century American physician, essayist and educator Austin O'Malley, probably with more wit than wisdom. Yet as the son of a Nobel Prize–winning physicist, I often feel the bite of truth in the aphorism. For that reason, I hesitated before writing this book. I did not relish poking at old wounds. I wanted neither to capitalize on my father's fame nor to build him another monument. Least of all did I want to speak ill of the dead. During my father's lifetime, silence was often my best answer to his prying, well-meaning queries; perhaps it still is.

Yet, over the years, relatives, friends, colleagues, seatmates on airplanes, persisted and insisted: "What was he like as a father?" "What was it like to live at Los Alamos while the atomic bomb was being built?" "What was it like to have Enrico Fermi, Niels Bohr, Robert Oppenheimer and all those other great scientists of that generation over for dinner?"

For many years, I didn't know what to say except that that was the way I grew up. That was the way we did things around our house. True, over the years, I kept notebooks, journals and diaries, but I never thought about them much. Like my friends, eventually I became curious. What *was* it like? E. M. Forster once commented, "How do I know what I think until I see what I say." I decided to find out what I thought.

The result lies in this book. It isn't a biography of my father. Others better equipped than I, especially in explaining his scientific work, perhaps will take on that task. Nor is this a true autobiography. I have left out many people, family, friends, teachers and incidents in my life that had little impact on my relationship with my father. This is a memoir; it's a portion of his life and mine, a window into both our lives. It's also a book about growing up in America, the son of an illustrious immigrant. It's about my coming of age, caught between and nourished by two cultures, at home in both, at ease in neither. Most of all, it's about a father and a son reaching out to each other, trying to touch, too often out of touch. For me, we were never more alone than when together.

In writing this book, I have relied primarily on my recollections, my notebooks and diaries, my correspondence with my father, and his autobiography. Working with such material is notoriously difficult. "History is a pack of tricks that we play on the dead," Voltaire wrote. The same applies—perhaps even more so—in a book like this: part history, part memory, part reflection. What follows portrays my father as I saw him. As I discovered in writing these pages, others experienced him quite differently.

Even such a personal book as a memoir is, in part, a communal effort. My wife, Elisabeth (Zaza) Bregman Segrè, my children, Francesca, Gino and Joel Segrè, and my sisters, Amelia Segrè Terkel and Fausta Segrè Walsby, contributed everything from stories and insights to cheers and punctuation. My mother, Elfriede Spiro Segrè, gave me memories and sustenance long ago. My father, my aunt, Lilli Spiro, and my stepmother, Rosa Mines

Segrè, provided memories and materials. Frances Bregman, Stephen Harrigan, Von and Patricia Hardesty, Adam Hochschild, James W. Kunetka, Robert Rafferty and Thomas Zigal read early drafts and offered valuable suggestions. Among the many friends who listened, questioned, suggested, urged me on, I'm particularly thankful to Carolyn Banks, Cindy Bonner, Dinah and Norman Chenven, David and Joan Hilgers, Sandra Lynn and Rick Brown, James Magnuson, members of the "Schedule 'C' Writers Group" in Austin, Texas, and Marc Pachter and the Washington, D.C., Area Biography Group. My agents, Anne Engel and Jean V. Naggar, and my editor, Kathryn Court, loved this project and saw it through. I'm grateful to all of them.

Atoms, Bombs
&
Eskimo
Kisses

CHAPTER 1

Son of Superman

I first discovered that I was the Son of Superman—or at least a superman—when I was eight. The revelation came at midday on a bright summer day in August 1945. "The noon news is next," I remember hearing from the chorus of radios in the apartments in the apple-green fourplex where we lived. A blue jay challenging me from a little stand of pines across the road sounded more interesting. I'm on my way to a doctor's appointment in Santa Fe and I'm thinking of the new comic books I will buy in town. I almost miss the lead news story, though it's now etched in my memory.

"A new bomb was dropped today on the Japanese city of Hiroshima," the newscaster was saying. His twangy, casual cowboy's voice, which I greatly admire, sounds stiff and sober, and he carefully enunciates "nee-oo," as if to emphasize the novelty and importance of his announcement. This is no ordinary bomb, he says; this one delivered the equivalent of 20,000 tons of TNT. A superbomb, I remember thinking. Superman or "the Golden Eagle" (another of my comic-book heroes) habitually snatched such devices from the clutches of sleazy-looking enemy spies and saboteurs or goggle-eyed mad scientists. The bomb on the radio, however, is real. Much of its development, I understand, must have taken place about a quarter of a mile from where we live. I have another revelation. My father made the bomb! I'm pleasantly surprised and pleased.

For a while I've had my suspicions. For nearly two years now, we have been living at Los Alamos, a secret Army post buried in the mountains of New Mexico. The nearest town, Santa Fe, is nearly forty miles away. Before that, we lived in Berkeley, California, where we appeared to be a normal family, leading a normal life. My father taught at the University of California; my mother took care of me and my baby sister, Amelia; I went to school and I played with my friends. To my parents' dismay, I also devoured comic books, especially the adventures of Superman.

Los Alamos is nothing like Berkeley. There's something peculiar about this town. I like it all right. I love watching the soldiers salute each other (and sometimes I imitate them); I dream of taking the wheel of the jeeps, the big Army trucks. It's fun playing bomber pilot down in the woods with my friends, and pelting each other with snowballs in the winter. And yet, this is a strange city. There aren't any drugstores or dime stores where I can buy ice cream and comic books. I have to get them at the military PX, where I sometimes see the soldiers drinking beer. There aren't any real playgrounds covered with grass or asphalt. In fact, the streets aren't even paved, and the jeeps and trucks and cars stir up clouds of dust that my mother complains about. A large part of the population—at least the men my father works with—consists of hyperintelligent beings with thick, un-American accents like my father's. Is this normal? Is this American? Is this even earthly? Superman's home planet of Krypton comes to mind. Am I the son of a superman?

But so far as I know, Superman was never a physicist, and that's what my father is. I know all about his work. Physicists fuss in their laboratories. In Berkeley, it was the cavernous basement in LeConte Hall on the University of California campus; here it's the Tech Area just down the road. A laboratory is a stuffy room cluttered with pumps, meters, gauges and yards of intertwining wiring that reminds me of the dishes of spaghetti that my mother sometimes serves. Physicists fiddle with their wiring and switches. They study their gauges and dials—especially the monotonous green lines on their oscilloscopes; they write numbers down in their notebooks and Greek letters on a blackboard. They calculate on their slide rules; they punch the keys on their adding machines. Then they argue about what their numbers and Greek letters mean.

I know that on Sundays physicists often hike in the mountains with their families. Hiking means a long walk in the woods, or across the meadows of the Valle Grande, or high up on narrow trails in the Sangre de Cristo Mountains. During hikes, for the most part, wives and children talk among themselves, and physicists talk among themselves. Sometimes physicists debate about how the war is going or discuss news about the laboratory, but mostly they seem to argue about "atoms" and "energies," "alpha particles" and "beta decay." They speak English, but also Italian and German. Occasionally they scribble numbers on handy scraps of paper and then argue some more. I like to pretend that they are talking in code; my mission is to decipher it.

That August afternoon, as the military bus winds down the switchbacks off the mesa, then past the pueblo of San Ildefonso, the black mesa, Espanola, the "camel rock," and then labors over the hill into the main plaza in Santa Fe, I keep thinking about the radio announcement and the superbomb. All the fussing with oscilloscopes and wires, all the arguing over the numbers and Greek letters, has amounted to something after all: a superweapon, the kind, as my comic-book heroes liked to say, that could blast our enemies to "Kingdom Come," the kind of weapon that could really end the war overnight. As the idea sinks in, another one looms larger: a superweapon is the product of supermen.

I have trouble associating my father with Superman, or even his everyday incarnation, Clark Kent. True, like Clark Kent, my father wears glasses, but there the resemblance ends. Clark Kent is tall, with a firm, almost jutting jaw. He wears suits that barely conceal his broad shoulders, powerful biceps, narrow waist. He speaks good American English in a deep, powerful man's voice —or so I imagine from the balloons in the comic strip.

My father is small—about five foot eight. His dark brown, almost black hair shows flecks of gray. He combs it straight back. I think he is handsome in a boyish sort of way. I like his wild bushy eyebrows. Much later I will discover that I have inherited them. He doesn't have a broad chest and rippling leg and arm muscles. In fact, at forty, he shows signs of softening in his middle. In Berkeley, he usually wore suits and ties to work. Here, in the mountains of New Mexico, he favors an old windbreaker or his Army-issue field jacket. No matter what he wears, however, he reminds me more of the brightest kid in my class, the "brain," the "teacher's pet," than of "the Man of Steel."

Like Clark Kent, for the most part my father is mild-mannered, but he is subject to fits of excitement and anger. His nickname among his Italian friends is "the Basilisk," a mythical fire-breathing dragon or serpent whose breath or even glance could prove fatal. When he isn't in his laboratory or talking physics with his friends, he reads a lot of books, recites poetry in Italian or German, and sporadically listens to the soap operas on the radio. Occasionally he takes me for jeep rides, and we go trout fishing together in the mountains—so long as I don't bother him too much and scare away the fish. On the few occasions when I present him to my friends, his thick Italian accent, with all those hard, rolling *r*'s, embarrasses me.

In subsequent days, as more news about the bomb and its development at Los Alamos comes out, I screw up my courage and ask him about the new weapon, how it works and why. I call him "Papà"—with the accent on the second *a*, Italian-style. *Pah-pàh*. Never the more familiar, more easygoing (to my ears, at least) American-style "Dad" or "Daddy." "Papà": it's as much a title, with overtones of head of the family, *paterfamilias*, lord and master over us all—my mother, my baby sisters and me—as it is a term of endearment. *Pah-pàh*. At times the two syllables sound to me like two quick pistol shots, or a whip cracking. When I mouth those syllables, they invite me more to attention, awe and obedience, than to playfulness or affection.

I approach him carefully, almost gingerly. He never seems to know quite how to talk to me, what to do with me. He asks prickly questions about what I know, what I'm learning at school. He doesn't seem too interested in what I'm thinking or feeling. I ask him about the bomb anyway. At first he seems proud and pleased at my interest. We are sitting in the little dining area that overlooks the street where we often watch his colleagues pass by on their way home from the lab. I can see that he means well, that he's in a good mood. He calls me "Claudietto" (Little Claudio).

"I'll explain the secret of the bomb to you," he promises. At first I listen eagerly. He talks to me in a mixture of Italian and English—English when he's at the hard parts and he thinks it will be easier for me to understand.

The trick is to slap two hunks of uranium together, he says. The heart of the device really isn't much larger than a cantaloupe. But already, no matter whether he's speaking in Italian or in English, I have trouble. I can't picture uranium, much less hunks of it stuck together. What does uranium look like? Is it soft, like gold? How are the hunks bound together? And how could a bomb look like a cantaloupe? At first, he tries to explain. Actually, I shouldn't imagine solid metal, he says. I should think of the atoms inside the metals and how they collide with each other. Those collisions can be controlled into what he calls a "chain reaction."

The more he explains, the more questions I ask and the more

impatient he becomes. I'm looking forward to the part I really want to hear about: the huge explosion, the fireball, bright as the sun, the thousands of Japanese blown up, the way I blow up enemy stick figures in the war scenes I sometimes draw when I play with my friends. My father never gets as far as the explosion. He keeps trying to explain about the chain reaction, and I don't really follow. I can picture the atoms, like billiard balls or my marbles colliding, but I can't see what that has to do with the explosion as bright as the sun, the mushroom cloud that rises up thousands of feet into the sky.

I sense that our conversation is like one of my kites. We got it off the ground, my father and I, but there are too many cross-winds, and now the kite is wheeling and zooming dangerously earthward. I sense his frustration. I wish I were older. When I'm older, as he often says, when I can "reason," I'll understand the things he wants to explain to me better. He'll feel more comfortable with me—and I with him, I decide.

Nevertheless, my father tries desperately to rescue the conversation. He brightens, as if he's found the key. He asks me—as he often does—about the math I've been doing at school. I get an odd feeling: it's as if he were inviting me to play, teaching me a new game. In the fall, as a fifth-grader, I'll be learning about fractions, I tell him.

"Oh. You know, if you multiply the numerator and the denominator by the same number, the value of the fraction doesn't change," he says.

He makes it sound as if he were one of my friends, revealing his secret hiding place down in the woods, or as if he were entrusting me with a secret code. My father pulls the emerald-green mechanical pencil from the breast pocket of his shirt, reaches for the nearest old envelope and writes down an example. "Four eighths. One half. Eight sixteenths." He records the numbers neatly one below the other, as if he were writing in his notebook at his lab or talking to one of his colleagues on a Sunday hike. "Isn't that pretty?" he says hopefully.

I look at the penciled numbers; I look at the divisor line. I don't see what's pretty about them, but I nod blankly. My father looks disappointed again. I know there's some mystery, some wonder that he wants me to understand and appreciate. For him, numbers are something to play with; numbers are fun. For me, at best, numbers are useful. I use them to add up the value of my comic books. I multiply my allowance and dream of how many comic books I can buy at the end of the month. That is all.

Finally, as if to put an end to our impasse, my father beckons. "Claudietto! *Vieni qua.* [Come here.] *Nasacocchia!*" That's the signal: time for an Eskimo kiss. His tone is peculiar, I remember, an odd mix of commanding and coaxing. Of course I obey him, as I always do. But that quick, playful rubbing of noses does nothing for my uneasiness. Of course he cares for me. I know that. Then why doesn't he know how to talk to me? Why does his affection seem as tentative, as fleeting as that instant when the tips of our noses touch, as evanescent as the atoms he studies—and sometimes as explosive. Also, would Superman or Golden Eagle rub noses with anyone?

As I grow older, my images of what Superman should look like, and what he should do, change. I no longer expect him to have muscles of steel, rescue children, stop wayward trains, bash crooks or fly fighter planes. As a teenager, I'm bespectacled, bookish-looking, a budding intellectual, with a reputation among my classmates for being a "brain." I now associate Superman with a powerful and original mind, one that reasons well, grasps ideas quickly, retains facts, ideas, books, lines of poetry. My father fits this image brilliantly, and he looms more powerful than ever. That is clear from the essay I wrote about him in the spring of 1951, when I was fourteen and attending a boarding school in Gstaad, Switzerland.

I'm tall and gangly. I wear navy-blue shorts and a matching

windbreaker with an École Privée Tournesol shoulder patch. I like my legs, long, solid, tanned. My glasses give me a serious, professorial look that masks the emotional cauldron of adolescence steaming within me.

My father, whom I see during vacations, wears double-breasted suits, Italian shoes, and sometimes bow ties. He slicks his hair back with Yardley's brilliantine and smells of lavender. For me to tour the Louvre with him as we did in February, to hear him discourse on artists, periods, styles, history, is dazzling. He seems to know so much. He talks so easily, so clearly and confidently, with so much authority, as if whatever he says is the final word, the truth. I understand that what he doesn't know (because occasionally he can't answer my questions) isn't worth knowing.

As I reread the essay, I remember how I felt when I wrote it. It looks the way my teachers have taught me to do it. My handwriting in the notebook is clear and neat. No mistakes; there can be none, for this is the final, the "good copy." My teachers would approve—both of my neatness and of what I wrote.

I even imagine myself singled out from the class as a model. I can hear my teachers, Monsieur Spohr or Monsieur Mayer, saying, "Look at Claudio's fine composition! Read it, please, to the class." I picture myself standing up, the model boy, "the first in the class," as my father had been, and reading loudly and confidently.

I push my courage to the limit. I imagine my father in the audience, listening. At the end, I can hear his "Bravo!"—distinct, but almost perfunctory. (In fact, I'm not sure that my father ever read or heard the essay.) "Bravo!," as if that were a formality, a courtesy—and then he would get on to more substantial matters. As a friend of his once remarked, "Segrè has the soul of a professor. He never stops teaching. He never stops giving examinations, either." So I imagine my father saying, "Your French is getting much better. Not many mistakes. Do you know Victor Hugo's poems?"

Looking back at the essay nearly four decades later, I wonder, did I believe what I wrote? Perhaps, I decide.

My Ideal Person

Me, I'd like to be like my father. I certainly have good reason to be proud of him because it isn't often that you find a man like him. It isn't just anyone who accomplishes some really important work in physics as he has. It isn't every day that you find a man who was present at the birth of a new age, the atomic age, and who will always be remembered in the history of physics as the man who discovered element 43, technetium, and who was the co-discoverer of several other elements. He has worked with some very famous men and he has known the most famous men in physics today. Now he is professor of physics at one of the largest and most famous universities in the world. No, you don't find a man like him every day.

His enormous intelligence always astonishes me. He seems to know everything that one can possibly imagine, whether it is history, literature, botany, mathematics, but most of all science, naturally, because that's his profession. It's really grand to have a walking encyclopedia like him at home! More than once I've felt how little my knowledge of the world is compared to his and always afterwards I've said to myself that I would study a little harder to diminish my ignorance. Finally, he serves as an inspiration. He gives me the thirst to drink at the fountain of knowledge.

But in addition to being a great scientist and a famous man, for me he is also a very good father. He is always concerned that I should be happy and he does everything he can to make me still more satisfied. I know very well that I'm a "special case" with two trips to Europe and one to Canada. It's very convenient to have a father like him in Europe because I have a very good guide in him. If I go into the Louvre with him, he explains to me the history of art by showing me examples of the different types of paintings. This is much more interesting than to listen to the tour guides say, "On the right, is a fresco by——done in 15—" in a monotone and who speak foreign languages badly. He always has to explain to me a bit of history which makes the tour even more interesting.

My father knows very well how to repair things. How many times has he done *"gewust wo"* (knowing where) which is his term for when he completes a particularly difficult job. He also teaches me to do repairs around the house. And his wise advice! How many times I wish I'd followed it instead of doing just the opposite!

Like all men in this world, my father is not perfect. He has his faults, but if I manage to become as good, as kind, and as knowledgeable as he is when I'm an adult, I will feel that I've accomplished something.

Over the years, I discover that a large proportion of the people I meet share my admiration for my father—including the Nobel Prize Committee when they award him (with Owen Chamberlain) the prize for physics in 1959 for his work on antimatter. I discover something else. I often feel invisible. At best, I'm a shadowy presence. I'm on display in a bright package marked "Son of Superman." Yet, I don't act like one. I can't talk knowledgeably about "proton scatterings" and "gamma rays." When I look at an anthill, I watch the ants crawling; I don't speculate on the efficiency of ant brain cells—as my father did, as a bright young physicist, when he went to the beach with his Italian colleagues Enrico Fermi and Franco Rasetti. If I can't say brilliant things, I have nothing to say. I feel I'm not there. I remember meeting one of my father's eminent colleagues one day. "How is your father?" he asks. His dark eyes look right through me. When I am a guest at the house of another, equally eminent colleague, my host remarks bluntly, "Your father will be here in about ten minutes. You and I have to talk now. When your father arrives, he and I will be very busy."

For a long time, I accept this shadow life when I am with my father. I barely notice it; when I do, I ignore it. It's simply part of being Son of Superman. I should be grateful, I tell myself. Think of all the opportunities I enjoy; think of the brilliant people I meet, the unique events that I attend, I tell myself. For a long time, for more than four decades, I convince myself that I'm grateful. Then, one day, in the spring of 1989, my father is finally, irrevocably gone. To my surprise, I don't seem to mourn; instead, like a volcano—or is it more like a nuclear blast?—I erupt.

When I get the news, I'm far away. I'd always imagined I would be; I prefer some space between my father and me, though half a continent seems excessive. He lives in Lafayette, California, high on a ridge of live oaks and pines in the hills east of San Francisco Bay. I live in Austin, Texas, on the faintest ripple of a hill among the bamboos and juniper at the edge of Lyndon Johnson's beloved Hill Country. "Lafayette" evokes the enlightened, cosmopolitan French noble, the hero of the two great revolutions of his day; "Austin" suggests some tough, saddle-worn settler who didn't have sense enough to make it across the continent.

What I didn't anticipate is that on a peaceful Saturday evening in the spring of 1989, the news would touch down so suddenly, so unexpectedly, like one of those Texas tornados. I'm relaxing on the couch, watching TV with my wife, Elisabeth (Zaza), when the phone rings. Over the long-distance lines from Berkeley, my son Gino's voice seems to hiss. For a college freshman, he sounds unusually grave and subdued.

"Nonno Emilio's dead," he says.

The hissing on the telephone reminds me of a pot of water ready to boil over, as if he's ready to burst into tears.

"When? How?" I'm stunned. Of course it's Gino, the bridge between father and son, who bears the sad news, I'm thinking.

"This afternoon. Around five o'clock."

At least the end came at the conclusion of a good day for my father. Gino, as he often did on a Saturday, had spent the day with his grandfather. I picture them in my father's wood-paneled study, which opens onto a large deck. Robins, sparrows, blue jays, squirrels chirp and chatter in the live oaks. Through the sliding glass doors, it looks like an aviary. My father and Gino ignore it, ignore the cluttered mosaic of photographs on the walls— physicists who were my father's masters, like Enrico Fermi and Pieter Zeeman; my mother; the Matterhorn; children and their spouses; grandchildren—snapshots from a life. Grandfather and grandson hunch over the computer screen, their eyes on the cursor, pulsing hypnotically. Gino is teaching my father a new program. Like a piano virtuoso's, Gino's fingers click rapidly over the keys. My father protests, "Wait, not so fast. Don't hurry." His *r*'s still roll thick and hard. "How did you do that?"

Late in the afternoon, my father and Rosa, my stepmother, drive Gino down the long, steep hill to Lafayette for the commuter train station to Berkeley. Coming down the corkscrewing road off the ridge and into the steel, concrete, neon and blacktop jungle of Lafayette, my father was fine, Gino says. It all happened after Gino had left on the train. As my father and Rosa often did, they went for a little walk. This time, instead of following the slopes, the curves, the sudden pitches around the Lafayette Reservoir, they parked the car down in the valley on the outskirts of town. They had just begun to walk when my father stiffened abruptly, grabbed his chest and collapsed. *Cascato secco* (dropped on the spot), like a dry tree limb snapping off. *Cascato secco:* it was one of his favorite epitaphs, pronounced with a childish glee—and with increasing frequency—over friends and colleagues. Now it applied to him. After eighty-four years, his heart had given out. April 22, 1989—before now a random date for our family—has become a milestone, an anniversary. He's gone.

The boiling in Gino's voice subsides and it becomes hushed. I put down the phone.

"He's gone," I tell Zaza, unsure what color, what weight I'm giving those two words. For years my father had thundered, admonished, even bantered about this moment, so often that it seemed improbable. Now it had come.

Zaza hugs me. I can feel her trying to stanch the pain with the warmth and softness of her body. Yet there's nothing for her to absorb. My eyes are dry. I feel empty, like one of those California reservoirs at midsummer, depleted and desiccated by the sun. "He's gone," I repeat. There's a finality about those words, honest yet unsentimental—also comfortably distant—that soothes me. Yet I keep wondering: When will the tears come? When will I feel numb or get a headache?

I need to break the news to my sisters. I'm five years older than Amelia, who lives in Israel; I'm eight years older than Fausta, who lives in England. To them, I'm "Coach." The name derives from our many ski outings together in the California Sierras, when I often coached them on their skiing technique. I like to think that as my sisters followed me admiringly, swooping and dipping down the ski slope, so they study my moves as I swoop and dip through life. Their eyes will be on me now, and I worry at my calm, my detachment.

I call Fausta in Bristol. "I'm sorry to wake you up, but I need to tell you, Papà died. He's gone." My words spew out, blunt, massive, brutal, like a football tackle plunging across an offensive line. I don't like the way I sound at all. This is not the Coach I know or like to imagine. Yet, in the back of my mind, I feel a certain pride. I know where that bluntness, that brutality comes from: it's him. In a situation like this, one that calls for tact, for sensitivity, my father would nod in agreement—then add stubbornly, "That may be so, but it's a fact, isn't it? He's dead. *Cascato secco*."

I call Amelia in Herzliya, near Tel Aviv. "Oh, no!"—I hear her genuine wail of grief, far more heartrending and humane than my "He's gone." Tonight the Coach seems to have deserted me.

I drift back to the living room. "Do you want to take a walk?" Zaza says.

"Yes." Maybe then I'll feel something. At least, maybe I'll understand what I feel.

Outside, it's clear and warm, a spring night with the scent of magnolia. Between the dark outlines of the oaks and pecans, the Texas stars, big and bright, glow against a dark satin sky.

He's gone, he's gone. The phrase reverberates in my mind. A weight lifts off my shoulders; I feel a sudden lightness. I'm puzzled. If there was a burden, I hadn't been aware of it in years. Then, unexpectedly, I erupt: "That bastard. He had it all. Even the way he died."

No terrible wasting away for him; none of the humiliating helplessness that had, in some cases, ravaged family, colleagues and friends. Nor, best of all, did his wonderful mind fail him. To the very end it remained as clear and powerful as always. To go instantly, in a favorite place, at the conclusion of a good day: I should be so lucky, I tell myself silently, sarcasm muffling rage—and uncertainty. Would I be so lucky?

Then, just as suddenly, the volcano in me subsides. I'm at one with the arching pecan trees and the live oaks, the scent of magnolia and honeysuckle. All is as it should be: a cycle completed, a life fulfilled. I wonder at this epiphany and I see that I'm the lucky one to have it. Once again, my father has set the example. Who else but a superman would complete his life so perfectly?

And yet my emotional rumblings don't dissipate easily. In subsequent days, I scan his obituaries. Nobel Prize–winning physicist in 1959 . . . co-discoverer of the anti-proton, evidence that antimatter, an antiuniverse exists . . . author of a host of pioneering works in nuclear physics . . . worked at Los Alamos Scientific Laboratory during World War II . . . faculty member at University of California, Berkeley, for nearly four decades . . . born in Tivoli, Italy, in 1905, the son of a wealthy Italian Jewish businessman . . . studied physics at the University of Rome . . . fled Italy for the United States in 1938 to escape Fascist racial persecution . . . student, friend, colleague of Enrico Fermi . . . married to Elfriede Spiro for thirty-four years, until her death in 1970 . . . survived by his second wife, Rosa Mines, three children and five grandchildren. All the parts of his life are there, stark as an anatomy manual: achievements, birth, lineage, survivors.

I glance at a few of the dozens of condolence letters from friends and colleagues, sometimes from distant admirers, total strangers. I sense their mourning, their feeling of loss, even in stock phrases such as "esteemed colleague" or "valued friend, wise and supportive." They think they know, I snort to myself. They don't know the half of it. But what is the half of it? I ask myself uncertainly. And why this raging grief of mine? That seems an odd way of mourning. Yet, when I think about it, my eruptions are not totally unexpected. For decades they have been building, perhaps from the time when he tried to explain the bomb to me at Los Alamos—perhaps even earlier.

I'm not even sure where to begin. How to untangle this peculiar mourning, this grief as rage, over a relationship that for more than half a century eluded and frustrated us both? It was a connection that often reminded me of those manzanita bushes in the mountains around Los Alamos: flourishing and vigorous, yet so often twisted, contorted into peculiar shapes. I suddenly feel I have so much to say. I can't stop talking and I don't know where to begin. Perhaps I should start with those childhood years on the earthly equivalent of Superman's Krypton: high in the mountains of New Mexico, at Los Alamos, among the supermen.

CHAPTER 2

The Beautiful Place

Going back to Los Alamos wasn't easy, I discovered. For nearly half a century after we left in 1946, I stayed away. I had no particular reason to go back; I felt no special attachment to the place—or that's what I thought. When people asked me, "What was it like to live there?" I shrugged. I heard myself answering as my father might have, with a nonchalant indifference, as if he were reviewing his data from an old experiment. Some boys grow up riding horses in Phoenix or flying kites on the Mall in Washington, D.C., I say; others remember going to the beach at Coney Island or picking apples near Wenatchee, Washington. I grew up playing Indians and Cowboys in Los Alamos, New Mexico. That's the way it was; that was the fact of the matter.

I see the disappointment, even incredulity, in my well-meaning interrogators' eyes. What was it like? How can I be so nonchalant? Am I hiding something? There must be a story. What was it like, with all those brilliant men—Fermi, Bohr, Bethe, Oppenheimer, just to name a few—around? With the atomic bomb being built? I shrug, but I'm uneasy. These are all people I met in my everyday life. To me, as a child, they were ordinary men, my father's colleagues. For the most part, I found them a trifle boring. Through time they've grown, swelled, stretched, taken on mythic proportions. They've become enshrined in history. When I read about them in books, they seem to belong to a different time, a different world—a heroic one that an ordinary mortal like me could not have shared. And so what can I say? What dare I say? The story of Los Alamos and the building of the atomic bomb has been told many times, in books, in movies, on television. What can I add? I was only a child, with a child's memory and a child's knowledge. I know nothing first hand of the science, or the policy decisions, or the personality conflicts. I cannot shed any new light on the Army's conflict with the scientists, or how Oppenheimer and General Groves somehow managed to pull off the entire scheme. Compared to my father, what can I add? What can I say? As so often, when confronted with my father, I feel speechless. I have nothing to say—or so it seems.

My father doesn't say much about Los Alamos either—at least not to me. Usually, with my father and me, as with so many parents and children, the demands of the present crowd out the musings on the past. There's my career to be planned, or a family visit to be arranged, or financial matters to be resolved. Perhaps I'm not persistent enough in asking him. I note how nostalgic he is about New Mexico and that period of his life; how often he likes to visit the Southwest, even when he is retired; how, from time to time, he likes to sport a bolo tie with a silver-and-turquoise pin. *"Posti belli,"* he likes to say mysteriously; "beautiful places." Yet, when I try to draw him out, he repeats, like an incantation, *"Posti belli."* His face lights with wonder, as if he can't quite believe his memories. If I press him, perhaps he recalls trout fishing in the San Antonio River, or hiking around Truchas Peak in the Sangre de Cristo Mountains. About his work, or about his colleagues, about how he felt when he saw the unearthly flash of the first atomic bomb test, he says very little. *Posti belli.* It's as if he could never adequately explain, or I could never grasp, any more than I understood the workings of the bomb when he first explained them to me as a child, the world encompassed within that phrase. The child in me whispers again, disappointed, "He doesn't know how to talk to me."

Finally, in the summer of 1993, I do go back to Los Alamos. I don't know quite what I expected to find. Perhaps merely a confirmation that the images I was carrying about in my head from those days—where our house was, where I had my "fort," where my friends and I played down in "the woods," the loop where I rode my first bike—were valid. From a distance I recognize the broad outlines of what I remember, the mesas, the dark Jemez Mountains in the background, the stands of pines, the signs for Bandelier National Monument, with its Indian ruins. Those primal shapes and colors cradle and comfort me. The mesas still sail like ship's hulls or submarines or whales, just as they did when I was a child. In the jungle of memory, the outlines of my boyhood, like some pre-Columbian temple ruin, appear intact, safe. But then, as the road begins to climb up to the Pajarito Plateau, my confidence wavers, my anxieties mount. Men and their machines have been swarming over the landscape, digging, slashing, scraping, leveling, smoothing, grading the cliffs. Where I remember hairpin turns, I see smooth ribbons of blacktop, six lanes wide in some places. The asphalt ribbon streams down from the mesa, roller-coasters over hills and down into washes to accommodate the commuter traffic that comes from as far as Santa Fe, about forty miles away. Where the old guardhouse used to be, where the snappy-looking MPs used to check our passes, there's now a small airport. At the crest of the mesa, I look in vain for the signs of an Army post. The olive-drab or camouflage trucks and cars are nowhere to be seen. Nor can I find the sets of squat, regular, military-style buildings, barracks, workshops, office buildings, churches, most of them a uniform green, as dark as the pines.

Instead, I am on the outskirts of yet another high-tech Sun

Belt town (population 17,600), bright and bustling with traffic lights and neon signs, gas stations, convenience stores, shopping centers, motels. The Los Alamos County Municipal Building now occupies the site of the old Tech Area next to Ashley Pond. The building, I note, sports a handsome municipal lawn—an inconceivable amenity when I lived here. The residential areas where we lived have all vanished. I'm startled, then unaccountably irritable. I feel as if something has been snatched away. But what did I expect to see after more than half a century? I ask myself. And where are the giants—or at least the traces of the giants—the atom splitters, the heroes who in this primal setting released such primal energies? I see only ordinary men and women browsing in the supermarket, filling their cars at the self-service gas stations, sipping coffee at the convenience store. I can hear my father's voice: "They've ruined everything." It's his all-purpose condemnation for any changes in a favorite place.

Until I visit the Los Alamos Historical Museum and the Bradbury Science Museum, I'm uneasy, disoriented amid the shopping malls and blinking neon signs. I could be anywhere in the United States. Wandering among the exhibits and memorabilia at the museums, I feel better. Fuller Lodge (one of the buildings from the original settlement on the mesa, an old boys' school), with its wonderful, rustic beamed ceilings and Indian rugs on the walls, is still there. The floors still creak. These days, in the main hall, where my mother and father occasionally took me to dinner and where I learned restaurant manners, two Chinese girls are practicing a Bach partita for piano and violin. That seems right, in tune with the Los Alamos I knew. But why does the Los Alamos Chamber of Commerce have an office in the Lodge? Should Los Alamos *have* a Chamber of Commerce?

With the old, grainy black-and-white film clips in the Bradbury Museum, I feel positively vindicated. My memories of the water tower, which I could see from my bedroom window, are not my fading delusions. Playing in "the woods"—the stands of pine on the edge of the housing projects—with my friends, or buying an ice cream and sneaking a look at comic books at the Commissary are real memories.

The images are a comfort; they are also a revelation. I study the familiar faces. They are my neighbors, my parents' friends, my friends' parents, all the people I knew as a child: there's "Oppie" (J. Robert Oppenheimer) in his porkpie hat; there's Enrico Fermi's stocky figure and his usual enigmatic smile; there's Victor Weisskopf, who used to come striding past our house at mealtimes, whistling a little three-note fanfare to alert his family that he was almost home; there's Kenneth Bainbridge—his daughter, Joan, blond and freckled, was in my class at school; and there's Julian Mack, whose daughter, Cornelia, had long brown braids.

I'm surprised at how young, how earnest the scientists look. These are the giants of the history books, the supermen of the documentaries and TV specials? I remember them wearing laboratory coats and sports shirts; yet the pictures often show them in coats and ties and double-breasted suits. I study the scientists poised over charts or pointing to a formula on the blackboard. I see them square-dancing or putting on amateur theatricals. I watch the images of the first bomb test at Alamogordo. In a way that I could not grasp as a child, I glimpse for the first time what a magical place Los Alamos really was, why my father murmured, "*Posti belli.*"

And what an astonishing story. In the middle of World War II, take an old boys' ranch in the middle of New Mexico. Populate it with the world's best scientific minds under a kind of loose military discipline. Tell them to build a weapon that will end the war and possibly change the future of the planet. Tell them to do it fast—in about twenty-eight months. They do it. The entire scheme succeeds beyond the organizer's wildest dreams. Looking back, it seems like a story out of another time, another place. I flash on one of my father's credos and frequent phrases: "high standards." Here's an entire community of people with his high standards.

As I wander among the old black-and-white still photographs, the newspaper clips, the period jukebox, government furniture and other memorabilia, the supermen take on more human proportions. I listen to familiar voices, old family friends, on tape or on a sound track—and laugh with them again as they reminisce. There was basically nothing wrong with the housing, John Manley says, "it just had a tendency to catch fire." My memories flow more easily. They bridge the gap between the heroic world enshrined in the books and the museum, and the mortal, everyday one of my childhood. I see how my comic book heroes, my discovery of hamburgers, the lonely fishing trips with my father, the disappearance of my Italian grandmother, could fit into that world after all. "What was it like?" Once again, I hear my friendly interlocutors over the years. Perhaps that voice of a six- or seven-year-old, too, deserves to be heard. Perhaps it will reduce the giants to human proportions and help explain how Los Alamos was possible. Perhaps I can finally grasp what my father meant by his Sibylline *"posti belli."*

I was six years old, going into second grade, when we left Berkeley for Los Alamos at the end of the school year in June 1943. For my age, I was on the tall side. My mother kept my hair short; it still had many blond highlights, though by then it was taking on the brown hues of the Berkeley hills during the summer. My timid, blue-green eyes peered curiously at the world which came into better focus shortly after I turned seven and began to wear glasses. Photographs of me in Berkeley a year or so earlier show me dressed as an elegant professor's son in velvet collar and felt hat, or standing on the terrace in bathrobe and slippers, with my hands behind my back, like a pensive European gentleman. By the time I was going to first grade, however, I looked much more like an American child. My mother dressed me democratically: in brightly colored cotton polo shirts and corduroy pants or blue jeans; even, on occasion, in bib overalls, as if I were a farmer's son.

I don't remember now how my parents broke the news to me

that we were moving. Probably they said very little. For security reasons, there was little that my father *could* say. Los Alamos was an administrative never-never land designed to make people figuratively "vanish into the desert." Los Alamos appeared on no map and its existence was not officially revealed until the first atomic bomb was dropped on Hiroshima. Its residents could not vote; the locale of their births and deaths was "Post Office Box 1663, Santa Fe, New Mexico."

Wherever we were going sounded intriguing to me because my parents assured me that I would find Indians there. With Indians must come cowboys and pioneers, I decided. Yet there was a war going on, I knew. Because of it, my parents, who didn't speak English the way real Americans did, had moved to Berkeley from a place called Europe—a distant land that was somehow much better than where we lived now. Because of the war, at school my classmates and I bought red savings stamps with the statue of the Minuteman on them. Because of the war, my friends and classmates had fathers, brothers, sometimes sisters who were in the Army or the Navy or the Air Corps. They knew how to drive tanks or fire big guns or pilot bombers; the sisters knew how to be nurses.

From time to time, I wondered what my own father was doing for the war effort. I knew he had been in the army in Italy. I had seen photographs of him in uniform. Yet, so far as I knew, he had nothing to do with the current conflict. He wore suits and sometimes bow ties. He walked a few blocks down the street to the university, where he taught classes, much as my first-grade teacher taught me. He worked in his laboratory. Yet when I heard that we were moving, I sensed that in the new place he would somehow be involved in the war. How the war, Indians and pioneers might mix I wasn't sure. I was certain, however, that my father, who knew so much, would make it happen.

I watched anxiously for clues. The trip did not begin auspiciously. Pioneers, I knew from first grade, rode horses and hauled their goods in covered wagons. I had to make do with squeezing into the backseat of an old navy-blue 1939 Chevrolet. Pioneers rolled westward across the plains. We headed east across the deserts of California, then the plateaus and mountains of Arizona and New Mexico. Pioneers fought Indians, who rode fast ponies and wore eagle feather war bonnets. The Indians that my parents pointed out looked merely sad, beaten and a little scruffy. Pioneers often stopped at trading posts and forts along the trail west. We stayed overnight in motels in sleepy, dull little oasis towns that broke the monotony of the desert.

My father seemed to enjoy the trip, as if he were witnessing what he had only imagined as a child. I learned much later from a cousin that when he had been my age my father loved to play Wild West and shared many of the fantasies that I did. Only the locale and names were different. Amid the vineyards and olive groves of the Tuscan countryside in the summer, during family visits to Florence, he galloped about as a character named "Arizona Bill," rescuing his cousin Giuliana, the lovely maiden "Melilla," from her brother Marco, the evil "Nerumo." Cowboy hero and lovely maiden burned the evil Nerumo in effigy and chanted, "*Nerumo che fece tanto fumo*" (Nerumo who made so much smoke). At other times, my father became an Indian. Nerumo recorded the occasion with a delightful sketch of my father in headdress and war paint.

In Santa Fe, my father marveled at the city's main plaza. At the time we arrived, it still looked straight out of the pages of Willa Cather's *Death Comes for the Archbishop* (which he had been reading as background for settling into his new home), he informed me. I had no idea, of course, who Willa Cather was, or exactly what archbishops did, or why; during free moments, my father kept his nose in that book with the cream-colored jacket and the brown lettering that reminded me of the trim on our house in Berkeley. At least the "death" in the title sounded intriguing. I imagined that perhaps there was some grand scene in the book in which someone (who? cowboys, Indians and pioneers were all brave and manly; only an outlaw, maybe Billy the Kid, could have done such a dastardly deed) stabbed the Archbishop. In the middle of the plaza, he reeled and twirled, jerked and twitched, finally collapsed, as my friends and I knew how to reel and twirl, jerk and twitch, before we collapsed and "died." Nevertheless, as I had been taught to do, I listened respectfully to my father. Meanwhile, my eyes roved around the plaza, took in the dark, coppery faces of the Indians and the olive skins of the Mexicans. I also noted what was missing: tonsured friars in brown cassocks, or, better yet, Spanish soldiers in breastplate and helmet. I didn't dare ask about the exact spot where the Archbishop collapsed.

At other times, in part thanks to my father's suggestions, my hopes of finding pioneers revived. "You be in charge of her," my father said when we first got in the car. He was pointing to the baby basket in the backseat. Inside the basket was my eight-month-old sister, Amelia. It was my job to be sure that she didn't spill out if we stopped suddenly, my father said. I also liked the way we carried our own water and made water stops, as the pioneers did. In those days before the interstate highway system was finished, we carried the water in a canvas bag attached to our front bumper. When we were thirsty, or my father wanted to stretch, he would cut the ignition and let the car decelerate naturally. We would roll to a stop on the shoulder of the road and get out. The desert's primal stillness would envelop us. Particularly in the early morning, it was as if the world had just been created and we were its first inhabitants, my father said. I liked imagining that as I tipped up the water bag and a little stream trickled down my throat. I didn't mind the faint odor of dust and burlap. The water tasted as fresh as if it had just been created.

I was still looking for the war. As we crossed the deserts of Southern California, my father had been teasing me about mirages. "Oh, look," he would say. "The water." There, through the windshield, just on the horizon, inundating the road, was a big lake; perhaps we could even go swimming, my eyes told me.

Yet, as the miles rolled by, the lake never materialized. When I complained, my father laughed. My mother, in German, the language of parental secrets, chided him. So, my father, like a scolded puppy, tried to redeem himself. He invited me to play by teaching me something "pretty": explaining why mirages occurred. I barely followed him. I was getting tired of being fooled.

Then, between Barstow and Needles, huge dust clouds appeared on the horizon. "There's the war. I told you," my father said. He sounded as if he were teasing again and I was ready for another mirage. Yet, as we approached, I made out the silhouettes of tanks, jeeps, armored cars through the dust clouds. Then there was no mistaking; these were real. I heard the rumble of the engines, saw the tank drivers peeping out of their turrets, and the soldiers in the jeeps and trucks. The men wore camouflage uniforms, carried rifles and radios. A military policeman stopped us while a tank crossed the road right in front of us.

I still didn't understand. I was wary of yet another one of my father's tricks. They reminded me of what sorcerers and magicians did in fairy tales. I looked at him suspiciously. In his glasses and his short-sleeved shirt he didn't look right for a magician. What was going on? So far as I knew, "the war" that my parents talked so much about was far away, overseas in that Europe that they also talked so much about. How could we have driven to Europe? An ocean lay between the continents; I knew that. What was going on, I asked. "It's the war," my father said. My mother shook her head, chided my father in German again, then reached over and gave me one of her rare hugs. This wasn't the war, she said; at least not yet. These soldiers were only practicing, she explained. Soon enough, they might be in the real one; some of them would probably die. I saw tears forming in her eyes. I was sure she was exaggerating about the soldiers dying—or if the soldiers died, it would only be for a little while. I waved at them, hiding my disappointment that they were only practicing for war. Vindicated, I glared at my father for leading me on with yet another mirage.

My hopes rose again during the last forty miles or so from Santa Fe to Los Alamos. This looked more like a landscape where I might find pioneers. Especially at the end, when we bumped along dirt roads, then around hairpin turns newly gouged out of the mesa. Big boulders dotted the road. There were no guardrails, and we could see real Indian ruins. After days of desert heat, the air felt heavenly. At 7,200 feet it was cool and dry. The wind rustled the pines. Late in the afternoon the sky darkened. Lightning flashed and thunderclouds roared. Rain poured down for half an hour, then the clouds vanished. The sun came out; the air smelled clean and fresh, of pine trees and sagebrush. As we drove through the settlement, my father pointed out the old Los Alamos boys' school that had once been the only settlement on the mesa. Around it, barracks and apartment houses, service buildings and Quonset huts were mushrooming. I saw jeeps and trucks and soldiers in uniform. This was no mirage. We were on a military post. We were going to live there, I realized. The war had arrived, just as my father had promised.

Our new home was not a log cabin, as I had imagined. In place of it, we had a new apartment at T-170C, on the top floor of the apple-green fourplex. There was much less space than in our two-story house in Berkeley: just a kitchen, a dining area, a living room, three bedrooms and a bathroom. Nor was there much of a neighborhood of the sort I knew on Spruce Street: no paved streets or sidewalks, no front lawns bordered by rosebushes and a holly tree, no backyards with fruit trees. But I liked the view from the window of my room. In Berkeley, I faced the stucco wall of the neighbor's house. Here I looked out at stands of pines and onto the dirt road below. I could see the water tower up the hill. I felt as if I were at summer camp. My mother worried about the woodstove that smoked up the kitchen. She got impatient that at such high altitudes water took so long to boil. My father explained why and invited me to stick my finger in the pan. Sure enough, though the water was bubbling, it was only lukewarm. I was mystified and delighted. I was going to like it here: a place where boiling water wasn't hot, where the war mixed with Indians. Krypton must be something like this, filled with such strange contradictions and juxtapositions. I glanced at my father with new respect. He still looked small and dark. He still wore his professorial glasses, and when he talked he seemed to know too much about everything. And yet, who else had brought us to this wonderful place? Who else had made it all happen?

My father came to love such a strange and wonderful land as much as I did, and yet we rarely talked about it. I even have trouble picturing him there. That's because I see him, remember him best, as many others saw him, in his later years. By then he was the cosmopolitan European gentleman, the world-class nuclear physicist, secure in his fame and reputation. By then he often wore tailor-made Italian suits. In conversation, he had a way of making declarations and pronouncements in a tone that left no room for response. Though he was never the kind to bow or dip over ladies' hands, people often claimed that there was an "Old World" air about him. Paris, London, Amsterdam, Berlin —later in life, Lagos, Rio de Janeiro, and Tokyo—were all familiar to him. He loved good food and good wine. How could this man who prided himself on coming from a "wealthy and cultivated" Italian Jewish family, as one of his obituaries put it, find himself at home at a secret military post in the mountains of New Mexico?

But of course, that's not the man who went to Los Alamos. The one I have trouble picturing is not the hero, enshrined in the pantheon of Nobel Prize winners. Then, it wasn't even clear to me that he was a superman. He was youngish, approaching middle age (he was thirty-eight when we left for Los Alamos). This man was thinner, with a slight build, dark hair and a temper like a coiled spring. He was also a world-class worrier (as he was throughout his life), a master at generating doubts and anxieties, a real *cacadubbi* his Italian friends and colleagues often said, relishing the scatological metaphor. For him, the focus was on the cloud—not the silver lining, which was likely to tarnish, anyway.

During that period of his life, he had reason to be gloomy. As a young physicist in Fascist Italy, he had predicted that Europe was headed for catastrophe. For once, his dark prognostications were fulfilled. In the summer of 1938, he was summarily fired from his position as a professor at the University of Palermo because he was Jewish. With his wife and young son, he fled to the United States. There he became an enemy alien with only a precarious research position to support his family.

As an adult, I imagined my own reactions to these shocks. What if I had been a refugee with tenuous job prospects and with a wife and young son to support? What if I had found myself an ocean and a continent away from parents and friends, all of whom faced a future dominated by the Nazis? What if I had moved to the wilds of an isolated mesa in the middle of New Mexico to live under military control, surrounded by a high wire fence, with my mail censored? What if I were building a super-bomb, a device that—if it worked—might end the war overnight? And how would I feel, knowing that if it worked, it would kill thousands of people, the innocent as well as the guilty? I came to admire him; I wanted to tell him so. I wanted to share with him my own memories of Los Alamos. It wasn't easy.

At the dinner table as a child, I listened to him a great deal. I learned what was important and what was not. (I generally fit into the latter category.) At times I wondered if my father was really there with us.

"What did you do at the lab today? Anything interesting happen?" my mother would say to him.

"Nothing much."

"But you must have done something?" she would persist.

"I went to get my mail. I saw Owen [Chamberlain]. I talked to Clyde [Wiegand]. I had lunch with people from my research group. I looked in on our experiment."

Always the facts. Always the chronology, as if he were reading from his datebook. Seldom what the facts meant, or what he felt about them. When I was older, I speculated about why he was so telegraphic. It would be easy and romantic to say that his head was among the atoms. He was thinking about his experiments. To a certain extent, especially during certain periods of his life (at Los Alamos, he and his colleagues worked six days a week), that was undoubtedly true.

Yet, as a child at Los Alamos, I sensed something else from watching my father: that knowing about things was more important—or at least much easier—than knowing about people, "hee-u-man relations," as he sometimes called them. In his mocking voice I heard contempt mixed with frustration at the complexities and uncertainties of human affairs. From time to time, he liked to quote Marie Curie: "In science, we must interest ourselves in things, not in people." Many years later, during his retirement years, my father wrote down and shared with me an imaginary conversation that he might have had with his own grandfather. In it the old man comments to the young Emilio, "You are lucky that you get on with plants, stones and natural objects, and that you can slightly dispense with mankind." But the "conversation" teeters with ambivalences. "Being able to 'slightly dispense with mankind' is a stroke of luck, but one has to pay even for that," my father replies equivocally. Even Fermi commented, "With science one can explain everything except oneself."

And yet, of course, my father did reminisce with me from time to time. We might be walking in the woods and something would trigger a memory of hikes in the mountains of New Mexico. A lemon tree in a nursery might recall the one that Oppenheimer sent him in his attempts to recruit my father for Los Alamos. An op-ed piece in the newspaper about the morality of developing nuclear weapons would enrage my father.

Long after we left the mesa in January 1946, he would return periodically for professional reasons. After his retirement in 1972, he went back because he loved the land, the desert, the mountains, the spaces, the solitude. For him the mountain air was crisp and clean, and he enjoyed watching the "ever-varying clouds." On summer afternoons, at precisely three o'clock, he liked to claim, thunderstorms crackled and roared and blew away the sultriness that had drifted up from the desert. On Sunday outings, he delighted in spotting deer, marmots, porcupines, wild turkeys. He learned to distinguish among the varieties of columbines. In the fall, he watched the aspens turn, and, as he had in Tivoli, the small town near Rome where he grew up, he sniffed the newly fallen leaves. As a family, we often harvested piñon nuts and mushrooms. In the spring, he tramped along the banks of the San Antonio, in the Valle Grande, or scrambled over the boulders along the Rio Grande to stalk the trout in his favorite fishing holes. In the winter, we skied on the nearby hills.

For him, as for many people, New Mexico truly was—quoting the state motto—a "Land of Enchantment," a place of magic and wonder. For example, while on a camping trip with my mother, he discovered a hot spring in the Sangre de Cristo Mountains. In the morning, just as he and my mother were about to take a bath, a band of Indians appeared out of the woods. In Spanish they politely asked the visitors not to desecrate this holy place. On that same trip, my parents chanced upon a young, newly married Navajo couple on horseback. My father, delighted by the bride's costume, pointed his camera to take her picture. She turned away, terrified. The camera, she feared, would steal her soul.

My father had a premonition about New Mexico, as he loved to recall. When the United States went to war with the Axis in 1941, my father, living in Berkeley, was still an Italian citizen and thus an enemy alien. Curfews and regulations so restricted his movements that he could not go to the movies at night. Following the Japanese attack on Pearl Harbor, the American government relocated Japanese Americans to camps in the interior of California and Arizona. My father wondered if the same fate awaited other aliens, like himself and my mother. One day, while leafing through an atlas, he called to my mother: "If they relocate us, here's where we'll spend the rest of the war," he said. His finger was pointing to Santa Fe, New Mexico. He was only about forty miles off. A year later, he was on his way to Los Alamos.

The laboratory where my father did some of his most important work had a special aura about it. The site was an old ranger's cabin in Pajarito Canyon, a few miles from the main laboratory. My father had practical reasons for choosing this isolated spot. His measurements needed to be very precise. He had to protect his instruments from any radiation that other experiments might be generating at the main laboratory. Yet he also loved the locale. It was accessible only by jeep. Indian caves, many of them containing pictoglyphs, marked the canyon walls. In season, the meadows bloomed with purple and yellow asters. An occasional rattlesnake slithered away at his approach. The cabin itself was located in a grove shaded by huge, broad-leaved trees. In the cabin, I noticed, was a nice cot where he could nap after lunch, or where he could spend the night if the experiment was at a critical stage. It was the sort of place over which my father waxed poetic. For him that usually meant recalling some classic passage from Italian literature. In this case, my father evoked the Italian Renaissance poet Ludovico Ariosto (1474–1533). In far-off "Arabia," Ariosto wrote, in "the shade of two mountains thick with ancient spruce and robust beeches, far from cities and villages," lay a dark, mysterious and magical cavern. For my father, the cabin in Pajarito Canyon was his cavern in Arabia, and one of the *posti belli* at Los Alamos that he most cherished.

Was that magical cavern, that most improbable of laboratories, actually the lair of a wicked sorcerer, a scientific Darth Vader? Had my father and his colleagues at Los Alamos, inadvertently, perhaps, done evil? Was working on the development of the atomic bomb immoral?

Such ideas never even crossed my mind when I was a child,

growing up in the shadow of the bomb. In my comic-book world of superheroes, he was one of the clean-cut researchers in white lab coats who produced the superweapon that allowed our side, the side of Goodness and Righteousness, to triumph. Nor, as an adult, do I have any doubts about the propriety of my father's work. I see images of stick figures in tattered striped uniforms of concentration-camp inmates peering out through barbed wire. I view pictures of thousands of bodies stacked like cordwood (among them, perhaps, my grandparents). I watch grainy black-and-white images of bulldozers filling huge pits; there's no question what the filler is: thousands and thousands of human corpses. I have no doubts: my father was involved in a righteous cause. In a dim way, I even envy him: what could be more ex-hilarating than to know that the fate of the world rests on your work—and that you are fighting the good fight?

Nor did my father have any doubts. "There are a lot of things to go to hell for, but working on the bomb isn't one of them," he would say, bristling, when the morality of working at Los Alamos came up, and he would add, as if he didn't really need to complete the thought, as if the proposition were self-evident, "It was because there was a man like Hitler." The Fascists and the Nazis had stripped him of his position, driven him from his homeland. They had murdered his mother and his German-Jewish in-laws. He and his colleagues *had* to succeed. Mussolini, in his eyes, was always something of a *buffone*, a clown, and Italy didn't have the organizational capabilities to produce an atomic bomb. The Germans did, however, and Hitler with a nuclear weapon was simply unthinkable. Undoubtedly one of my father's regrets was that the bomb was ready too late to be employed against Germany. Should it have been used against the Japanese? Was it really necessary? Couldn't the Japanese have somehow been warned? My father hated questions like that. For the most part, he dodged them and afterward grumbled at the "fool" or the "idiot"—usually a journalist or perhaps a student with radical sympathies—for posing the questions in the first place. Nevertheless, he left Los Alamos in 1946, when the war was over, and he never again engaged in weapons work. Those who did were rarely in his good graces.

I sometimes try to imagine that call to the good fight. I think of the great scientists at Los Alamos, the heroes of the Manhattan Project, appealing to each other to serve the noble cause. I want to imagine a scene with the dignity and high seriousness of an eighteenth-century neoclassical French or Italian play, like those of the Italian playwright Vittorio Alfieri, whom my father often quoted. In my imaginary scene, the heroes, full of manly admiration for each other's past deeds, address each other in grand, heartfelt speeches. They appeal to each other with words like "honor," "duty," "country," "sacrifice." I know that I'm imagining. As a child I often overheard my father and his colleagues speak to each other from the heart. What I heard was not "noble friend" or "faithful comrade"; more often than not, it was "fool," "idiot," "imbecile" (referring to a colleague not present). I also recall my father's favorite story of the eminent physicist greeting two colleagues at a conference. "Your paper was absolutely the worst one I have ever heard," the eminent physicist said to one colleague. Then he turned to the other: "I'd forgotten about yours. It was even worse."

I imagine that when my father got the call to Los Alamos, he welcomed it. During his first years at the Radiation Laboratory in Berkeley, from the time he emigrated in 1938 to the time we left for Los Alamos in 1943, he often felt estranged, unappreciated, the immigrant, the social outsider. In Rome, in the early 1930s, he had enjoyed the company of a band of dedicated brothers, the group of students and young researchers with whom he had worked under Fermi's direction, "the boys of the Via Panisperna." For them, doing physics was "like being in love," my father would often say reminiscently. Berkeley was different. In 1940, Berkeley was a provincial university, one of the last stops on the Southern Pacific train line west from Chicago. At the Radiation Laboratory, my father and the director, Ernest O. Lawrence, were not always in harmony. "*Il grande* Ernest Orlando," my father grumbled sarcastically from time to time in later years. Energetic, enthusiastic, expansive Lawrence, the inventor of the cyclotron, impressed my father as more of a promoter than a scientist. Lawrence, in turn, during those early days in Berkeley, had his doubts about my father's talents for academic research. He might do better as a physicist in industry, Lawrence suggested.

When the war broke out, my father, like many of his colleagues, joined a group that looked into military applications of research. But it was one thing to continue working at Berkeley for a cause he undoubtedly sympathized with. It was quite another to pull up roots again, to move to New Mexico for an indefinite period, to devote himself to a project that might or might not succeed. My father, the *cacadubbi*, was one to think not twice but twenty times before he accepted an offer like that. Nor was the man who recruited my father for Los Alamos the type who could insinuate himself easily into his confidence. J. Robert Oppenheimer, who became the scientific director at Los Alamos, and in 1953 was the subject of a Cold War security investigation, always appeared gaunt and ascetic. For many people that was part of his romantic charm. Here was a man who was not only a brilliant theoretical physicist but also a humanist and philosopher. He read Indian philosophy, and when he saw the first bomb explosion at Trinity remembered a line from the Hindu scripture, the *Bhagavad-Gita*. On the rare occasions when as a child I saw him in Los Alamos, I always thought that his wife or his mother should feed him a little more—maybe some extra carrots or another bowl of cereal.

My father admired Oppenheimer as "the fastest thinker I've ever met" and a man with an "iron memory." My father also viewed him as a pretentious man who deliberately spoke in an obscure and abstruse fashion. Fermi, my father loved to crow,

once attended one of Oppenheimer's theoretical seminars and walked out at the end shaking his head. When my father asked why, Fermi said laconically, "I didn't understand a thing except for the last sentence: 'And this is Fermi's theory of beta decay.' "

As for Oppenheimer's much-vaunted reputation as a humanist, in private my father jeered. Perhaps Oppenheimer read Indian philosophy and religion, but his French was atrocious and when he read Petrarch's sonnets in Italian he held the book upside down. Oppenheimer also had a reputation for arrogance that often "stung scientific colleagues where they were most sensitive," my father noted. Finally, the two men differed on politics. Oppenheimer had a reputation as a "fellow traveler" who sympathized with the Soviet Union. Moreover, to my father's great chagrin, Oppenheimer may have suspected my father of pro-Fascist leanings, simply because he, like all Italian state employees (including university professors) had to join the Fascist Party as a condition of employment.

Nevertheless, in 1942, Oppenheimer invited my father to lunch at Eagle's Nest, his Spanish-style home in the Berkeley hills. There, over a sumptuous lunch of chicken livers and wild rice, he appealed to my father to work at Los Alamos. How did Oppenheimer do it? How did he manage to put aside his own lightning mind and his streak of arrogance? Where did he find the patience and charm to win over the Basilisk?

I always wanted to ask Oppenheimer about that lunch. My last opportunity came in the 1960s at a party at my father's house in Lafayette. By then, I realized with a start, it was too late. What I saw that evening was the shell of a superman—a man so worn, so tired, so gaunt (mostly from the ordeal of the security investigation, his friends said) that nothing would have revived him. I heard an old man speaking softly, very carefully, as if he were afraid that his words might shatter. The only trace of the vaunted humanist was his insistence on speaking atrocious French, although the guest of honor spoke perfectly serviceable English.

There was one clue to Oppenheimer's charm and patience: his obvious concern for his wife, Kitty. His eye always seemed to be on her, making sure that she had a drink, that she was circulating among the guests and having a good time.

I can only imagine, then, what transpired at that lunch at Eagle's Nest in 1942 between the two physicists. I can only imagine—and wince: my father (probably anticipating what Oppenheimer had in mind) in one of his anxious, prickly moods; glowering, suspicious, his bushy eyebrows knitted into a frown. I can hear that honesty and candor that my father prided himself on, and that many others admired in him: "But you don't *really* know Italian, Robert. Why do you pretend that you read Petrarch?" I can imagine my father's restless mind, darting here and there, showering Oppenheimer with dozens of jabs and doubts about the feasibility of the Manhattan Project, about the hundreds of problems that would arise, about the apparent solutions that were sure to go awry. I imagine Oppenheimer doing with my father what I often did in later life—searching patiently for the arguments, then the phrases, the key words that would somehow soothe, pacify, perhaps flatter. Maybe, at that moment, the lines from my neoclassical play, the high-minded words like "honor," "duty," "country," even grand phrases like "the fate of civilization," did creep into the conversation after all. I imagine the storm clouds gradually receding from my father's face, the tension in his eyebrows fading, his head nodding in grudging agreement, his fists unclenching, opening, and finally a cautious commitment that he would "think it over."

"The high point of Oppenheimer's scientific career?" my father would say in later years. "Director at Los Alamos." In that phrase, I thought I heard sarcasm, contempt. Once again, my father, brandishing his honesty like a sword, was skewering a colleague, deflating a war hero, a fellow superman. In my father's world, real scientists who served as directors were the equivalent of real men who ate quiche.

But then, my father would surprise me. "Think of it! Soothing all those prima donnas—some even worse than me," he would add impishly. *"Non è mica poco, sai."* (That's not so little, you know.) It was one of his pronouncements—the kind to which there was no rejoinder. For once, I was glad that I had none.

Ironically, atop this mesa in the mountains of New Mexico, my father felt at home. He was a member of the elite, one of General Groves's "crackpot foreign" scientists, the flower of European and American physics at that time. The "senior" ones, many of them in their early forties, included Nobel Prize winners like Fermi and Niels Bohr. The "younger" ones, often in their early thirties, comprised at least seven future Nobel Prize winners, including my father: Owen Chamberlain, Richard Feynman, Isidor Rabi, Edwin McMillan, Luis Alvarez and Felix Bloch.

For my father, Los Alamos had even more familiar associations. At times it appeared like a bit of Rome and the laboratory on Via Panisperna transported to the mountains of New Mexico. Italians like Fermi and Bruno Rossi, and non-Italians, like Hans Bethe, who had also worked in Rome, were all there. In short, although the immediate task at Los Alamos was to build a bomb, it was a great place to talk physics, as remarkable and absorbing as Via Panisperna had been.

An enchanted place, a dedicated band of brothers, a righteous cause, a great place to talk physics—what more could a man want? Reading about Los Alamos as an adult, watching the movies at the Bradbury Museum, I'm reminded that Los Alamos was no futuristic city on Krypton.

Like all boomtowns, Los Alamos was ugly, feverish, improvised. At times the mesa's water supply was uncertain. Jerry-built houses, Quonset huts, trailers, sprawled among the stands of pine, juniper and aspen. A jungle of unpaved and nameless—for secrecy—streets linked the housing areas, the Commissary (for grocery shopping), the PX and the Tech Areas, where the research was done. Life was spartan. There was only one telephone line (furnished by the Forest Service) in 1943 and only three until 1945.

Like all boomtowns, Los Alamos was high-strung, a community filled with contradictions, a social oxymoron. Los Alamos was a dream scientific community behind barbed wire; it was an intellectual Eden created to build a device that would release a hell. It was at once a military post and a community, a gold-rush community whose chief asset was mining people's brains. As a community, it approached utopia: no rich, no poor, no in-laws, no handicapped, no unemployed, as a recent documentary has described it. The original plan for "thirty scientists" soon increased tenfold. At its wartime peak, between 1943 and 1945, Los Alamos had a laboratory staff of about three thousand. The quest for "the force from which the sun draws its energy," as President Truman eventually put it, meant long hours, unrelenting work pressures, a desperate need to succeed. "We worked and worked and worked all the time, and then on Saturday and Sunday, when we were really exhausted, we went fishing. I learned the meaning of the Sabbath there," my father reminisced in later years.

The feverish pace took its toll on the scientists and their families. The travel restrictions and the quasi-military surroundings generated a sense of claustrophobia. "We were too many of a kind, too close to one another, too unavoidable even during relaxation hours," Laura Fermi recalled. In these close quarters, questions of rank, of prestige, of who got which kind of housing in which neighborhood, escalated into major confrontations. Wives, especially, became gossipy, frustrated, depressed. Some took to drink. Yet the stress, the hardships, the cramped community also forged bonds, many of which lasted for a lifetime. "We didn't have telephones, we didn't have the bright lights, but I don't think I shall ever live in a community that had such deep roots of cooperation and friendship," declared Elsie McMillan, the wife of one of my father's colleagues, Nobel laureate Edwin McMillan.

My father generally dismissed the material and psychological hardships of living at Los Alamos. He had been raised in Tivoli, a small town in the hills just east of Rome, on boiled beef and endive soup. Only "sissies," as he called them, would grumble about Los Alamos's hardships. The dust from the traffic on the dirt roads and the sooty clouds from coal furnaces in the winter were nothing compared to the beauty of the drifting clouds or the jagged outlines of the Sangre de Cristos. So what if the water system was "two strings of holes held together by rust," as the joke went at the time. So what if the water tasted muddy or a little rusty. So what if, as happened shortly before Christmas, 1945, the pipes froze and the community had to be resupplied by water truck. So what if, like other families, my parents and I formed a mini–bucket brigade and filled our bathtub with the day's supply. Why was I whining, why were people complaining about a water shortage? my father gibed, as we passed the buckets down the line. We were swimming in water! If I didn't believe him, then I should calculate the number of liters available per person at Los Alamos and compare that to the supply of a typical European city.

From time to time, the restrictions of garrison-style living irritated him. He had come to the United States to escape censorship, to be free to express himself and to travel about where he pleased, he said. Yet at Los Alamos he lived within a series of fences, the mail was censored (though the Army insisted otherwise), he had no telephone. He was under military authority, and security personnel kept an eye on him and his colleagues. He was particularly contemptuous of the security measures. Paradoxically, as he liked to point out, until he and my mother were naturalized in 1944 he was an enemy alien, the citizen of an Axis power; yet he was entrusted with the most vital of military secrets. Security, of course, was necessary, but it was a matter of honor and commitment, most effective when self-imposed. Meanwhile, General Groves's rules and regulations often appeared ludicrous. The scientists needed to communicate with each other, and there was little the Army could do to control it. As my father gleefully pointed out, any time he and his colleagues wanted to speak freely, they took a hike in the mountains. As a double insurance of privacy—or when it was inconvenient to leave the post—all they had to do was to speak their native languages.

For my father, the dust, the censorship, the occasional water shortages were only nuisances. So far as he was concerned, he was living in an enchanted place, with a dedicated band of brothers—mostly physicists—fighting the good fight. What more could a man want? I understood my father's cryptic murmur when someone mentioned Los Alamos: *Posti belli.*

CHAPTER 3

War Heroes

At Los Alamos, my father and I shared a common fascination: the war. It was always there, like a bass accompaniment to our lives. In those pre-television days, the war to me meant mostly long columns of black type and grainy photographs in newspapers; or wider pages of type and bigger, grainy photographs in books and magazines. The war was also brightly colored posters at school and at the post office and colorful ads in the magazines. Occasionally the images took on sound and movement in the rare times when my parents took me to the movies.

But mostly we heard about the war. Listening to the news was a family ritual. At noon and in the evenings we gathered around the radio in the little alcove just off the kitchen that served as a dining area. The window overlooked the street. We could watch my father's colleagues walking by on their way home from the lab. "There goes Vicki [Weisskopf]. There goes Bob [Brode]," my father would announce. His own bulletins (occasionally spiced with a snide remark or appraisal) overrode those of the newscaster: "I see 'the great X' approaching." " 'Count Y' is late today." "There goes the Ugly Poodle."

My father and I didn't see eye to eye about the war. To me,

the news always sounded hopeful. Our side was winning. "The
Allies made new gains today on the Pacific front as American
bombers swept over . . . In the European theater, Allied tanks
blasted German positions near . . ." the newscaster twanged. My
father shook his head. During the dark, early days of the war, he
followed Allied reverses incredulously. With such an arsenal,
with thousands of planes and tanks, ships and guns, millions of
men and supplies, the Allies *had* to prevail in the long run. As
the tide turned in their favor, he became impatient. Temporary
reverses, like the Battle of the Bulge during the winter of 1944,
appalled him. Why was it taking so long? But then, he philoso-
phized, as he had learned from his year of military service in
Italy, generals were bound to be mediocre or incompetent; otherwise, they would have chosen another calling. When he was
stationed in Spoleto, he recalled, his superiors looked dashing in
their uniforms; they rode splendidly on horseback. "But just ask
them about calculating the trajectory of a cannon shell . . ." he
snorted. "They always asked me." He sounded as if he expected
the Allied generals to turn to him, too.

I regarded his attitudes as vaguely unpatriotic—and his ex-
pertise as more than a little suspect. I had seen photographs of
him in uniform. The tall hats, the high black shining boots, the
stiff collars of Italian military uniforms of the early 1920s looked
old-fashioned, out of style, as manly as operetta costumes. I much
preferred the American uniforms that I saw all around me: the
overseas caps, the snappy Eisenhower jackets. I also remembered
the revelation—and my humiliation—before my kindergarten
teacher when we still lived in Berkeley. My father had been a
general, I boasted confidently to her when my mother invited
Miss Stewart to tea one afternoon. My mother looked shocked
and a little embarrassed; he had been a lieutenant, training to be
an officer, she corrected. He had been too young to serve in
World War I. So, I concluded privately, what could he know
about war?

For my father the war represented gloom and doom, impatience and frustration. For me the war was a daily adventure, an opportunity for heroism. In my war, the "good guys," the right side, the Yanks, the American side (with some help from their allies) battled from victory to victory. Day by day we fought toward the great time—a dim and distant one—when we would finally win. Then the war would be over. I had doubts that I could bring my father over to my point of view. I discovered gradually, as most children do, that he had his world, as I had mine. At points—while we listened to the news or when we went on a Sunday outing, for example—our worlds overlapped. Much of the time, however, we went our separate ways. Unless we were talking about schoolwork, especially about math, my father didn't often seem to be curious about my world—including my contribution to the war effort.

At school, at home, at play, I conscientiously did my part for our side. I bought red victory stamps with the engraving of the Minuteman statue on them; I learned the virtues of victory gardens and at home urged my mother to save fats. From posters and magazine advertisements, I became alert to the dangers of spies and saboteurs and reminded everyone that "Loose lips sink ships." To the tune of "My Bonnie Lies Over the Ocean," I lustily sang songs like:

> A jeep lost its driver in battle,
> Kept on fighting enemy tanks.
> It pushed them all down in a canyon,
> And then gave three cheers for the Yanks.

> CHORUS: Buy jeeps, Oh buy jeeps,
> And bring back my soldier to me, to me.
> Buy jeeps, oh buy jeeps,
> And bring back my soldier to me.

I also practiced combat. To my chagrin and that of my friends, we couldn't actually fight the war like real soldiers, so we battled the enemy in our imaginations. At school and at home, we drew battle scenes in which two-dimensional fighter planes—recognizably American by the big stars on their fuselages—strafed and bombed German tanks—recognizable by the swastikas on the turrets. There was no doubt what happened to the enemy. Our dotted lines traced the stream of bullets from the swooping aircraft to the tank; squiggly lines indicated explosions. For good measure, as we drew, we added sound effects: *"Neeyyarr"* as the plane swooped down on the enemy; *"Aaaahhhhh"* as the machine guns blazed; *"Puuh-puuh,"* as the tank exploded. Sometimes, as a variation, we made up super weapons. We drew complicated ray guns with fancy trigger mechanisms and special sights; we sketched out machines that looked suspiciously like ordinary cardboard boxes, yet mysteriously emanated death rays. We drew superbombs—or, rather, the glorious explosion that was their product. Such bombs, we knew, were designed by goggle-eyed mad scientists nothing like our fathers.

In "the woods," the stands of pines, bushes and boulders at the edge of the housing developments, we became our war heroes, American GIs or British Tommies. We blasted Nazis and "Japs," and, rarely, because we weren't sure who they were, Italian Fascists. We mimed dramatic deaths, in our imaginations a hundred times better than the best efforts of any Hollywood stuntman. In B-24 Liberators or B-17 Flying Fortresses or B-29 Superfortresses we flew imaginary high-altitude bombing runs over Germany or Japan. From the crests of the highest boulders—the scale was probably one foot of boulder for every 5,000 feet of imaginary altitude—we heaved our bomb loads of rocks, shot-putter-style, yelling, "Bombs away!"

When World War II became tiresome, we switched to the wars of the frontier, to Indians and Cowboys. We rode with the cavalry. We charged after Indians. Ours, of course, had nothing to do with the rather dull and peaceable ones we met in our everyday lives, the ones who worked as maids or technical help or did construction work. Leaping over logs, hurtling down from boulders, we charged after imaginary horse-mounted Sioux and Apaches, Cheyenne and Comanches, with long, trailing war bonnets of eagle feathers.

When I wasn't playing or drawing my war, I was reading about it. I devoured patriotic boys' adventure stories. My favorites were *Barry Blake of the Flying Fortresses* and *Dave Dawson at Dunkirk*. Like Barry Blake, as a patriotic young American, I dreamed of volunteering for the Army Air Corps. Naturally, as Barry did, I wanted to become a fighter pilot. If I had been rejected, as he was, I would have been happy to settle for piloting a B-17 Flying Fortress on bombing missions over Germany. When that tour was over, I would have transferred to the Pacific. There, as Barry did, I would have cleverly spotted and destroyed camouflaged secret Japanese military installations. Of course, I might have been wounded on that mission—such things happened. In compensation, I would have been proud to accept the medal that Barry Blake was awarded. Unlike Barry, however, I was not interested in the beautiful blond, blue-eyed hospital nurse whom he met while he was convalescing. I would not have accepted her invitation to "compare notes when the war is over."

I loved flying heroes like Barry Blake best, but I also admired the American Commando Dave Dawson and his British counterpart and chum, Freddy Farmer. I was confident that I, too, would have escaped miraculously from Dunkirk and then gone on to outwit the Nazis in North Africa.

As best I could, I trained for war, prepared for it, by studying the world around me. After all, I lived on a military post. I knew all about uniforms, ranks and insignias. I watched with pride when my pediatrician, Dr. Henry Barnett, appeared for the first time with captain's double bars in place of a lieutenant's single ones. To my mother's embarrassment, on the rare occasions when we went out to dinner I gawked at the uniforms, the campaign ribbons and the medals of fellow diners. I reveled in code names and the mysterious Los Alamos post office box address. I knew, for example, about the code names for prominent Los

Alamos scientists. I realized that "Nicholas Baker" was really Niels Bohr, the old man who spoke so softly that, like everyone else, I barely understood him; and that "Henry Farmer" was Enrico Fermi, Giulio's father, who drove an old black Plymouth sedan. (If my father had a code name, so far as I know he never had occasion to use it.) If anyone asked me where I lived or what my address was, I knew how to answer tersely: "Post Office Box 1663, Santa Fe, New Mexico." But I also knew the other euphemisms for Los Alamos, such as "the Hill." Occasionally that put me into conspiracy with strangers. Once, a woman asked me where I lived. When I answered with the post office box, she smiled and then nodded conspiratorially. "Oh, you live on the Hill. I work there."

I was particularly proud of my pass, which was required to get past the guard posts at the main entrances to Los Alamos. My first pass wasn't much to look at: a little white card with an identifying mug shot stapled to it, a few typewritten particulars, my clumsy childish signature at the bottom. (Later, passes were enclosed in plastic.) Unlike my father, who, I noticed, always looked bored or annoyed when the MPs at the guardhouse scanned his pass, I loved to show mine. I liked it especially when the guards gave me a quick glance to make sure that I was really me. In contrast to my father's scowl, I usually gave the MPs a friendly nod or even a salute, as Barry Blake or Dave Dawson might have.

My hunger for adventure and my training to be a hero eventually paid off— at least *I* thought so. Ironically, my pass provided the occasion. It happened one Sunday, when we'd left on an outing with the Fermis. As we approached the guardhouse at the main gate, I realized that I'd done something I'd never done before: I'd left my pass at home. My father grumbled, erupted. I was seven years old, he complained. Couldn't I even remember my pass? He glared accusingly at me, then at my mother in the backseat. Fermi, calm, impassive as always, appeared amused at the scene. As usual, the Basilisk was smoking and flaming. "Emi-

lio, *non ti scaldare tanto* [literally, Don't heat up so much]," Laura
Fermi said in her gentle, sweet voice.

Fermi stopped the car. What to do? Rather than go back to
the apartment, my father decided, they would smuggle me in and
out. He invited me to climb into the trunk of the car. I could
hardly wait. Not only would I redeem myself, but this was a deed
worthy of a Barry Blake or a Freddy Farmer. Over my mother's
protests, my father got out of the car and opened the trunk, and
I climbed in. I curled up next to the snow chains, the spare tire
and the old newspapers, rags and tools. "As long as he can
breathe in there," my father muttered and slammed down the
trunk lid. "*Can* you breathe in there?" His voice sounded flat,
muffled and a long way off. I tried taking a couple of deep
breaths. "Yes." Except for the gasoline smell, the air seemed
abundant. The car started up. In the dark I bumped along until
we came to the main gate. I held my breath. I could hear the
murmuring of voices as the guard checked the passes. Then the
car lurched down the road, around several turns, and came to a
stop. Mission accomplished, I thought; this was the moment
when Dave Dawson or Freddy Farmer got a firm handshake and
a sharp salute from his commanding officer—and perhaps a hint
of a medal to come. I got my father's stony face when he opened
the trunk. "Don't do it again," he said. Shame-faced, I promised
not to. Secretly I was delighted; I knew how Dave Dawson or
Freddy Farmer felt when his mission had been successfully
completed.

While I hoped that my father was noticing my contributions
to the war effort, I also watched for his. It wasn't easy to find
them. He didn't wear a uniform. He didn't seem to have much
to do with the soldiers—except to grumble from time to time
about "how stupid the military is." At times, however, I knew
he drove jeeps—my favorite military vehicle. More than the big
two-by-four trucks with canvas tops, the olive-drab Army buses
on which I rode to Santa Fe, the bulldozers that cleared a building site or scraped the roads, the pickups, the dump trucks and

water trucks, I loved jeeps. I often watched them on my way to school or the PX. Jeeps were casual, jaunty; they could scat around corners and roar down the unpaved roads, raising hell-for-leather clouds of dust. You could screech to a stop; jump out of them without opening and closing doors. When you were speeding down the road, you could nonchalantly rest your foot on the little running board and lean on your knee while the wind rushed through your hair. A jeep engine rumbled hoarsely, a wonderful restless, impatient, high-strung sound.

I talked so much about jeeps that one afternoon, to my surprise, my father showed up in front of our apartment at the wheel of one. He was even wearing his khaki combat jacket and his dark glasses. Never mind that they weren't the famous teardrop aviator's glasses; never mind that he had no insignia on his jacket; never mind that he told me to hold on tight and not to stick my foot out on the running board; never mind that he seemed annoyed that I was wearing my imitation soldier's cap and was sure that I would lose it; never mind that he took me to his laboratory in Pajarito Canyon, then left me for a while to check his experiment. I watched him proudly, enviously, as he absentmindedly shifted the gears and we wheeled down the dusty road. I didn't know what else he might be doing to win the war. Driving a jeep was enough for me.

In my imaginary world of war, my heroes were sometimes hurt or wounded. From my reading, I knew that heroes like Barry Blake might feel a searing sensation in one leg or a shoulder as a stray bullet grazed them. Despite their heroic struggles to keep their crippled bomber aloft, they passed out. When they woke up in the hospital, family, friends and the commanding officer surrounded the hero. The commanding officer, of course, finding it hard to keep sentiment and duty separate, said something cryptic and gruff, like "Well, Barry, that was a close one. Next time, be more careful. Anyway, the President wanted you to have this."

And with family, friends and blond, blue-eyed nurse beaming, the commanding officer pinned the medal to the hero's pajama top and gave him a firm handshake.

Somehow, my real-life adventures never turned out that way. For example, there was the time when what I intended as a bit of commando training went awry. Los Alamos was forever under construction, and in front of our fourplex were shiny sheet-metal pipes that were destined for the roofs. The pipes, about four feet in diameter, lay on their side. At one end, they were flanged where they would be secured to the roof. The flanges were razor sharp; the pipes shiny and smooth. As part of my commando training I decided that I had to balance on the pipe. My mother, standing on the porch, warned me not to. I negotiated the length of the pipe, anyway. She begged me to come in for lunch. "Just one more time," I told her. That last time, when I reached the end with the flange, I slipped and fell. I got up, guilty but triumphant. I knew my arm had brushed against that sharp flange, but I was certain that nothing had happened. Then I looked. A long, surgical gash, from just below my wrist to my elbow, split my forearm. I was bleeding profusely. My father was at work. My mother had the presence of mind to apply a tourniquet or I might have bled to death. Fortunately, our car was there and the hospital was only a few blocks away.

When I woke up, I realized I was in the hospital. The afternoon had somehow disappeared and it was evening. My left arm was swathed in bandages and I couldn't move it. My mother and father were watching me. I smiled weakly, as Barry Blake might have done. They did not smile back. They asked me how I was. I nodded casually, the way a hero might have done. My father didn't seem to notice. Instead, he explained that the doctors had given me an anesthetic and sewn up the cut. Then he launched into an interrogation. How could I have been so stupid as to play around that pipe? I thought of telling him about the commando training. Seeing his sullen and angry face, I thought better of it. I was fine, I said, and promptly threw up. When I had finished, my mother looked more grim and anxious than ever, but my father's face relaxed. A little smile of delight, of discovery played around his mouth. "Oh, *poverino* [poor little thing]," he said, to my surprise. I felt uneasy. From the way he was looking at me, it was as if I were a little monkey and he a medical researcher. He had made a breakthrough in his experiment. "Don't worry," he said. "It's only the ether—the anesthetic, you know. Don't worry, your sickness will pass." Comforted and relieved at this news, I promptly threw up again.

Twenty-five stitches were required to close the cut. Once the bandages and the cast came off, once the scar had healed, I came to appreciate that number. Like the long, meandering scar itself, the number impressed children and adults alike. There was another unexpected dividend. My parents entrusted me with a new mission. I was susceptible to the growth of keloids, a kind of scar tissue. To arrest the growth, I needed radiation treatment. For several months afterward, I got to ride the big olive-drab military bus alone to Santa Fe for my biweekly appointments with the radiologist.

The pipe episode, at least, had the potential of contributing to my development as a soldier, patriot and war hero. Other adventures, like the ringworm episode, had no such value, real or potential. Betsy Allen, our neighbor, who was about my age, caught the ringworm from her cat. My parents warned me not to play with Betsy until she had healed. I played with Betsy; I got ringworm. Naturally my parents were annoyed. Again my father comforted me as best he knew how. What I had on my head was nothing more fearful than a fungus, he explained. His eyes lighted up. It was like the rings of mushrooms that we found in the forests or in the meadows on our Sunday walks, he assured me. The fungus would die when it was deprived of its nutritive environment—the hair on my head, all of it, he said.

I didn't want all my hair shaved off, I protested. Even if I didn't, that's what would happen, my father predicted. He looked at me as if I were foolish to try to defy a perfectly natural process.

Anyway, my hair would grow back, he said. In the end, my father was right. For a while, the doctors treated the ringworm with salves, but they weren't effective. My head was shaved. For several weeks, I went to school with a sort of linen grandmother's nightcap. It had drawstrings, so that it fit snugly. Later I got a corduroy cap with a bill. As a special dispensation, I was allowed to wear it in class at school. The cap, however, did not fit as well as the grandmother's nightcap, and my classmates, especially during recess, had a way of rushing by and accidentally brushing against me—or, rather, against my cap. At best I had to reset it; at worst, it went flying into the dirt. I knew what was coming: a humiliating chorus of "Baldy, Baldy" or, even worse, "Baldy Four-eyes."

Imponderables, I discovered, also blocked my path to heroism—or at least the appearance of heroism. My heroes were tall, lean and lantern-jawed. They had broad shoulders and piercing eyes. For my age, I was tall and lean. I was too young for broad shoulders, but at least I could aspire to growing them. My eyes, however, were not and never would be piercing, any more than my father's were. Like him, I needed glasses. So I discovered during a routine eye screening at school when I was seven. I became a "four-eyes." My first pair of glasses came in a little brown cardboard box from Santa Fe. When I put them on for the first time, the little circle of gnats on the yellow kitchen wall clock became a ring of numbers. "Well, now you look like a little professor," Mrs. Perry, our neighbor downstairs, announced cheerfully when she first saw me.

I hated that professorial look. I wanted to look like a commando, not like my father. I hated the way the frames on my glasses faded from a clear flesh color to that of old parchment, or old mummy fingers, as I thought of them. Circles of old mummy fingers around my eyes did nothing to enhance my appearance, I decided. With glasses, I felt more vulnerable and fragile, and I had to be careful. When I got into fights, which was rare, I had to take my glasses off. At least then my opponent looked fuzzy and soft, easy to crush or pinch or knock over. To my father's irritation, my glasses also had a way of breaking. When the lens shattered, there was nothing to do but get another one. When the frame broke, my father patiently mended it with the help of acetone and rubber bands. No matter what the damage, or the source of it, he grumbled and glowered when he had to deal with it.

Why had this humiliation of glasses been visited on me? I was being punished, I concluded. My parents encouraged me to read and I loved books, especially my war adventure stories. At night, even after my mother had kissed me goodnight, I sometimes guiltily turned the reading lamp back on and darted a few more pages ahead. All that reading, especially late at night when I was supposed to be asleep, strained my eyes—or so I understood. All that sneak reading—together with the poor print of the comic books, my parents said—transformed me from a potential Barry Blake or a Dave Dawson into a four-eyes and a little professor. The comparison to my father did not ease my humiliation.

As the war dragged on, my father became more impatient about bringing it to an end. He appeared to be working harder than ever. Occasionally he would be gone overnight, yet I saw him nearly every day. He was often home for lunch and usually for dinner. Nevertheless, I sensed that, for the most part, he was more interested in his work than in me.

I did not know what it was that so absorbed him, but I did know where he worked. The Tech Area, near the center of the post, was a cluster of unassuming, green, two-story buildings behind a Cyclone fence topped by barbed wire. Only once did I go inside the fence. That was when I was given a small initial dose of radiation to retard the growth of the scar tissue on my left arm, the one I'd sliced open on the pipe.

Whatever my father was doing in his laboratory did not strike me as very interesting. Electronic equipment—meters, gauges, wires, oscilloscopes, cords—cluttered the rooms. Everything looked makeshift or half finished. My father's colleagues, some of them graduate students from Berkeley, greeted me cheerfully enough. In their rumpled lab coats, or in their shirtsleeves, with pencils and pens stuffed in their breast pockets, they looked haggard and scruffy. They twisted the dials on their oscilloscopes or hooked up one wire to another; they jotted numbers in their notebooks and on their yellow pads. Their work did not seem in the least as glamorous as, say, that of the MP in his snappy uniform, checking passes at the gate. Only when the first bomb was actually dropped on Hiroshima, August 6, 1945, did I realize that while my friends and I had been drawing superbombs, my father and his colleagues had been building one.

What his role had been remained hazy to me. I had a hard time connecting the clutter of oscilloscopes and wiring, the adding machines and the Greek letters on the blackboard at his lab, the seemingly endless conversations with his colleagues on his Sunday outings, with the explosion brighter than a thousand suns. Only as an adult did I finally grasp what he had done.

Briefly put, his research was critical in determining the nature of the fissionable or explosive material in the bomb. The atomic bomb derived its explosive energy from unleashing the forces of the atom. The theoretical basis for such a weapon had been known since the turn of the century, when physicists Henri Becquerel and Marie Curie discovered radioactivity, the spontaneous, uncontrollable breakdown of the nucleus of an atom with the emission of particles and rays. Atoms were no longer immutable and perhaps not impenetrable. If there was natural radioactivity, could it also be induced? scientists wondered. Could atoms be transformed, "artificial radioactivity" be created, new elements formed, by bombarding atoms with particles such as neutrons or protons? Fermi and "the boys of the Via Panisperna" were among the many physicists who followed this line of research. Lawrence's cyclotron at Berkeley was one of the tools for carrying out these experiments.

In exploring the properties of various elements, scientists also discovered that certain ones, like uranium, are highly unstable when they are bombarded. The nuclei of certain forms of uranium split into two more or less equal parts, a process known as fission. This results in a small loss of mass and a tremendous burst of energy, much as Einstein had predicted when he argued in his theory of relativity that mass and energy are related. Moreover, the uranium fission initiates a chain reaction. As each uranium atom splits under bombardment, it releases neutron "bullets," which in turn strike other nuclei and liberate still more neutrons. In a fraction of a second, billions of neutrons can be produced as bullets. This is what happens in an uncontrolled chain reaction. The explosion of an atomic bomb is a chain reaction.

The goal at Los Alamos was to create a weapon based on these principles. The fissionable material, or "fuel," had already been decided upon: uranium 235 or plutonium 239. Enormous problems remained to be resolved, however. How much fissionable material would be needed? How pure would it have to be? How should it be arranged? What density, what shape, what mass were necessary for the device to explode at the right time? How was the bomb to be triggered?

This was where my father's research was critical. First in Palermo and then at Berkeley, he had studied artificial radioactivity. His work had focused on natural or spontaneous fission—naturally occurring fission without neutron bombardment—in uranium and plutonium. The measurements were difficult because of the small samples he had to work with. At Los Alamos, during the fall of 1943, he continued this research. The work was critical in determining how pure the fissionable material had to be and the nature of the "gun" mechanism that would start the chain reaction. With his group of coworkers, most of them graduate students or recent Ph.D.s, my father found that the spontaneous fission rate for natural uranium was about the same as it had been in Berkeley. For U-235, however, the rate was much higher. By December 1943, my father had a hunch. He theorized that cosmic rays at that altitude—Los Alamos was at 7,200 feet; Berkeley at sea level—made the difference. Shield out the stray neutrons and the U-235 bomb core could be purified less rigorously than had been assumed. Pre-detonation would be less likely. The gun that assembled the U-235 to critical mass would need less muzzle velocity and could be significantly shorter and lighter than had been anticipated. The device could easily be loaded into a four-engine B-29 bomber.

Was there anything heroic about this work? What could be courageous or valiant about twisting a few dials, monitoring some mysterious clicks, scribbling in notebooks, calculating with a slide rule? I didn't really find out until I reached high school and took physics myself.

I dreaded the sessions in the labs. I remembered my father working in his lab at LeConte and the Los Alamos Tech Area. I knew what I was supposed to do in my lab: I would hook up this apparatus to that and read the dials, record the numbers, do some simple calculations. Yet I tended to procrastinate, to be too careful. How could you trust those dials, those numbers? I wondered. What did they mean? I knew what they were supposed to mean—at least according to my teachers and my textbook. The laws of gravity or electricity or magnetism were at work. The steel ball rolling faster and faster down the inclined plane and the needle swinging on the voltmeter proved it. Yet my faith in these signs was tenuous. Like a peasant listening to his priest, I believed because I was told to. The only law I really had any faith in was Murphy's. Sure enough, whatever could go wrong with my experiments usually did. My steel ball never rolled as fast as it was supposed to; the needle on my voltmeter never twitched in the right direction. To spend a lifetime fumbling about in such uncertainty and disbelief appeared inconceivable to me. I didn't have the audacity, persistence, determination, precision to persevere in such a world. My father did. Thanks to these qualities, step by step, he and his colleagues built a device that ended the war and revolutionized human history. That, I concluded, showed true grit and I admired it.

I often pondered where my father got these qualities. What carried him through an enterprise like his research at Los Alamos? Was he inherently a precise and careful man? Not really, I thought, although he aspired to be. He often admired colleagues who were far more careful and precise than he was.

"You should see how Clyde [Wiegand] put together that bit of apparatus," he would say. "Really clean, exact, all the wiring just right."

Around the house, around his family, however, he liked to give the impression that he was precise. "Please get the garden scissors out of the cabinet," my mother would say to him. "Which shelf or which drawer?" my father would answer, mostly to heckle her. "The cabinet in the garage, you know," my mother would say. "But is it the third from the top or the second from the bottom? And is it on the right or the left?" my father would reply. In exasperation, my mother would often fetch the garden scissors herself. Or my father would go to the grocery store for my mother or, after she died, for my stepmother. "Please get what I need for duck à l'orange," my stepmother once told him. He came back with precisely one duck and one orange.

How much of his success was due to persistence and determination? He often credited his achievements to those qualities. Many of his colleagues, beginning with Fermi, of course, were much more gifted than he was, he said. They had better, faster, sharper minds; their intuitions sprouted good ideas like mushrooms after a rain in the forest; their talent for mathematics far outclassed his. To compensate for all these shortcomings, he said, he had his modest talent. The rest was mostly persistence, perseverance, hard work.

He never entirely convinced me. Persistence and determination? Those were the virtues of a drudge, of a drone, not of a brilliant, active, restless mind like his, and I remembered how his face lit up when he first tried to explain how the atomic bomb worked. I recalled how he looked at the refraction of light in a pitcher of water or the brilliant colors of a rainbow after a storm at Los Alamos. "Isn't that pretty?" he would say. He meant the colors or the magic way a stick or a glass stirring rod looked bent in the water. But he meant something else. He knew why the rainbow appeared, why the stick looked bent, and that, too, for him, was "pretty." At the bottom of it all, I concluded, was something simple and basic: he was curious, as any child is naturally curious. He loved knowing how and why the natural world around him worked, and he dared to find out. That was why he plunged ahead with his dials and his notebooks; why he fussed so carefully with his apparatus; why he faced the frustrations of dead ends and failed experiments. He succeeded, I decided, because inside the man, the eminent researcher, the Nobel laureate, was the child who dared to ask why.

Among my war heroes at Los Alamos, women did not rank high. They did not fly fighters or go on commando raids. For the war effort, they did the sorts of things that women, mothers, girls were supposed to do: they bandaged and cared for the wounded men, as the nurse in the Barry Blake story did; they taught second and third grade, as my teachers, Mrs. Hillhouse and Mrs. Marshak, did; they riveted together destroyers and cargo ships, as I knew some of my friends' mothers had done before they moved to Los Alamos; they saved fats and planted victory gardens and gave their children dimes to buy savings stamps, as my mother did. Although it did not occur to me at the time, they also served at Los Alamos—as my mother did.

When wives arrived at Los Alamos, when they discovered the high fence around the post, the garrison-style living, the forty miles that might have been four hundred between the mesa and Santa Fe, some broke down and cried. Others took to drink. My mother did neither. She rarely cried. That would have violated her sense of self-discipline, of toughness, of being able to take life's hard knocks and surprises. Nor would she have considered taking to the bottle. In my mother's world, one did not do these things. But what she thought of Los Alamos, I couldn't say, for my mother's life seemed to be made up of things she did not say, especially about herself. "Here we're doing the usual things," her letters, always sent regularly to me, noted regularly in later life. "*What* usual things? Most of all, how do you *feel* about them?" I often felt like shouting at her.

I have few pictures of her from Los Alamos. In my mind's eye, I see her, a woman of medium height, with gray eyes, wearing a blouse, a skirt, an apron. Her dark brown hair is up. She was heavier then than in later life, ample around the hips, with the substance of someone you can count on. She doesn't smile often. She's constantly moving around the house, doing. There's my father's shirt to be ironed or his socks to be mended, the kitchen to be swept, dishes to be washed, my father's papers to be filed, a translation to be done from her native German into English. For a while at Los Alamos, she worked as a secretary for my father's research group. With him, she compiled a current isotope chart, a Segrè Chart, as it was called. Of course, there was lunch and dinner to be taken care of (my father often said she deserved the Nobel Prize for cooking), and someone had to keep an eye on her baby daughter, Amelia, and find time to read to her son from the book of Bible stories. In the evenings after dinner, at last, she allowed herself to sit down in the living room with my father and have a cigarette while he puffed on his pipe or on a cigar.

I also hear her clearly, the deference in her voice, as in "I'll ask Papà." I sense her admiration for her brilliant, clever husband, her gratitude that he stole time from his important work to take their son fishing: "Isn't that nice of him?" In those phrases, I can hear her trying to convince me, as she did all her life, that I should appreciate how fortunate I am to have such a brilliant "Papà." If I whine or groan that "fishing's no fun," or if I complain that the hikes are always too long, I hear her toughness, her self-reliance, her discipline. "Stop complaining. You'll just have to make do." I know my father admires her for these traits, for this tough love that she has for me.

Making do was nothing new to her. She was used to sudden shocks, to being uprooted and starting all over. Los Alamos was her third major move in less than a decade. She grew up in Poland, the daughter of a middle-class grain merchant. Her family was German and Jewish; the world around them was Polish and Catholic. She completed her secondary-school education with taunts of "Jew" echoing in her head. In January 1933, Hitler became chancellor of Germany. For the next dozen years she had to reckon with that fact. A few months after Hitler came to power, she left Nazi Germany for Fascist Italy, where she made a new life as a secretary and translator.

In Rome, she met a dark-haired, intense young physicist, subject to outbursts of temper, named Emilio Segrè. She was a brunette with short hair and hazel eyes, pretty enough to turn the heads of Fascist Party bigwigs like old Marshal Emilio De Bono, who followed her on the street one day. The intense young physicist admired her vigor, her intelligence and her ability to jump into icy cold lakes when they hiked in the Dolomites. He courted her, invited her on trips to the hilltowns outside Rome, taught her to play bocce. He courted her, but not always with honeyed words. He was nearly thirty; she was twenty-seven. He was ready for marriage, he said. He was also convinced that Fascist Italy was no place to raise a family; nor, for that matter, was a Europe in which Hitler might prevail. "We've got to pull up stakes, we've got to get out of here," he announced. Though I don't know if he told my mother this at the time, he complained that his Italian girlfriends did not find such talk romantic. "Oh, no, Mamma, Papà, *il caffè*," he used to say, mocking them. They couldn't leave Mamma and Papà; they couldn't give up their cappuccino in bed in the morning. The young German refugee woman, Elfriede Spiro, showed no such reluctance. She had to pull up stakes again and she had the strength and courage to do

so. In February 1936 she married the temperamental physicist
and aspiring university professor. In March of the following year,
she bore him a blond, blue-eyed son. To distinguish him from
her husband's nephew (also named Claudio), hers was nicknamed
Claudio "Il Gotico" (the Goth).

In 1938, while traveling to Berkeley alone for a brief summer's
research trip, he was fired from his job as a professor at the
University of Palermo because he was Jewish. From the United
States he cabled my mother to leave Italy immediately. "If you
believe that it's necessary to take the Big Step, you have my full
support," she cabled in reply in German; then, in Italian, in a
letter, "If we have to start over, I'll be beside you with all my
support." Other than that, I have no record of what my mother
thought, of her doubts and fears about once again starting over,
of her anguish about leaving behind her family in Germany. (My
two aunts survived the war, but my grandparents perished in a
concentration camp.) It was another occasion for my mother not
to say things, especially about herself.

Dutifully she packed and with her Aryan-looking baby boy
sailed from Palermo during the height of the Munich crisis.
Czechoslovakia was partitioned. In news photographs of the day,
Hitler, Mussolini and British Prime Minister Neville Chamberlain glared at the cameras like gangsters or backroom abortion-
ists. War appeared imminent. My father in California read the
papers, terrified that the ship would be interned at Gibraltar for
the duration of the conflict. The crisis blew over, the ship landed
safely in New York. For once, my father's gloom and pessimism
were justified and might well have saved her life and mine, my
mother often intimated. So, with her husband and a new baby,
my mother settled first in a provincial university town, Berkeley,
California, on the shores of the Pacific, on the western edge of
America; then, in 1943, shortly after she had borne a baby daughter, she moved again, this time to a secret military post in the
mountains of New Mexico. It was one of those states in the far
West of America, one of the ones that bordered on Mexico, she
might have written to her relatives.

It was not an easy move. In Berkeley, she had a modest, but attractive two-story, four-bedroom house, cream-colored with dark brown trim; she had a garden in which apple, apricot and plum trees bloomed white and pink in the spring; rose bushes and camellias bordered the sloping front lawn, where her son was forever rolling around and getting grass stains on his jeans. In Los Alamos, she had an upstairs three-bedroom apartment with paper-thin walls. For a garden there was the raw land cleared away by the Army bulldozers. In Berkeley, she had a real gas stove. At Los Alamos, she fussed dutifully—and only briefly—with a Black Beauty woodstove; then, as most wives did, she made do with electric hot plates. In Berkeley, there was always plenty of running water. There were telephones and dentists, a dry cleaner and convenient grocery shopping. Eventually these amenities reached Los Alamos—but it took time. In Berkeley, where she had a piano, her son drifted off to sleep at night listening to her wrestle with Bach's inventions, Xavier Xarwenka's "Scarf Dance" and, most lyrical of all, Chopin's preludes. In the preludes, she seemed to let out a warmth, a sweetness and lyricism that she seldom permitted herself in her daily life. At Los Alamos, there was no piano at home.

How did she do it? How did she make those moves, from continent to continent, from country to country, from university town to military outpost? How did she cope with hot plates to cook on and with no telephone? In memory, when I hear my mother's voice, it is saying, in her native German, *Man muss* (one must), or, as I once heard her insist with a French bellboy who balked at handling our baggage, *il faut*. With my mother, duty always seemed to be calling. Undoubtedly, her "Prussian upbringing"—as my father called it—explained a good deal. He teased her about it; he was also proud of her sense of duty and order, and delighted when my sisters and I showed signs of it. "The girls have a good sense of *Pflicht* [duty]." So he wrote on a Swiss elementary-school admissions application one year when we were abroad on one of his sabbatical leaves. He wanted to write "a Prussian sense of duty," but knowing how much that would have infuriated my mother, thought better of it. For her, such a phrase stirred girlhood memories of taking walks while holding a stick flat against her back so that she would stand up straight. Perhaps because of such experiences, my mother rarely talked about her childhood; perhaps that was why her life was so often filled with things she did not talk about.

My mother always made do, and managed to care for us all. Settling in Los Alamos was not as alien as moving to Krypton. There was a lively musical life—mostly amateur. Edward Teller, for example, was known for practicing the piano late at night. A low-power radio station began broadcasting on Christmas Eve, 1943. It drew on several of the scientists' excellent classical music record collections, including Oppenheimer's. Occasionally there were live performances. Perhaps Los Alamos was an American Army outpost, and there were lots of gum-chewing American soldiers around; but there were also plenty of German, British, Italian accents that she recognized, friends she had met in Berkeley or even in Italy. In such a young (the average age at Los Alamos was twenty-six) and high-spirited community, parties were plentiful. There were also regular social activities such as square-dancing sessions, though my father was never one for parties, and my mother probably dismissed square-dancing as "too American." Nor was my mother much of a joiner or an activist. She heard how Edward Teller's wife, Mici, and some other neighborhood women, intent on saving trees as part of a playground for their children, sat down in front of an invading Army bulldozer. "Exaggerated," my mother sniffed of the protest. She frowned on the inevitable gossip in such a tight community, claimed to be above it. She probably savored morsels now and then anyway, and passed them around: who had been drinking too much at a party, or was said to be drinking too much; who had an impossible ego; who was blowing up little privileges—or lack of them—out of all proportion. As my father did, she loved the mountains around Los Alamos, the wildflowers, the icy lakes and streams, the skiing in the winter. She did not share his passion for trout fishing, which she found boring and solitary.

What she thought about the explosion at Hiroshima, the fruit of her husband's work, I don't know. Probably she shared his satisfaction and relief. The device had worked, but it had been a close thing. Probably, like him, she was disappointed that the bomb was not turned against the Nazis, who had exacted such a terrible price on her and her family.

What she thought about her bespectacled son—bright, inquisitive, enthusiastic (especially about anything that had to do with war and the military)—I don't know. She was there to listen to him when he came home from school. Her face lit up at moments like the one when he explained enthusiastically that he was learning to alphabetize words. Better that, she probably thought, than all his talk about the model airplanes and ships that he glued together out of pine wood kits; better if he had drawn fewer war pictures and talked less of uniforms and medals. She'd had enough of that in her childhood and had spent a good part of her life reaping the consequences. Better if he listened to her more attentively. If only he had, he might have avoided the ringworm episode and especially the gash on his arm.

Nor do I know what she thought about her son's relationship with his father. She had a hard time bringing the two together, and that troubled her. At least they went off fishing and took an occasional jeep ride. At least, the father showed an interest in his son's schoolwork. She spent time reading aloud to the boy. It was one of the ways she knew how to be warm and comforting to him. Her husband had little time or patience for that sort of thing. He was absorbed in his work, important work. Anyway, she had her baby daughter to think of, and by 1944 she was pregnant again. My mother made do; with her, there was always something to do, something else to be done.

CHAPTER 4

All-American Boy

When we lived in Los Alamos, my parents often spoke of another never-never land. It was called Europe. I'd first heard about it when we still lived in Berkeley. "These California lupins are almost as beautiful as those around Tivoli," my father would say on spring Sundays when we walked through splashes of wild-flowers in the hills. Or: "This Bob Hope. I don't understand him. He isn't funny like Petrolini [an Italian comedian] or Charlie Chaplin," he would complain at a movie or during a radio program.

"Those *frankfurters*," my mother would correct me, whenever I asked for a hot dog. "They taste like boiled rubber," she would mutter, making a face as if she were biting into a piece of old tire.

And so it went. In Europe, oranges were juicier, wines had more bouquet, music was deeper, blackberries more succulent, mushrooms more aromatic. In Europe, people were better educated, had better manners, were more sincere. They didn't chew gum and drawl and say, "Glad to meet you," when they really weren't. Even the buildings in Europe were more original. After all, my parents pointed out, Berkeley's famous landmark—the

64

university's trademark—the Campanile, was only an imitation of an Italian bell tower, like Saint Mark's in Venice.

Yet when I was alone or at school or with my friends, I looked carefully at the lupins and poppies on the Berkeley hillsides; I thought they were lovely. I laughed at Bob Hope and Danny Kaye. I savored the taste of hot dogs and peppermint gum, and I thought my parents' European friends were as boring as their American ones. It was as if I lived in two different worlds. With my parents, my family, I was sure that my world at home, or in Europe, was much better. When I was with my teachers, my friends, the American way beckoned. Los Alamos was no different. I was forever trying to figure out who we were as a family — or, at least, who we were not.

We were not, for example, like our neighbors in apartment T-170. We shared the upstairs floor—and thus a porch—with the Allens, but not their standards of decorum and public morals. On sunny days, my mother sometimes blocked off the stairway with a little gate and the upstairs porch turned into an ideal playpen. There, my two-year-old sister, Amelia, pranced around in the buff. This did not sit well with Mrs. Allen, a short, chubby woman who moved with a slight waddle. When she looked at me, she always squinted through her left eye, as if to save herself the energy of opening the right one. When she saw my sister in all her pristine glory, however, Mrs. Allen opened both eyes and offered some neighborly observations to my mother. Passing Indian and "Meskin" youths sometimes pointed at my sister, then giggled among themselves and jabbered to each other in Spanish, Mrs. Allen told my mother. In Mrs. Allen's view, this was the wrong sort of exposure if a little girl was to grow up to become a lady.

On another occasion, I threatened her daughter Betsy's morals by exposing her to the dreaded "*f* word." The problem was, which *f* word? *I* claimed that when I blamed Betsy for giving me ringworm, I'd said nothing more than "*Pfui! Pfui! schäm' dich!* [Yuck, yuck, shame on you!],*" a German nursery rhyme that I'd learned from my mother. The Allens, however, were convinced that I'd used a very different *f* word, a staple in the vocabulary of virtually every soldier on the post, they indicated delicately. My father did not understand. Annoyed and bewildered, he finally turned to an American colleague and old friend from Berkeley, Robert Brode—in my father's view, an authority on American cultural arcana. *"Pfui!,"* Bob assured my father, violated no canons of taste and breached no public decorum—at least in English. On the other hand, if I'd used the *f* word, I really shouldn't have—at least not in English. Which term had I used? In what language? In a halfhearted way, my father quizzed me. He explained the differences in terminology, as if he weren't too sure himself. He then strongly urged me to find a different playmate.

Nor were we like the Olmsteads, who lived directly below us. In the first place, they had four children. In my parents' view, that was too many, even if they were all close to my age and provided me with a wide choice of playmates. Also, in my parents' opinion, Mrs. Olmstead wore too much makeup. Her thin, pale skin hugged her high cheekbones, which she accentuated with blush. She used eye shadow and eyeliner and made her mouth too red with lipstick. She reminded me of the women on the covers of the movie magazines she read. Her husband, Tom, was very good-looking, I thought—good-looking enough to be one of General Claire Chennault's "Flying Tigers" fighter aces. In fact, the dark leather jacket that Tom often wore reminded me of the kind I'd seen real Flying Tigers pilots wearing when I came across their photographs. I also liked the way Tom sometimes winked at me when I saw him drinking a beer at the PX. Tom, however, had a habit of drinking more than one beer and staying out late—or so I understood from my parents. His good looks, his Flying Tigers jacket and his friendly wink did not, in my parents' view, justify his penchant for coming home at three o'clock in the morning to practice his trombone.

Nor were we like the Perrys, who lived downstairs in apartment B. My parents appreciated the Perrys. My father called them *"brava gente"* (good people). They had only two children. They did not drink—not even coffee or tea. They did not attend wild parties. Mrs. Perry did not wear makeup, and she suggested that my mother read Bible stories to me from *Egermeier's Bible Story Book.* When I sliced my arm and my mother had to rush me to the hospital, Mrs. Perry was the one who helped my mother tie the tourniquet. "Just lean against me," Mrs. Perry said very calmly, as we climbed in the car, and I knew from her voice that everything would be all right.

Nevertheless, we differed with the Perrys on how to spend Sundays. We dressed in our old clothes and went for a hike. The Perrys dressed literally in their Sunday best and attended religious services. Their denomination was a new one to me, and it sounded grand: the Church of Jesus Christ of Latter-Day Saints. After church, they often had visitors—usually elderly gentlemen with white hair, in dark suits. That part of their Sunday appealed to me less. I was allowed to invite the Perrys' oldest son, Douglas, on one of our Sunday outings. Once. After that, Mrs. Perry asked that he not be invited again—"never on Sunday," she said.

But were we like the Fermis? That was tricky. They were Europeans, even Italians, and yet they didn't do things the way we did.

"You know what Giulio Fermi did the other day?" I overheard my mother say to my father one evening as they were sitting in the living room. Giulio, Enrico Fermi's son, was about my age and a friend of mine, so I pricked up my ears. My mother's fingers flew back and forth over the sock she was darning. My father was reading the newspaper and smoking a cigar. "First of all, he calls himself 'Jud,' " my mother said incredulously. She repeated, " 'Jud.' It sounds like 'mud.' " Her voice sounded flat and gooey, as if she'd just stepped in some. "Anyway, 'Jud' came home with a friend of his, yelling, 'Pass the eats! Pass the eats!' Can you imagine? Yelling at his mother like that? She told him, 'That's no way to talk. Ask politely.' He was more polite, but he

still said, 'Pass the eats.' That's not even English, is it?" My
mother sounded appalled, yet uncertain. She looked at my father,
always the source of knowledge, but she also stole a glance
at me.

I shook my head authoritatively. English was one area, at least,
in which I knew something, sometimes even more than my father. "Pass the eats" was incorrect, of course. Yet secretly I admired Giulio's courage at using such a racy (to my ears)
expression—and at calling himself Jud. I didn't like the rhyme
with "mud," but it sounded more terse, masculine, American,
than Giulio—safer, too. What teachers did to his name when
they first encountered it on a class roster was even worse than
what they did to mine. The clear, singing vowels of Giulio were
transmuted into grunts and moans: "Gew-leeo" or "Goo-ee-
leeo." The most I'd dared call myself was Claude, but no fighter
pilot would have a name like that. I also liked Giulio because he
was growing tall, fast. Soon he would overshadow his stocky father. I found this comforting. If Jud and I didn't know much, or
used American slang, or violated parental standards in other
ways, at least we could grow faster and taller than our parents.

My father puffed on his cigar. "Fermi's become so American
that he votes Republican. He also studies the comics. He says it
helps him understand American culture," he said. I still remember the condescension in my father's voice. It was one of those
rare occasions when he didn't refer to Fermi with respect, even
awe. Instantly I felt sympathy with Giulio's father, who normally
didn't pay much attention to me. At least he was trying to be
American. My parents, it seemed to me, were not—and they
were proud of it.

I never knew quite what to do. Even if the way we did things
at home was different, "European," my parents certainly never
objected to my playing with American children. There weren't
many others at Los Alamos, anyway, except a handful who were
the sons and daughters of British visitors. Besides, even they, like
all the children of new immigrants, like me, like Giulio Fermi,

took on the trappings of Americans. So I was free to play with Frankie or Gladys or Mary or Diane Olmstead from downstairs, even if their father did practice the trombone at irregular hours; or with Dimas Chavez, who lived just up the hill, spoke better Spanish than English, and whose father was a maintenance worker. Of course, I could play with them. My parents had fled Europe so that I would be free to play with any kid I liked. Yet there was an unspoken message: I could play with them, as long as I didn't forget our way, the right way, the best way, the European way, of doing things.

Even if I wasn't always sure how to behave, I liked going to other children's houses. It was a little like exploring foreign, maybe even enemy territory, as a secret agent would. I never knew how much to tell my parents of my discoveries. They often asked me about what I'd done at my friend's house—or, at least, my mother did. My mother's comments, like her disapproval of Giulio Fermi's slang, produced awkward moments. I learned when to tell part of the story and when to maintain a discreet silence.

I told my parents about Billy Hunter, my best friend in third grade. He was small, dark, thoughtful. But I didn't tell them that his parents were divorced—something that I knew people in my family did not do. I also passed lightly over my observations of Billy's teenage sister, known as "Peaches." I was sure that my parents would not approve of her any more than they approved of Mrs. Olmstead, for Peaches, too, wore bright lipstick and painted her nails a fire-engine red. Peaches wore bobby sox and a man's shirt with the shirttails trailing across her small and shapely buttocks; she listened to Big Band music on the radio, like that of Glenn Miller, and hummed a song that went, "Chickery chick, chilla, chilla, chickalaroma inna bananica, bollica wollica can't you see, chickery chick is me"—definitely not my mother's musical taste, which defined "good music" as the classics.

I did tell my parents about my friend Neil Marcus—or at least part of the story. He was pale, sleepy-looking and shy. Like me, he wore glasses. It was a long time before he invited me over to play at his house. The first time, I remember, was around Christmas. There was snow on the ground and I worried—as my mother had taught me—that my black rubber galoshes might drip on the floor when I took them off just inside the door.

What we did at Neil's house was not unusual. Board games like Monopoly, Parchesi and checkers were all familiar to me. So were the model airplanes, miniatures in plastic, or in pine wood, of American B-17 and B-25 bombers, German Messerschmitts, British Spitfires, and Japanese Zero fighters. I had models like them myself. I knew how to simulate aerial dogfights and bombing raids and how to argue loudly about who had shot down whom first. I knew that Neil's father was a doctor—an occupation that my parents approved of.

I noticed, however, that it was Christmastime and there was no tree in Neil's living room, as we had in ours. I asked him why. "We're Jewish," Neil explained.

I nodded, as if I knew all about religion. I did. In Berkeley, we lived just down the street from a Presbyterian church. On Sundays, when I mowed the front lawn, I watched people dressed in their best clothes file into the church. I pushed the lawn mower back and forth to the strains of the organ and the choir singing "Rock of Ages." When I asked my mother about what people did in church and why we didn't go, she said that it was a waste of time. People were supposed to be finding God; instead, they spent their time gossiping and socializing. I also knew that we were not Mormons like the Perrys. On the other hand, on Mrs. Perry's recommendation, my mother read to me about the "Israel-eets"—as she called them—from the crimson-covered collection of Bible stories for children. I knew enough to write "Protestant" beside the blank next to "religious preference" when I filled out forms at school. When I told my parents that, they looked at each other and my father shrugged, as if that was all right with him. So, when I returned from Neil

Marcus's house and told my parents that he didn't have a Christmas tree, I expected another shrug from my father. Instead, he turned to my mother and spoke to her in German, the parental code that I couldn't break. Being Jewish, I sensed, was one of those topics that invited silence.

Who *was* I like? Where *did* I belong? Was Europe really so much better? At Los Alamos I began to develop my own opinions about Europe and Europeans. So far as I knew, most of them were physicists. No matter who they were, Italians like Fermi and Bruno Rossi, Germans like Hans Bethe, Austrians like Victor Weisskopf, Swiss like Hans Staub, or Hungarians like Edward Teller, all had thick accents. I assumed that when they were in Europe, in that wondrous land, they looked less scruffy than the way I saw them. I doubted that they'd pay any more attention to me, even if I met them in Europe. Most of them—at least the men—had little to say to me, a child of six or seven, except to pat me on the head. Few even bothered to raise old chestnuts like what I was doing in school, or what my hobbies were. And what could I say to them? What did I know about physics or poetry or politics, anyway?

To me, it appeared that they viewed the world from a distance; they watched the world instead of being in it. With their mechanical pencils, they were forever scribbling on the backs of envelopes or napkins and talking in Greek—at least the letters were Greek ("If sigma stands for the scattering cross section, then . . ."). They scrawled their mysterious formulas. Their world, it seemed to me, was as distant as another galaxy. But at least I could picture a galaxy—space, darkness, burning stars. The world of the Greek letters and the formulas on the envelopes was nothing I could even imagine.

At times I wondered: were there other kinds of Europeans, like the Indians and the construction workers that I met, the Okies and the Texans and the Mexicans? Occasionally I heard about faithful maids who had worked for my mother in Italy. I knew about "Lella" (Elia Palma), a tough peasant woman from the Abruzzi. She had skin the color of varnished oak and a gold-toothed smile. In photographs, she holds me aloft with all the pride involved in showing off a trophy or presenting a crown prince to the populace. My mother admired maids and sitters like Lella because they were even better at darning socks and turning men's shirt collars than she was. Yet Lella, I learned to my surprise, couldn't read. Was it possible, then, that not all Europeans were as learned and refined as my parents claimed?

Nevertheless, the screen of European cultural superiority was not fine enough to keep bits of Americana from seeping into our lives. Watermelon, for example. I'd heard a lot about it; I'd read about it in school, but we never ate it at home. At last, at a picnic, I saw the dark green melons with the bright red meat and the hundreds of little black seeds that were so much fun to spit. Proudly I devoured piece after piece after piece, as if by filling myself up with this strange new American food, I might transmute myself into an all-American boy. I met my third-grade teacher, Mrs. Marshak. I ate ten pieces, I announced to her, proud of my gargantuan capacity. Would I get sick? I asked her. Secretly I wondered if she saw any change in me, if somehow I now appeared more American. If I did, she gave no sign of having noticed. No—she smiled—even ten pieces were not likely to make me sick, and she expected to see me in class in the morning.

 I also discovered hamburgers. My friends and classmates often talked about them. I was sure I knew what they were: they had something to do with the city of Hamburg in Germany. Yet, so far as I knew, I'd never actually eaten one. The great occasion came at last when I went to Santa Fe for one of my radiation treatments for the scar on my arm. I sometimes had permission to buy lunch for myself on those trips. At a Woolworth's, I set myself on a stool at the lunch counter as if this were something I did every day. Next to me was a boy my own age. His off-key nasal twang, like a twelve-string guitar with a few strings loose, thrilled me. Its resonances suggested the depths of Oklahoma or Texas or Tennessee or—in my parents' eyes—some other cultural Siberia. "Ah'll have uh hamburger," he said. "Ah'll have wun, too," I twanged casually in chorus. When my hamburger arrived, I picked through the mushy white bun, the obscurantist layer of onion and lettuce, the smudge of mustard and mayonnaise, to the heart of the matter: a dab of fried ground beef. I was thunderstruck: my mother made these at home quite frequently, and she made them better. She just called them "beef patties."

Another bit of Americana, but one to which my family was becoming addicted, was the soap opera. We heard the soaps on the radio, during the noon hour, just before the news. My father became quite a fan of *Jezebel* and *The Woman in White*. I hated the melodramatic organ music that ushered in or concluded each scene. I recognized many of the *Jezebel* plots from the Bible stories that my mother read to me. I much preferred the Good Book's plagues and wars to the soap opera's interminable romantic crises. My father, on the other hand, particularly relished wicked Queen Jezebel and the way she thwarted the romance between Caleb, her bodyguard, and one of her handmaidens. One day my father came home to lunch radiant and chuckling to himself. Niels Bohr had returned from a trip to Washington that morning. He had asked to be brought "up-to-date." That meant he wanted to know about the progress of my father's work, of course—but Bohr also inquired pointedly about the *Jezebel* episodes he had missed.

Another American joy was reading comic books, a delight all the sweeter because it was usually done on the sly at my friends' houses. My parents had warned me that reading comic books would further strain my eyes; I sensed that they were more concerned with my cultural degeneration than my visual one. I read the comics anyway, collected them, cherished them. In addition to admiring Superman, I was a great fan of the Golden Eagle. Tall, lanky, square-jawed, with the profile of a classical Greek bust, Golden Eagle, like Superman, was a young, courageous, resourceful and patriotic white male. His chief occupation was leaping into the cockpit of his custom P-51 Mustang fighter with the golden eagle markings. Into the skies he roared in quest of German or Japanese spies and saboteurs, whom he always thwarted in the nick of time. I longed to be as handsome, brave, courageous and American as Golden Eagle. Even more, I longed to be at the controls of his P-51.

Sometimes, when I was visiting at a friend's house, I would come across a particular toy that I liked, or a shirt or a book that I admired. "Where'd you get this?" I would say. The answer would come: "Oh, my grandmother gave it to me. She lives in Fort Wayne." Or I would notice a photograph of my friend with an older woman. "Oh, that's my grandmother in Pocatello. We always visit her in the summer." I noted the ambivalence in my friends' voices, the ennui of a seven-year-old, as if grandmothers were among life's inevitable burdens. I also noted their half-smothered smiles of anticipation. I imagined the grandmother's arrival: the hugs, the "My, how you've grown!" the presents. I envied my friends. I couldn't quite explain my feelings. Los Alamos, I sensed, was not quite Earth. My friends had relatives in such earthbound locales as Fort Wayne and Pocatello. For me not to have a grandmother in a similar town seemed not only unearthly but vaguely un-American. Not to have a grandmother at all left me with a sense of emptiness.

When my friends asked me about my grandparents, I didn't know what to say. I felt a hole in our family world, a crater. As a child, I wondered how that void came to be. My father, who usually had explanations for everything, who often tore into painful and intimate stories with the delicacy of a jackhammer operator, rarely talked about what had happened to his mother. I found out only later, piecing together the story from various relatives.

My paternal grandmother, Amelia Treves Segrè, filled my father's childhood the way she filled the living room of my father's last house on Quail Ridge Road in Lafayette. No visitor could help noticing or remarking on the huge oval framed portrait of her that hung over the fireplace: a white-haired woman seated in a rattan chair. She is not particularly handsome, and the artist has rendered her in soft shades of wisteria and chalky whites. He has undoubtedly muted the lines of her mannish face, whose nose is too large and pronounced, the eyebrows too heavy, the cheekbones too wide, as if by a trick of nature, though she belonged to the opposite sex, the daughter were a clone of the father. Yet the woman's face radiates an unmistakably feminine air of intelligence, sweetness and tranquillity. She belongs to a settled, civilized world of late Victorian Italy—of an Italy before the "Great War." It's a world that seems utterly disconnected from the one that eventually destroyed her, as if time had made a sudden, unexpected lurch, skipping some vital period in between.

"She was kind, intelligent, very sweet. She had a luminous smile that revealed dazzling white teeth. Her hair, which turned white when she was very young, crowned her fresh face. Her personality was gentle, made to love and give herself totally to those whom she loved: her father, my mother, her beloved [husband] Peppo," recalled her niece Silvia Treves Levi Vidale.

"She was a saint, a kind of Madonna," one of the old hands who worked at my grandfather's paper mills for more than half a century assured me about my grandmother. "I'm a Christian and I believe in another world, in a heaven. I believe that Signora Amelia went directly to Paradise. How we all cried when we heard what happened to her."

Saints come in many varieties. If my grandmother was one, she certainly did not fit the model of radical firebrand. If anything, she epitomized the Victorian ideal of how a woman, through sweetness and gentleness, could overcome the rough and crude manners of her man.

"Peppo, have some of this egg," my grandmother would say (according to the old mill hand).

"No. I don't want to. Leave me alone," my grandfather, who was a big man and had a reputation for gruffness, would bluster.

"Peppo, have some of this egg."

In the end, he ate his egg. Sweetness and gentleness, patience and modesty triumphed, like the North Wind and the Sun in Aesop's fable.

More than a decade separated my father from his older brothers, Angelo and Marco. By the time my father was born, my grandmother was free to dedicate herself to him, and he reveled in the care and affection that she lavished on him. He recalled the way she first encouraged him to explore the natural world and taught him French. He was especially proud of her as a *persona colta* (educated person). She had studied French, drawing, music. She also knew English fairly well. She read widely from the books at hand in the family library, from Tolstoy, D'Annunzio, Maeterlinck, Turgenev, Oscar Wilde and Shakespeare, the tastes of an Italian middle-class family of the period.

My grandmother combined sweetness with wisdom, with an understanding of the complexities of human relationships. Her cousins and nieces in the Treves family often came from Florence to Tivoli to consult with her about their personal problems. My grandmother's reputation extended far beyond her family circle. After World War II the city of Tivoli named a street after her. (And not after my grandfather, who, according to my father, was a far greater material benefactor to the city.)

My father was never a great fan of saints and humanitarians. "Saint Francis's influence on the world was nothing compared to that of the inventors of the atomic bomb," he announced loftily from time to time. When he heard that my sister Amelia was doing an eighth-grade history report on a great historical figure and had chosen Gandhi, he appeared irritated. "Why don't you choose some great scientist?" he said.

How could the son of a woman known for her gentleness and courtesy, and of a father who, for all his bluff manners, enjoyed dealing with people, talk that way? I asked myself in frustration. At times, I was sure his outbursts were no more than the explosions of an *enfant terrible* who relished his moment in the limelight. Perhaps a few more spankings as a child would have set matters straight.

At other times, I sensed genuine disappointment, even fear, in my father's voice. In dealing with people, I decided, his mind operated on certain false assumptions—or perhaps they were only hopes. One was that the world of men was a rational one, and that other minds worked like his. They would consider all the consequences of an act before making a decision. From experience, the man, of course, knew better. The world rarely measured up to his standards of intelligence and rationality. My grandmother's fate was the most terrible example of that failure—an example that haunted my father all his life.

My grandmother's fate was as ironic as it was tragic. Her chief flaw, according to my father, was her indecision—a trait that he, too, exhibited. Yet my grandmother's flaw may also have stemmed in part from her upbringing, from the education of most women of her class at that time. *"Mia figlia non ha volontà* [My daughter has no will of her own]." So my great-grandmother's generation boasted of their daughters, a niece observed.

During the summer of 1943, the Fascist government collapsed and in September the Germans occupied Rome. My grandmother apparently sensed what was coming. At the end of September, she wrote a letter to her three sons. In it, she gave instructions about the disposition of certain pieces of jewelry and personal effects. She also appealed to her children to remain close and united as a family and "in the faith of our ancestors."

Two weeks later, October 16, 1943, the Germans carried out their infamous roundup of Roman Jews. My grandparents had been warned ahead of time. In fact, they were down in the street in front of their apartment at Corso Vittorio Emanuele 229, ready to make their escape when my grandmother hesitated about something she had left behind. Finally she went back into the house to get it. By the time she came out again, my grandfather had been spirited to safety—and the Germans, with their guns, their steel helmets, their dogs, pounced on a white-haired lady of seventy-six, known for her sweetness, her good temper and for "not having a will of her own." In the Jewish section of the Verano Cemetery in Rome beside my grandfather's marker is one for my grandmother. "The Lord gave and the Lord hath taken away; blessed be the name of the Lord" reads the inscription from Job 1:21, followed by the birthdate, July 27, 1867. There is no death date, for we don't know whether she even reached her intended final destination: Auschwitz. In June 1944, when the Allies captured Rome, my father found out what had happened to her. "Nazi *und* murder" nightmares, as he called them, haunted him periodically for the rest of his life.

Throughout my childhood I felt my grandmother's absence. It was as if my father and I, diametrically across from each other, were both circling a huge pit. I wanted to fill that pit. I wanted to have a grandmother or a grandfather in Pocatello or Fort Wayne, so that I could be like my American friends. Yet my questions to my parents generally met with silences as deep as the pit. Having grandparents around was one of those American ways of doing things—one we didn't talk about.

Like other boys, I went fishing with my father. Because it sounded American, I liked to tell my friends that I went; I never told them much about the going. As so many things were with my father, fishing was a learning experience. So I learned: how to dig worms out of the soft earth in the meadows of the Valle Grande, or how to stalk and trap grasshoppers. I learned how to ignore their desperate wriggling, the scratching of their powerful legs against my palms, enough so that I could stuff the insects into a matchbox. I mastered the art of baiting hooks with my live bait: how to open the box just enough so that the grasshopper's head crept out and I could grab it with my thumb and forefinger, then insert the hook into the thorax. I also learned how to impale wriggling worms or bright red salmon eggs on the sharp little barbed hook at the end of my fishing line, how to cast and how to untangle my line from treacherous bushes and rocks. I mastered the art of cleaning a trout and pan-frying it with sage.

I also learned about my father's fishing style—and thus about his values. On the one hand, my father admired elegance and style; he favored friends and colleagues who were urbane and sophisticated. He also could be utterly pragmatic. If what physicists sometimes call "brute force" methods were called for in his research, he used them shamelessly. The same applied to fishing, as he indicated in some of his favorite fishing stories. To my father's private glee, for example, Fermi, normally the great pragmatist, developed peculiar theories about the way fish *should* behave. He insisted on using tackle that was appropriate for lakes, but not for mountain streams, and he persisted fruitlessly "with an obstinacy that would have been ruinous in science." Another eminent colleague was a dry-fly purist. I remember how my father and I met him along a trout stream one day. I watched the elegance of his casts, the perfect way his line alighted on the surface of a quiet pool. I also remember the way he politely sneered at my father's suggestion that the trout were going for grasshoppers. At the end of the day, we came upon the colleague again. His casting was still breathtaking, his hands clean, his creel empty. Naturally, my father, his fingers stained from the "tobacco juice" of the grasshoppers, had caught his limit.

Fishing was supposed to be fun. So I understood from my father, from my friends. Father-and-son fishing was supposed to be especially fun—or so my friends said. Fathers and sons got away together, left wives, mothers, women behind. Fathers told sons stories, perhaps gave sons a taste of the burning rotgut sensation of whiskey. They sat around campfires and slept out under the stars. Father and son returned home in triumph, reeking of fish, campfires and mud.

With my father and me, none of this seemed to happen. In the first place, we seldom left the women behind. My mother went along. My father bought her a fly rod, similar to his own. He showed her about dry flies and how to cast. It made no difference. She usually passed the time reading a book or sunning herself. At times she simply balked, insisted on doing something else. Then my father would grumble and sulk, with the air of an injured little boy: "Mamma is preventing me from going fishing."

When my father and I did go alone together, he would find a convenient spot, a big rock or perhaps a little sandbar, or a clearing in the brush, not too far from our starting point—usually where we had left the car. "This looks like a good spot," he would say. "You try right here. I bet you there are some big ones in that hole over there," and he would point to the nearest pool. "I'm going upstream (or downstream) for a while." Then he would scramble out of sight over a pile of boulders or disappear through the brush.

I felt rooted to the spot. I thought of horses that I'd seen tethered or hobbled, or dogs tied while the owner went into a store. There wasn't much to do except to try my luck. I would eye the deep pools where my father said the big ones were waiting. Occasionally I glimpsed their shadows or the flash of their scales in the sun. I also noted that the pool was usually just beyond the reach of my line, or hemmed in by overhanging branches or a submerged log. I noticed the tricky current or the eddy that was bound to sweep my line under some boulder. With a shrug, I would dutifully cast out toward the pool, troll my glittering little spinner among the darting shadows of the fish. On a good day I would hook one that was large enough for me to actually keep; more likely I caught small ones that I had to throw back. Most of the time, however, after half a dozen casts, the brush or the trees or the current would exact its price. I would get my line tangled in a branch or in a rapid; I would lose my spinner or break my leader or run out of bait. There wasn't much for me to do then except sit and wait for my father's return.

For a while, I would watch a bird, or listen to the river, or to the wind in the pines or the aspens. I would take in the endless reach of the sky, the ages of the rocks and the trees. I would listen for the call of a wild turkey or perhaps a deer rustling through the brush. My father loved this solitude, found it comforting, I knew. I, too, gave myself up to it, let Nature and the boundless universe cradle me. Or I imagined myself an Indian boy living alone off the land, on trout and berries. I was no "sissy." Like my mother, I was tough. I didn't need my father; I didn't need anyone. But I also wondered if living the Indian boy's life might not be a little lonely, even frightening.

About that time, I would usually see my father wandering back, working his way over the rocks and through the brush, trying this spot and that, like an animal grazing or hunting. Occasionally he would wave, but most of the time he appeared intent on his fishing. Eventually he would reach me and open his creel. If he'd had any luck—and he usually had—I glimpsed half a dozen trout, sleek, silver and black, sometimes wrapped in an old rag or grasses so that they wouldn't stick together. He would flash a smile of pride, perhaps ask me in a perfunctory way if I'd had any luck, and then say, "Well, it's time to go back," and head down the trail or over the boulders toward the car. Like an obedient, faithful puppy, I would trot along behind. More than three decades later, when I was forty-something, my father and I had one of those father-son conversations that we never had on the fishing trips. I found myself shouting at him as if to fill in the silences at last. My father appeared bewildered. But we *had* gone fishing together, he protested. He had the photographs to prove it. But the only ones he could find were of me alone on my rock.

By the spring of 1945, as I was finishing third grade, the war was winding down. Every day on the noon news, we heard that in

Europe the Allies were racing across Germany toward Berlin. In May came VE day. The Germans surrendered; the war in Europe ended. If my parents felt relief and satisfaction, perhaps even vengeance, they kept their feelings private. Meanwhile, the war continued in the Pacific, where the Americans captured island after island and began bombing Japan regularly. For as long as I could remember, people had been talking about the day when the war would end. That great day would be coming soon, I sensed.

I noticed that my father was gone for a few days in May, and again in July. His absences had to do with his work, my mother said. He had been "in the desert," my father said. I wondered why physicists did their work in the desert. Did his job have something to do with the ending of the war?

I wondered how wars ended. Did the enemies just stop fighting one day? Or was there one grand final battle, or one super bombing raid—the kind I sometimes drew in my war pictures—when our side, the American side, blew up all our enemies? How would people feel on the day the war ended?

It would be like recess at school, I decided. I would run around yelling and screaming, pushing and hitting, as my friends and I did when we first raced out into the school yard. I had a toy gun that fired paper rolls and made a noise like caps exploding. I would certainly shoot that. I pictured a grand, all-American picnic. Grownups—maybe even my mother and father—would relax. The most important leaders, like the President and the generals, would give fiery speeches. People would sing songs, wave American flags. At night the sky would fill with exploding, cascading fireworks. I would gorge myself with watermelon and hot dogs. At the picnic, my mother (my father would be busy talking to his colleagues) would order me to calm down, to behave myself. But from her voice, from the way she turned back to talking with the other mothers, I'd know that she didn't really mean it. I imagined there would be a parade with heroes in uniform, wearing their medals. They would look something like

Barry Blake or Dave Dawson. They would all be young, handsome, with shining white teeth. They wouldn't wear glasses, as
I did.

And then the great day arrived. The week before, came the
news of the atomic bombs, first on Hiroshima on August 6, then
on Nagasaki on August 9. At last, late in the afternoon of August
14, the official word came over the radio: "The Japanese have
surrendered. The Second World War has come to an end." The
radio announcer's voice sounded unusually deep, solemn, final,
as if the President or, somehow, even God had given him the
word. This was the great day. I could see that people were gathering outside in the street. I wanted to wear shorts and tennis
shoes. My mother made me put on blue jeans or patched corduroys and the brown high-topped shoes I hated. "We live in
the mountains," she reminded me. Even in the middle of August,
it could be cold.

Like our neighbors, the Allens, my parents and I gathered
outside on our porch, just at the top of the stairs. I leaned over
the balcony, looked down on the Olmsteads and the Perrys, on
the families in the other complexes down the street. I had my
cap gun. Everybody was screaming, "Yay, the war's over! The
war's over!" Like everyone else, I yelled, "The war's over!" I
held my cap gun over my head, as if the noise would be too
much for my ears. "The war's over!" I yelled. To augment the
sound of my gun, I also yelled: "*Bang!*" I yelled again: "Yay, the
war's over!" For good measure, I added, "And we won!"

My parents watched approvingly. I knew it was what they and
their friends wanted to hear. I knew it was what the neighbors'
kids were yelling, what the radio, like a broken record, announced over and over. I knew I was yelling what I should be
yelling, but secretly I had my doubts.

War had provided me and my friends with many grand adventures. In the woods we had flown fighter planes, raided Berlin, driven tanks and commanded battleships. We smeared our
faces with a little dirt and like commandos snuck up on each

other. But we knew that war was bad; peace was good. Our parents and teachers said so; the President said so; the heroes in my adventure books said so. Too many people, civilians and soldiers, men, women and even children, who had nothing to do with the fighting, got hurt or even killed. In magazines I had seen pictures of bombed cities. In some cases, nothing was left except the bare walls of buildings, and sometimes not even those—just piles of scattered, broken bricks.

"Yay, the war's over!" Even my mother yelled a bit. "Hooray! The war is over!" My mother, in a plain skirt and cotton blouse, looked genuinely happy. My father smiled, too, the way the smartest kid in the class would.

But this was the great day! I wanted them to scream, to dance, to sing, to jump around. I set the example. I shrieked wildly, hysterically. I jumped up and down. I fired my gun. The more I fired it, the sillier I felt. This great day called for resonant, thunderous bangs, for ear-shattering booms that rolled and echoed off the mountain peaks. But now that I listened, I heard only *Pop! Pop!*

"The war's over! The war's over!" I screamed a couple of dozen times. My throat began to feel dry and scratchy; it hurt. My father looked bored; my mother had stopped yelling. There didn't seem to be anything more to do or to say. I glanced at the stand of pine trees across the street, at the outline of the water tower up the hill. We were still here, still in the mountains, in the wilds of New Mexico. I wondered if I'd been screaming at nothing more than the trees, the wind and the peaks. Now my father looked annoyed; my mother looked ready to go inside. Where was the picnic, the grand celebration, the parade of heroes, the President? Inside we went, my mother to washing some dishes, my father to reading the newspaper and doing calculations with his slide rule. The war was over and life went on, I discovered.

At least I was happy about one thing: the war had come to an all-American ending. We, the Americans, the good guys, invented the super weapon, the atomic bomb. With one grand and terrible blast, we had crushed our enemies.

But the more I thought about that all-American ending, the more questions I had. The super weapon, I knew, had been created in large part right here, in Los Alamos, where I was living. Yet this was no all-American project. I thought of my father; I thought of all the people I knew who worked with him. They were nothing like the all-American heroes I had pictured at a victory parade. Instead of crisp uniforms, they wore rumpled suits or jackets; some were balding, like Fermi, and many wore glasses, like my father.

Bit by bit, I learned about what my father had been doing. The more I learned, the less all-American it sounded. In May, I learned long afterward, he had witnessed a practice test of the bomb with conventional explosives. Then, on July 15, he had been at Alamogordo for the first real bomb test.

It had been hot in the desert, he said. He had seen many scorpions and Gila monsters. The night before, there had been a tremendous thunderstorm. Halfway through the night, he had been awakened by an unearthly noise. When he got up to investigate, he found dozens of frogs croaking love songs to one another in a mudhole. Real all-American heroes wouldn't pay attention to frogs in a mudhole, I decided.

But then I pictured him at the test site. There, like a commando, he lay flat on the sand, next to his teacher, his colleague, his old friend, Enrico Fermi. They were about nine miles from "ground zero." I imagined my father's suspense and anxiety; I wondered if he had been afraid. That single test of July 15, I knew, was the culmination of years of grueling work. If the test failed, there could be no repetition. The flash of the explosion, even through dark glasses, appeared many times brighter than the sun, he commented. It "flabbergasted" him, he said later. "Flabbergasted." From the way he rolled out all the syllables, I knew that what he had seen was more than a flash of lightning, more than a peek at the sun, more than anything I could imagine.

For a moment, he was afraid that the explosion might set fire to the atmosphere and finish off the Earth. Calculations had shown that this was not possible—and yet "one can always make errors," he commented. He wished that the bomb had been ready in time to use against Hitler and the Nazis.

What impressed him most of all struck me as odd. More than the blast, he remembered Fermi's behavior. Other scientists who witnessed the explosion laughed joyously that the test had succeeded; others cried. Many looked somber and lapsed into silence, as if suddenly realizing what they had unleashed. For Fermi, the test was, first and foremost, an experiment. The goal was to measure light, radiation, shock wave from the blast. Fermi concentrated on the latter and with the simplest apparatus possible: some bits of paper. Immediately after the explosion, he stood up and released them in the air. When the shock wave reached him, the little shreds were displaced a few centimeters. From that displacement, he calculated the energy of the explosion. His answer closely approximated the official calculation done with far more sophisticated means. So absorbed was he that he was not aware of the tremendous roar of the blast, his wife wrote later.

I pondered the great day when the war ended for some time afterward. I was glad the war was over and that we had won. Still, I felt disappointed—even cheated. I wished I'd seen at least one ruined building or a dead soldier—preferably an enemy one. I had drawn so many pictures of aerial dogfights and of burning tanks that I wished I'd seen at least one real one. I saw pictures of the big victory parades in New York and I was sorry I missed them. I wondered what it would be like without the great drumbeat of the war in the background of our lives. What new games would I play? In place of war scenes, what new pictures would I draw?

Most of all, I wasn't sure anymore about all-American heroes. Were there any like them in real life? Could it be that the real heroes who brought the war to an end were more like my father,

with his delight over lovesick frogs, or like Fermi, testing the
shock wave of the first nuclear blast with his bits of paper? But
they didn't look like heroes; nor did they act like them. Besides,
I was an ordinary kid. I couldn't imagine living among real
heroes.

Did my father ever think much about the long-term effects of
his work? Did it trouble him, perhaps even haunt him? Was he
proud of having ushered in a new era—the atomic age—of having affected the lives of millions of people? What did it feel like
to know that you were one of the architects of a new historical
epoch?

As a child, I didn't know enough to ask such questions; as an
adult, I rarely risked them. I knew that he found them pretentious and overblown; they irritated and embarrassed him.
"*Discorsi a pera* [literally, 'pear-shaped talk']" he would snort
sometimes, as if he considered any exchanges or conversations
on such matters intellectually obese. What was there to think?
What happened, happened; that was that. Real scientists didn't
fill their heads with such high-flown thoughts.

Of course, he did answer those big questions—in his way. As
I skim the pages of his autobiography, his voice, impatient, terse,
irritable, even belligerent, echoes in my head. I see how gener-
alized, how evasive his replies are, as if they weren't worth his
time. What about his thoughts during those days immediately
following the first nuclear blast? "I did not jot them down at the
time and recollections would probably be distorted," he replies.
"I certainly rejoiced in the success that crowned years of heavy
work, and I was relieved by the ending of the war." Beyond that,
he was mostly concerned with the moment, with the progress of
the war and with personal plans for his immediate future.

Time didn't mellow him with regard to these questions. Even
after four decades, his thoughts on the nuclear age, on politicians
and the political impact of the bomb, on the hopes and fears of

the time, tumble out scattered, superficial, as if he couldn't be bothered to collect and shape them. "It seems to me that most developments were unpredictable and often depend on accidents," he writes. "Politicians do not come out well as far as intelligence and farsightedness are concerned, and they often acted on erroneous information," he pronounces. "Many scientists, like everybody else, nurtured illusions about the farsightedness, intelligence, and reasonableness of their fellow men," he declares. "There was optimism for the future in the sense that one trusted mankind's rationality more than was warranted." The bomb "possibly had the beneficial effect of preventing major wars between the superpowers by inspiring mutual terror."

Even as an adult, I got no more out of him. What was the point of speculating? he retorted when I tried to draw him out about, for example, alternative ways the bomb might have been used against the Japanese. Sometimes, imagining paths not taken, speculating about what might have been, was helpful in clarifying what did happen, I would say. But there are no data, he would object. At times, it seemed to me, he considered his ideas as so many data points. Looking back on his "more general ideas" about the postwar nuclear age, he noted that they "evolved with time," and added that they "should always be dated in reporting them." Were ideas merely data? Wasn't it natural, human, to reflect on the human condition and what he had done to change it? I objected. "I'm no poet. I'm no philosopher," he protested. At other times, he abruptly switched the subject; I watched him go back to shuffling his papers or to reading his book. Sometimes there were simply the silences.

I knew that in raising those big questions I was poaching on a restricted area, his private preserve. That voice, impatient, contemptuous, evasive, even outraged, was intended to keep me out. And yet, even as a child, I sensed that that voice masked something. Although I couldn't articulate it at the time, I detected skepticism, mistrust, even fear. What could a superman be afraid of? I wondered. That what he might say might not be original?

That it might sound flat, lame, banal? That it wouldn't compare with the best of the philosophers, poets and wise men? Was my father intimidated when he applied his own high standards to himself? Or was he afraid of sharing his touch of misanthropy, his fears about the unpredictability of things, with me, his son? Was he afraid I would think less of him? I knew only that it was best to avoid those questions—the ones that led to pear-shaped talk.

In February 1946 we left Los Alamos for Berkeley, where my father had accepted a position in the Physics Department. My mother and sisters flew back. My father wanted me to drive with him. I wasn't eager to do so. The old 1939 Chevrolet sedan was the same one we had driven from Berkeley to Los Alamos. Its navy-blue paint was now faded and scratched and blotched. The car radio faded in and out, and the button that activated the heater usually did so only in theory. From Los Alamos to Berkeley was a long trip—more than eight hundred miles, nearly three days of driving—and in those days no interstates swooshed and curved through the deserts and mountains. It was winter. I wondered if driving with my father would be like our fishing trips together. I hinted that I would prefer to go with my mother and my sisters. Yet my father kept insisting that I drive with him. I wasn't sure why. At the middle of our first day on the road, I found out.

One of the pillars of my father's routine throughout his life was a nap after lunch. "*Mi metto a panza per aria* [literally, 'I'm going belly-up']," he would announce at home. At his office at the university, he claimed that he would sometimes put out a sign that declared, "The Professor is studying." Then he would doze off for a quarter of an hour or twenty minutes.

After lunch on the first day, I discovered that he had no intention of varying his routine. Nor, apparently, did it occur to him to stop the car. "You drive for a while," he said. I couldn't believe my ears, but he stopped the car. We moved the driver's seat forward so that I could reach the gas pedal, and I was firmly and carefully briefed on my mission. I was to stay in the right lane and not to exceed the thirty-five-mile-an-hour speed limit, still in effect after the war. I was not to pass any other cars. I was not to try to shift gears. Satisfied that I knew my mission and that I would not deviate from my instructions, my father retired to the passenger seat for his nap. For three afternoons in a row, for perhaps fifteen minutes, I was king of the road.

For months I didn't stop talking about it to my friends.

"My father let me drive the car back from New Mexico."

"Oh, sure he did!"

"He did so."

"I bet. He just let you steer a little. My father lets me do that too, but he always keeps his hands on the wheel."

"Oh yeah, well, mine didn't have his hands on the wheel. He was taking a nap."

"Liar." But I could see the envy in their eyes.

I don't know how my mother found out.

"Emilio, no! You didn't," she protested.

"I needed my little nap," my father said.

His voice sounded firm, decisive, matter-of-fact, as if he'd faced a problem and found a practical solution. He glanced at me; he did not wink, but I saw a wisp of a smile. For a moment, "Papà" disappeared and I glimpsed my father's face as the bright, mischievous child he must have been. I saw the *enfant terrible* signaling to his partner and chum after an escapade: "We did it, didn't we!" For once, I really wanted to do *nasacocchia*, to rub noses Eskimo-style with my father. For once, I sold out my dreams of becoming an all-American boy.

CHAPTER 5

American Primitives

When I tell people—unless they are New Yorkers—that I grew up in Berkeley, I hear a murmured "Oh, Berkeley." Voices hush with deference, respect; eyes scrutinize me curiously, as if my dual heritage, my hybrid roots, Berkeley–Los Alamos, must have produced a truly remarkable specimen. After growing up in such communities, how could I not be brilliant, ultrasophisticated, refined, cosmopolitan, a man of the world? My father didn't see things that way. On the contrary, his fear was that my sisters and I would grow up to be real American primitives, barbarians—even in a town like Berkeley.

Of course, the Berkeley my family and I returned to in 1946, the city I grew up in until I left for college in 1953, was nothing like the Berkeley of today. These days Berkeley is synonymous with cultural mecca (and gourmet's ghetto), the home of a world-class university, a model of progressive—some might say radical—municipal government and politics. In today's Berkeley, bookstores and Parisian- or Roman-style cafés and cappuccino bars surround the campus on three sides. Specialty food shops cater to the most fastidious taste in pasta or chocolate. The City Council has been known

to officially challenge American government policy toward
Cuba or the People's Republic of China, and to decree that
Columbus Day should be celebrated as Native Americans'
Day.

The Berkeley I knew in the late 1940s was quite different. It
was a sleepy, provincial university town, blessed with a magnificent climate and a spectacular natural setting overlooking San
Francisco Bay. The air, untainted by smog, tear gas, or burning
luxury housing developments in the nearby Oakland hills,
smelled clean and fresh with hints of ocean spray. In the spring,
golden poppies danced on the slopes behind Memorial Stadium
and splashes of lupins, like secret underground springs, erupted
on the hillsides. As I remember them, "the people" in those days
were mostly middle-class whites, with sprinklings of Asians and
African Americans. "The people" then ran small businesses, it
seemed to me. When they took to the streets, it was to go to
work or to school, to go shopping or to a ball game. They
seemed content to ingest nothing stronger than a little beer while
they fished in the Bay off the Berkeley Pier or played softball
and roasted hot dogs in Tilden Park. To get a cappuccino or an
espresso, you had to cross the Bay Bridge to San Francisco's
Italian colony in North Beach or come to our house. For *The
New York Times* to arrive in the morning with your coffee
was unheard of. The Berkeley City Council focused primarily
on municipal taxes and street repairs, and even professors could
usually afford to buy their own homes. As my father did, many
of the faculty walked to work. In those days, the senior ones
still wore gentlemanly dark suits and hats; they tipped their
hats politely to women, as our neighbor, Walter Mulford, a professor of forestry, did to my mother when he met her on the
street.

My father regarded this quiet university town in far-off California dubiously. For him, it was certainly better, especially from
the point of view of career and research, than going back to Italy.
Yet, as for settling in a cultural center, he wondered if he was

much better off, if his family was much better off, than we had been in the wilds of New Mexico.

I couldn't understand his diffidence. From him and from my mother, I understood vaguely the importance of something called "culture" and that people who possessed it were desirable. As an eight-year-old, even I understood that in this regard, Los Alamos, for all its magic, had its drawbacks. My father's colleagues might be brilliant, sophisticated, worldly. They might speak half a dozen languages, play the violin or the piano at the level of a gifted amateur; they might develop a taste for Indian artifacts and archaeology and flock to nearby pueblos like San Ildefonso or Santa Clara for the dances. Yet there was no escaping that we were living on an Army post atop a remote mesa in New Mexico.

But what was wrong with Berkeley? At the university, educated, cultured people like my father gathered, did their work. I discovered a big public library, and bookstores near the campus. On the campus, my mother often went to hear concerts or recitals or to see a play or an art exhibit. And if Berkeley wasn't enough, San Francisco, just across the Bay, beckoned—a big city teeming with strange ethnic neighborhoods. Sometimes my mother went to the San Francisco opera or the symphony, or she took me to some art exhibit at the De Young Museum in Golden Gate Park. And yet, from time to time, as my father checked on my growth, on my intellectual progress—as he might check on one of his experiments, I thought—he regarded me doubtfully. As I often heard, growing up in Berkeley could not compare with growing up in Italy, especially in Tivoli.

"In Tivoli, we used to . . ." or "When we still lived in Tivoli . . ." my father would begin from time to time. In his voice I always heard nostalgia, regret for an Eden forsaken, a Paradise

Lost. Tivoli, I discovered, was the little town perched on olive-clad hills about twenty miles northeast of Rome where my father spent his boyhood. Tivoli was the home of the world-famous gardens of Villa d'Este, an old Benedictine monastery transformed in the sixteenth century as a residence for Cardinal Ippolito II d'Este. Artists from Franz Liszt to Gabriele d'Annunzio marveled at the cascades and fountains, the fern-filled grottos, the dark and somber cypresses, the ever-changing play of sun, shadow and water. No less charming, my father said, were the terraced hillsides of Villa Gregoriana, the tangle of Tivoli's medieval quarter, the fragmented columns of the Roman Tempio di Veste. Down the hill, half a dozen miles toward Rome, loomed the walls of Hadrian's Villa. Near there was a restaurant where you could eat outside under a pergola of grapevines. During the heat of the summer, at midday, or in the cool evenings, you could sip the chilled white wines of the nearby Roman *castelli*, the hill towns famous for their local vintages. In August, the grapes on the arbor ripened. They were known as *pizzutello*, a white oval-shaped variety unique to Tivoli. You could reach up and break off small bunches and nibble at them. The Signora who owned the restaurant didn't mind, as long as you didn't take too many.

His secret dream, my father claimed, was to retire to Tivoli —to carry the mail. What better occupation was there in the world? he often declared. The mailman's life was tranquil and routine, healthful and secure, and Tivoli was the ideal place to make the daily rounds. Trudging up and down the hills provided plenty of exercise. The vineyards and vegetable gardens on the terraced hillsides, the lush bamboo thickets along the banks of the Aniene River, the silver and gray of the olive groves afforded breathtaking views. In the winter, of course, he would have to bundle up against the north winds and the rain, but in the summer, when the rest of the Roman *campagna* was an inferno, Tivoli remained cool, and the *pizzutello* dripped down from the vines in Biblical abundance. What else could one want? On the rare occasions when he played charades, my father donned a little paper hat with "Poste Tiburtine" lettered on it. With a large symbolic mailbag—often the largest woman's handbag that was readily available—slung over his shoulder, he marched happily up and down, to the bewilderment of the other players.

When I listened to his stories, Tivoli sounded much grander than the sunburned hills and pungent eucalyptus groves of Berkeley. I hid behind our garage and ducked below our back porch; I pictured my father playing hide-and-seek among Roman temples and columns, or in the maze of streets in Tivoli's medieval quarter. With my friends, I ran through the sprinklers on our front lawn; he splashed among the fountains of the Villa d'Este with his friend, the gardener's son. Like him, I built forts and tree houses, but our neighborhood was never used as a movie set, as the Villa d'Este had been. Nor could my friends and I boast of having disrupted the film crew's shooting schedule by accidentally setting off some fireworks, as my father did.

I listened and I compared: Berkeley, barely three generations removed from the days of the "Wild West," with Tivoli, the Tibur of the Romans; my schooling, my teachers with his. Among his teachers, he always remembered Signorina (Enotria) Maggini, who eventually received a national award for her years of dedication to the children of Tivoli. She tutored him privately when he was six or seven years old. She took him on long walks along the dusty country road to Carciano, the next village over the hill from Tivoli. Along the way, she picked up a rock or pointed out a flower or a Roman ruin and turned the object into a mini-lesson on geology, biology or history.

I thought of my own and my sisters' childhood mentors, the Miss Lobbs, the Miss Connollys, the Miss Reynolds, and dozens of other dedicated American public-school teachers, mostly white-haired, mostly "Miss." My sisters and I never strolled one-on-one with our teachers. We were young recruits at the orders of our gentle drill sergeants: "Now, class, let's open our books to page . . ." Schooling like that, I sensed, would never measure up to my father's.

My doubts were confirmed in the letters that my father wrote home from a visit to Italy in 1947—his first after the war. In the process of settling my grandfather's estate, my father had had occasion to sift through old family papers in Rome. There he confronted "the layers of almost a century of culture" that had made him "a living encyclopedia, as you call me," he wrote to my mother. He reflected on "how complex the education of a European is and how many ingredients went into it, at least in my case." Meanwhile, he concluded, "Claudio and sisters are being raised on such a simple and primitive diet that they'll grow up to be barbarians."

Growing up in Berkeley, I wondered if I was missing out in another way. My father often reminisced about how things were *a casa* (at home), when he was a child. My Italian friends still often say to me, "*Salutami tutti a casa* [Say hello to everyone at home]." When I thought of "everyone" at home, I always felt uncomfortable. Of course, there were my parents and my sisters. And no one else. For my father, *a casa* meant a houseful of people, the extended family. Not only his parents and his brothers, but his Uncle Claudio.

A casa also meant relatives coming to visit him in Tivoli or in Rome. He, in turn, visited relatives during the summer. Usually in August, the Segrè and Treves families gathered at the Ligurian beach resorts of Viareggio or Forte dei Marmi. Sometimes other families would join the party at the Pensione Barsottelli Pini. Among them were families like the Ginzburgs. Their son, Leone, later became well known as an anti-Fascist martyr and the husband of the writer Natalia Ginzburg. In those days, around 1910, Viareggio had not yet become a concrete jungle, and a magnificent pine grove dominated the town. Giacomo Puccini roared around in his motorboat and dreamed up new operatic melodies; everyone knew where the poet and dramatist Gabriele D'Annunzio's villa was located—and gossiped about which new mistress was in residence. The long summer days were filled with swimming, eating huge quantities of grapes and taking long walks in the pine grove.

In September, the Segrè and Treves families moved to Marignolle, a sixteenth-century villa in the hills just above Florence. Even today the setting is magnificent. The grounds include a formal Italian garden and a splendid view over the olive groves and vineyards of the Tuscan hills.

For children, Marignolle was a paradise. Beyond the grounds of the villa were the estate lands. My father's cousins, Silvia and Marcella, were a few years older and took care of him. He was "a bit wild," he admitted, whereas his cousins appeared severe, even prudish. They were used to iron-willed English governesses, but he enjoyed the protective wing of his mother and his teacher, Signorina Maggini. But generally, at Marignolle, the cousins had a good time together. The older ones organized a secret postal service, complete with Lilliputian stamps and envelopes. Soon the younger ones began to receive orders by mail to collect certain objects and deposit them by a fishpond on the grounds of the villa. The game came to a climax one night after dark when everyone met secretly at the pond and the evening ended in a fireworks display.

Yet, when I listened carefully to my father, I also heard discordant voices within him. At first, during that initial postwar visit to Italy in 1947, my father was ecstatic. Being in Italy "was even better than going trout fishing," he rhapsodized in a letter to my mother. He loved visiting Tivoli again. Lunch at Hadrian's Villa "beneath one of those pergolas and with one of those wines from the Castelli that I miss so much in America" convinced him that "here people live a hundred times better than in California and if one were retired, he would have to come back here instantly." The "familiar faces" of family, friends, colleagues delighted and comforted him. Old schoolmates greeted him warmly and praised him as a model scientist, "which tickles my vanity." The "loneliness that I speak of from time to time in Berkeley" evaporated.

By the end of the summer, he had changed his tune. Neither twenty years of Fascism nor the war years had lessened Italy's bureaucratic confusion and inefficiency. "For example, it's impossible to send a telegram from the central railroad station in Rome!!" he wrote furiously. "By now I'm convinced that it wouldn't be a bad idea to go back to America and that perhaps this country is more for vacations and for enjoying life than anything else."

For the rest of his life, my father returned to Italy many times, but he never really went back. Certainly temptations were not lacking. As he became well known, he received many alluring proposals. The Italian government offered him a university chair, back pay for the years following his dismissal in 1938, and a pension. He often lectured in Rome and occasionally gave a course. After he retired, he taught there once or twice for an academic year, but he never stayed permanently. Although he sometimes talked about it, he never bought land or a house or an apartment. For him, Italy remained a mirage, so perfect from afar, so imperfect from close up.

I noticed that, unlike my father, my mother never really looked back to Europe. For her, there was nothing there, nothing in her native Germany or in Italy. Her parents disappeared at Auschwitz. Only her older sister, my Aunt Edith, miraculously survived the war in Germany (she had a Gentile husband) and continued to live there. The rest of my mother's relatives scattered from England to South Africa to Israel. Nor did my mother look to Italy. Italians had welcomed her as a young refugee woman and she spoke the language fluently. Rome evoked memories of meeting my father and their days of courtship. But over the years Rome also acquired other associations. The Eternal City became synonymous with eternal family feuds between my father and his brothers, quarrels that poisoned my father's life and hers. Tivoli, which had so many happy memories for my father, to my mother only meant a dull little suburb of Rome where she knew no one and where time creaked by. For my mother, "home" became simply the place where she lived longest, where she tended her husband, her children, her house and her garden. That proved to be, first, Berkeley, and then its suburban extension, Lafayette.

Despite my parents' ambivalences about Europe, in Berkeley, as in Los Alamos, I understood that in our family we were proudly not-American. At school I might hear about immigrant melting pots and joining mainstreams. That wasn't for us. Take food, for instance. The school lunch that my mother lovingly packed for me every day failed the ultimate test. In the cafeteria, no fellow fifth-grader grabbed the best parts and wolfed them down. With me, my friends knew, they could not hope for even a forlorn peanut-butter-and-jelly sandwich, for my father had an aversion to peanut butter, and my mother generally catered to his tastes. My battered metal lunch box, the color of a Granny Smith apple, was more likely to contain my mother's culinary memories from her own childhood, like liverwurst on rye, or cream cheese and radishes on pumpernickel. In place of gooey American chocolate cake, or angel food cake, I found my father's favorite *buccellato*, an Italian aniseed cake that reminded me of a dried-out bagel. At home the joke was to take a little nibble, then clutch your throat, as if you were choking, and scream, "Water! Water!" At school, my classmates sniffed, "I wouldn't feed that stuff to a horse." Or they likened the aniseeds to so many crushed ants. The raisins on top of my mother's *stollen*, a German Christmas yeast cake, invited comments like "Why are you eating those little rabbit turds?"

When my friends came to my house for a meal, they were always apprehensive. "Stew" to my good old American friends meant plain old stewed beef swimming in a brown sauce with potatoes, onions and carrots thrown in. At my house—to my friends' repressed horror—"stew" meant stewed beef literally dripping with a "green sauce" (*salsa verde*) of minced onions, capers and parsley. That was the way my father had eaten it at home in Tivoli, and that was the way my mother's great culinary mentor, Lella (Elia) Palma, the peasant maid from the Abruzzi who cared for me as a baby, made it.

Or take the houses we lived in. On the outside, they looked acceptably American, modest professors' homes within walking distance of the Berkeley campus. What we did in front and in back of them also looked appropriately American. In the little front yard of the shingled cottage at 2532A Piedmont Avenue, the house that my parents first rented when they arrived in 1938, my father, in white shorts, a T-shirt and sandals, washed the 1939 navy-blue Chevrolet sedan. As old snapshots show, he was ably assisted by his three-year-old blond, blue-eyed son. On the sloping lawn, in front of the two-story cream-colored stucco house at 1617 Spruce Street where my parents moved in 1940, my friends and I rolled over and over down to the sidewalk, totally ignoring maternal warnings against getting grass stains on our clothes. Down the driveway I raced on my tricycle, my wagon or my roller skates. A few years later, the front steps provided a natural backboard for an aspiring baseball player like me to practice my moves.

In the backyard on Spruce Street, my parents strolled up and down the little brick paths that marked the different flower beds and vegetable patches. They studied the fruit trees—the apple, the Japanese plum, the apricot—discussed what needed to be cut and trimmed and pruned, what vegetables were to be planted, and where the dahlias or the nasturtiums or the daisies were to go. Though the plans were often joint, their execution was largely my mother's work. In an old blouse or shirt, an old skirt or blue jeans, and her battered gardening shoes, she dug and watered, trimmed and planted. Sometimes, on Sundays, my father would get up from his lecture notes to dig and trim a bit himself.

Inside our houses, however, the visitor encountered a different world. I remember Spruce Street best. Certainly, the oilcloth-covered kitchen table where we often ate was suitably American. And the upright piano in the living room was nothing out of the ordinary. Yet nobody among my friends had Italian custom-made walnut sideboards in the dining room or a matching round dining table. Nobody else I knew set the mail on an eighteenth-century Boulle table with its inlays of brass, tortoiseshell and unburnished gold set in ebony. No friend of mine had his uncle's paintings—pleasant, French Impressionist–style landscapes and still lifes of Sicily or the Florentine countryside—hanging on the walls. None of my friends dried themselves with the likes of those rough, monogrammed linen towels that hung in our bathroom.

Nor were we American in the language that we spoke— or, rather, the languages. Most of the time, we spoke Italian. That was my father's native tongue and my mother had learned it so well that only as an adult could I detect her slight accent. German was my mother's original language. My father had learned German when he did postgraduate research in Hamburg. I noticed how my mother glided through the syllables, as if she had found a natural way of expressing herself at last. Neverthe-less, German evoked too many painful associations from her past. She spoke it reluctantly, occasionally with friends, and in spo-radic bursts at home with my father as the language of parental secrets.

Finally there was English in its family variants. (French, for us, remained a secondary language, serviceable in France or where nothing else seemed to work.) There was my good Amer-ican English and that of my sisters. Our soft, mushy *r*'s, like commercial white bread, blended perfectly with those of our friends at school.

Then there was my father's English. When he talked to gas station attendants or my teachers, I winced, I cringed, I looked out windows or pretended to be absorbed in my comic book. Despite more than half a century of living in the United States, his *r*'s sounded like grinding millstones, and no amount of practice saying "Rear Admiral Byrd wrote a report covering his travels in the southern part of the Earth" ever softened them. He also persisted in a bullheaded Italian penchant for enunciating all English syllables, especially if the word was unfamiliar. On the rare occasions when I tried to correct him, he bridled. The syllables were there, weren't they? he protested, and then muttered that English was an impossible language. People always sounded as if they were chewing potatoes. No wonder the sound track at American movies was incomprehensible, he claimed. But his vanity was pricked, and he would challenge me to explain an abstruse word in English or an unusual Italian expression. Eventually he made peace with his accent, even reveled in it when he realized that many people found it charming. As a child, I much preferred listening to my mother ask the gas station attendant to fill the tank, or to have her talk to my teachers. She didn't know as many elegant and literary words as my father, but no one had trouble understanding her.

Nor were we American in the guests who came to our house for dinner or a party. I noted the contrasts between the elegance and education of my parents' European friends and their American ones. One of my father's dearest friends was Dr. Giacomo Ancona. He had been a physician at the Italian royal court. Small and cheerful, with his gray, curly hair combed straight back, he always exuded elegance. His expensive Italian shoes, his understated gray suits and dark ties, the dark, shiny new cars he always drove epitomized for me what it meant to be "educated" and "cultured." His wife, Alma, pale, gray-haired, aristocratic, complemented him. I could never imagine their doing anything as mundane as taking out the garbage or brushing their teeth.

Others, like Tanya and Walter Ury, possessed a dry wit, charm and spirit in the face of enormous personal trials. Tanya, small, slim, conscious of her refined good looks, was a concert pianist. She had given up her career for marriage and had become a well-known piano teacher in the Bay Area. Occasionally

she gave recitals, and she taught my mother. Walter, always
tan, always smiling, always soft-spoken, had headed a major
department-store chain in Germany. After the Nazis confiscated
it, he made the best of running a small jewelry store in a San
Francisco Bay Area suburb. To me, these people never quite
belonged in American society. Their accents, their wry wit, their
casual and easy references to a culture and a world that my parents knew, set them apart. As a child, I wondered if they would
ever go back to Europe. By the time I was an adult, I realized
that, like my parents, they never would, that the longer they
stayed, the more they fitted into the landscape—as those who
never quite belonged.

My parents, of course, also made American friends. Colleagues and their wives like Robert and Bernice Brode, Francis
A. (Pan) and Henrietta Jenkins, A. C. (Carl) and Betty Helmholz,
Donald and Millicent Cooksey and many others became lifelong
friends. They helped my parents decipher the mysteries and
pleasures of their adopted country. *Persone civili* (civilized people)
or *persone per bene* (decent people), my father used to say, as if it
were a miracle to find them among Americans. Yet when I sometimes overheard telephone conversations that began "Say, Pan!"
or "Say, Bob!" and I could hear a distant, metallic voice saying
"Hi, Eh-meal-eeoo" or "Hello Uhlfreeda," I winced. How could
they be friends when they couldn't even pronounce one another's
names? How could they begin to find things in common? Only
later, looking back, as one by one the old friends passed away,
did I realize that those relationships were deep and lasting precisely because they transcended labels. Real friends were not
"Europeans" or "Americans"; they were simply friends.

So, I understood, we were not like American primitives. But
then, why were we not at least like most other European immigrants? As a child, I learned that we had nothing in common,
for example, with fishermen's families in San Francisco's North

Beach or with poor Jews or Italians from the ethnic communities in New York or Boston or Philadelphia. I also noticed that we didn't know any of the restaurant owners, car dealers and politicians whose families had first come to San Francisco at the turn of the century. On those rare occasions when I wandered in and out of the North Beach delicatessens, cafés and bookstores with my parents, I knew that the Italian I heard was not correct—or, at least, it wasn't like the language I heard at home. I sensed my parents' discomfort, their disapproval, just as they disapproved of garage mechanics or restaurant waitresses who said "ain't" or "they is." When my father had to deal with such people, he appeared to be in pain, as if he'd stubbed his toe.

In fact, my parents had little in common with the classical turn-of-the-century European immigrants. My mother and father never crossed the Atlantic in steerage. They never landed bewildered, confused, unable to speak the language, at Ellis Island. They never crowded into tenements in Manhattan's Lower East Side or San Francisco's "Little Italy." They never struggled for financial security. My parents booked a comfortable passage across the Atlantic and then took the train to Berkeley. They had enough money to buy their own home. My father had at least a temporary position doing research at the University of California's Radiation Laboratory.

What set us apart from the DiMaggios and Aliotos, the Gianninis and Ghirardellis and the other pillars of the Italian-American community? "*È una persona colta,*" my father used to say with a nod of approval. "He (or she) is well-educated, a person of culture," or sometimes, he or she "belonged to a certain (intellectual) circle." His grandmother Egle or his uncles, Gino and Claudio, were "people of culture," he reminded my sisters and me.

"*È una persona colta.*" The epithet irritated and frightened me. What exactly did it mean to be a "cultured" or "cultivated" person—in English, my father used those terms interchangeably? As a child, I imagined people with minds that glowed like cul-

tured pearls; I pictured special brains, sown with bits of knowledge. To be a *persona colta* did you have to know physics? Recite
long passages from Dante or Petrarch? Rattle off the succession
of medieval popes the way I knew baseball players? Understand
world politics? Could an artist be a *persona colta?* What about a
philosopher or a theologian? (My father seemed dubious about
them. What they studied and concluded was mostly "chatter,"
he said.) What was this "certain circle" or circles that my father
hinted at? To me, it sounded like an exclusive club. Who belonged to it? How could you join? I wanted names; I wanted a
membership list. As a child, an adolescent, a young adult, I often
wondered whether I would know enough to be admitted to the
Club. If so, would I join it?

For a long time, I did not realize how much of my father's
intellectual elitism had rubbed off on me. As a young instructor,
just beginning my academic career, I came to a rude awakening.
In San Francisco one evening, I attended a gathering of Italian
Americans with an old friend and colleague who studied immigrant communities. I came from an immigrant family; I was an
Italian American, I told myself. Yet, in my professorial gray suit,
I felt stiff and ill at ease, almost a foreigner, listening to the
conversations, half in Italian, half in English, about homemade
wine and Sicilian grandmothers' aniseed cookie recipes. Where
was the talk about Petrarch and Dante, or Manzoni and Leo-
pardi? I asked myself. What about Verdi and Monteverdi? Was
anyone a fan of Caravaggio and what did they think about the
origins of Fascism? I sipped jug wine, nibbled at the aniseed
cookies and said very little, but my silence did not conceal my
discomfort. Afterward, my friend told me several people had remarked about me, "He's not one of us. He's a snob."

As a child I had been eager to join the mainstream of American
life, even at the risk of growing up barbarian.

Miss Reynolds, my fifth-grade teacher, seemed to think I was doing well in my efforts to join in. "Claude has already in eight days found his place in the class and has made some fine contributions. We're privileged to have him with us," she commented on my report card at the end of January 1946. I was an "unusually fine student," my "quick mind grasps an idea immediately" and I had a sense of humor that was "delightful," Miss Reynolds wrote. I was "specially interested in U.S. history at this time" and was "writing chapters" for a book of my own.

Such comments pleased my parents; they horrified me. They were just one more sign of my failure to join American fifth-grade social life. At Los Alamos, I had skipped fourth grade, so I was a year younger than most of my classmates. When we first returned to Berkeley, for a month or so, before my birthday in March, I was "eight and in the fifth grade." I announced this to my classmates with an air of innocence, as if I couldn't help it. What I hoped was that if they didn't like me, at least I would amaze and impress them with my intellectual brilliance, as I impressed my teacher and my parents. Instead, I developed a reputation as a "four-eyes," a "teacher's pet." In lieu of achieving my dream of turning into an average, normal, all-American boy, I was well on my way to becoming a "brain," a "bookworm," perhaps a professor, like my father.

My name was another perpetual thorn with my classmates. It was all good and well for my father to honor his Zio Claudio, an uncle who had often substituted for his father. That didn't make things any easier for me. "Claudio": in Italy, the vowels ring out, round and full, a vocal monument to my great uncle's energy, spirit and compassion. In the United States, the vowels dribbled out from between clenched teeth with all the élan of a leaky faucet. Even today, garage mechanics and dry-cleaning clerks stumble over them. Cocktail party guests—unless they are European or Latin American—appear startled by the sudden dissonance in the normal music of English, as if I've suddenly struck some awful chords. For my childhood friends, with names like "Mike" or "Joe" or "Bob" or "Jim"—names encompassed within a manly grunt—mine was an embarrassment.

I should anglicize my name to "Claude," my father suggested. I wavered because I still remembered my run-in with the principal's secretary when I was in first grade. Since the United States was at war with Fascist Italy and my father was legally an enemy alien, Miss Curry probably felt it was her patriotic duty to raise my consciousness as an American.

"What's your name?" she asked one morning when I was in the office on an errand. She peered at me over her rimless glasses. They reminded me of two chips of ice.

"Claudio," I replied.

"Your name is Claude," she declared. Her voice and her white hair made me think of the white pepper I'd just been learning about in class. "You are American like the rest of us."

I was seething; I should know what my name is, I wanted to tell her, but I knew that Miss Curry's spicy temperament matched her surname. "Claude" was more in harmony with the music of English, but the sound also reminded me too easily of the name's derivation. "Claude. It. and Sp. Claudio. Lame," reads the dictionary section on "Common English Names." I fluctuated back and forth. In junior high, I settled on "Claudio."

One road to social acceptance might have been through Cub Scouts—especially if my father had become a leader, so that my friends would have commented respectfully, "*His* father is the Cub Scout Master." With my father, there was no danger of that. Yet, to my surprise, probably under duress, he did accompany me to the organizational meeting in the John Greenleaf Whittier University Elementary School auditorium. Cub Scout meetings, I discovered that night, were an exciting mixture of solemn flag salutes, pledges of allegiance and awards ceremonies, interspersed with delicious mini-riots. Mr. Brudney, the Cub Scout Master, was much given to raising his arms over his head like a boxing champion and encouraging us Cub Scouts to emit earsplitting yells. These only made my father's face darken and his teeth clench. At the end of the meeting, a beaming, enthusiastic Mr. Brudney approached my father to ask what he could contribute to the life of the pack. But one look at my father and

Mr. Brudney first asked about my mother. Could she, for example, serve as a den mother? No, my father told Mr. Brudney. She had two small children to take care of. As for himself, perhaps "sometime" he could take the boys on a hike. From his voice, I understood that that "sometime" would not materialize in any future that he or Mr. Brudney or I could foresee.

Secretly I was relieved. Our Sunday outings in the Bay Area were no different from those that I remembered from Los Alamos. In place of the Valle Grande or the Sangre de Cristos, we now tramped through the woods at the base of Mount Tamalpais in Marin County, or up the mountain trails of Mount Diablo, or through the damp, prehistoric gloom of the redwood forests near Santa Cruz. My father talked to his friends usually in some non-American language, or he poked around at the base of the live oaks after mushrooms. My mother chatted with the other wives, or herded my sisters along. Cub Scout songs, or spirit, or cheers, or plain old childish savagery had no place in this order of things. My father would never lead a Cub Scout hike, I knew—and he never did.

For me to complain to my father about my humiliations as a non-American grammar school and junior high school outcast was pointless. In the first place, although he accepted that I would be growing up American, to his mind some distance between me and my primitive peers might be beneficial. Anyway, school, in his opinion, had nothing to do with acculturation or developing social skills. As he once wrote in his neat, clear handwriting on the back of a mimeographed PTA notice about a "social adjustment class" for parents and children, "School is for learning. Why don't you study mathematics instead of social adjustment?" School for him was also about being the best student, the "first in the class." When he went to school, everyone knew who was first in the class, he used to say. What was wrong with that? Intellect should be recognized, not buried in some kind of democratic socialization process. At my age in school, he was not always the first, though he always ranked near the top, he said.

From time to time, after he became famous, he occasionally encountered some former classmates who came to congratulate him after a speech or a ceremony to honor him. With unabashed glee, he would say afterward, "You know who that was? He used to be first in the class." Or, in a patronizing tone: "So-and-So is a good lawyer now (or a respected doctor). He used to be first in the class." My father also joked about a mythical boy with red hair and thick glasses who was the most brilliant in the class. *He* should be my model—not some baseball or football star, my father said.

But I didn't want to be a goggle-eyed professor. I wanted to be a baseball or football star, so that I could impress my classmates. So I read the sports page in the newspaper and talked sports at home. My parents were mystified. For them "sports" meant hiking and swimming, skiing, mountaineering and perhaps a little tennis. For me, for my classmates, of course, first and foremost, sports meant shining heroically on the playground; bashing softballs on long, looping drives to the Cyclone fence; hurling footballs on a wobbly arc to a teammate far down the field—or smashing into the nearest classmate with the excuse of throwing a block; or, with a satisfying "swish," banking basketballs through a net. Sports also meant displaying an encyclopedic knowledge of local athletic teams, college and professional—a knowledge, it seemed to me, that approached that of my father's grasp of physics.

On my first day at school in Berkeley, a number of my new classmates asked me which team I had supported in the previous World Series. I had no idea what my choices were. At Los Alamos, the community's isolation and my parents' indifference left me abysmally ignorant. I wasn't even sure what the World Series was. I heard St. Louis and decided in their favor. Fortunately, no one asked me why; fortunately, explaining my preference seemed less relevant than having one.

Nor did I have any idea how to play football. The first day at recess, I was the new boy. Since my skills were indeterminate, I was told, "You be in the line." At first I had no idea what that meant. There was, I understood, the dim goal of tagging or, better yet, wrestling the enemy ball carrier to the ground. When our side had the ball, I was supposed to be protecting our ball carrier by knocking over everyone on the other side. I did what the other boys did. I pushed and shoved and elbowed the boy opposite me. He did the same to me. We argued violently about whether we were holding each other. On the next play, I was determined to go him one better. I did. "Hey, See-gray!" he screamed, more in outrage than in pain. "Don't you know anything about football? You're not supposed to grab the other guy's nuts."

My father might disapprove of my passion for sports, he might sneer and shake his head, half in contempt, half in bewilderment. Nevertheless, during fifth and sixth grades and during three years of junior high school, when I wasn't in class, doing my homework, practicing piano, going to Cub Scouts, I was out on the playground or out in the street in front of my house honing my athletic skills. Sports was my way of joining and making friends. Sports, I realized much later, was also a way to be me. When I was around my father, it wasn't easy for me to speak, to be myself. He valued learning, information; with me, these commodities were always in short supply—or so I thought. So what could I say? Since I had so little to say, at least I could do something with my body. On the playground, in the gym, I could hear myself panting, feel my legs aching and my shirt clinging to my sweaty back. I could smell my sweaty feet. I could feel me.

At times, I longed to share with my father that world as a junior high athlete. It was a hard, dusty, abrasive one. From time to time, I played on grass fields, but for the most part the surface was blacktop. When I fell I tore off skin from knees and elbows and forearms, ripped T-shirts and sneakers. The balls were hard, too: playground footballs, basketballs and softballs with tough rubberized exteriors, sometimes real baseballs with horsehide covers and red stitching. I was forever grabbing, snatching, hugging, hurtling balls: I cradled football "bullet passes" into my stomach (the idea revolted me); I tried to embrace basketballs, hard as old-fashioned cannonballs; baseballs stung my palm, even with a glove on. If I didn't catch them right, I bent a finger, bruised an arm or a leg when the ball bounced off me.

Neither my father nor my mother spent much time watching me play. So far as I remember, for example, they never cheered me as a pitcher or first baseman on my Cub Scouts baseball team. That was just as well. In the first place, I would have been embarrassed. If I was an American primitive, so was my father, I discovered—at least, when it came to sports. There his encyclopedic knowledge ended. He didn't even know the rules of the games, let alone their strategy and tactics. Stan Musial, Ted Williams, the Oakland Oaks, the San Francisco Seals, even the University of California Golden Bears were all alien to him. Nor did he know how to clap and whistle and stamp, how to yell "Go, Will!" or "Atta boy, Bob!" as real American parents did. If he had come to a game, I was afraid that his patience, usually in short supply, would quickly have reached its limits. I imagined him shifting restlessly, complaining loudly that he didn't understand what was going on, as he did when he sat through a concert or attended an American movie. And what could he yell? I imagined my blushing at something like "*Forza, Claudio!* [Go, Claudio!]"—though, secretly, I would have been happy even with that.

Actually, I was glad that he didn't come, for as an athlete I rarely shone the way I wanted to. I was always the last chosen: "See-gray, line." In football, I had no brute force for blocking or leading interference, but since I never got my hands on the ball, I couldn't fumble it or throw a pass interception. In baseball, it was "See-gray, right field, bat last." Most batters were right-handed, so they seldom hit to right field. Therefore, my chances of dropping a fly ball or letting a grounder roll through my legs were minimized. As for batting last, it just meant that the school bell would ring or the game would break up before I had too many opportunities to strike out. Only in basketball, where I had the advantage of height, did the team captains eye me with a flicker of interest.

Nevertheless, I persisted in my pursuit of athletic prowess— and I had my moments of glory. My grandest moment came in junior high school, when I lived the stuff of baseball legends. On that April day, in seventh-period gym class, clad in our institutional gray gym shorts and white T-shirts emblazoned with "Garfield J.H.," we were shivering our way through a squad game. My team was behind, four to one, but the bases were loaded. The bell to end the period was about to ring. I was at bat. I had read about such dramas in the sports pages, heard them unfold over the radio, even written about them for English class.

"C'mon, Claude boy. You can do it!" my team captain yelled. As usual, he had chosen me last, but now his voice carried all the fervor of a convert in the midst of a religious experience. The ball came at me about waist-high, a pitch luscious as a ripe mango. I swung as hard as I could. I felt the thick end of the bat connect solidly with the ball. I glimpsed the surprise on the faces of the outfielders as the ball arced over their heads. As I dashed around the bases, I heard my teammates cheering:

"Home run! Home run! Grand slam! Grand slam! Atta boy, Claude! Way to go!"

As I crossed the plate, I knew that as far as my classmates were concerned, my days as an American primitive were over.

At home that night, around the oilcloth-covered table in the kitchen, for once I decided to answer my mother's usual "What did you do today in school?"

"I hit a home run in gym. A grand slam!"

I kept my voice level, thin, factual, as I had heard my father do so often. It disturbed the silence minimally.

"Home run? Grand slam?" my father said. I savored the moment. Suddenly he was revealed in all his ignorance, an utter barbarian in his understanding of one of the foundations of American culture. He looked genuinely puzzled. "Oh, like Babe Ruth."

"Who is Babe Ruth?" My mother's voice had that edge of anxiety when she didn't know what she thought she should know. She forced a smile, and quickly changed the subject: "Bravo! How did you do in English today? You're such a good writer."

But my father couldn't leave well enough alone. "You don't know Babe Ruth?" he needled her. "Babe Ruth? *Il famoso giocatore di foot-boll* [The famous football player]?"

CHAPTER 6

People of the Book

In one way, at least, I was sure that I was solidly mainstream American. As I wrote on school forms under "religion," I was "Claude Segrè, Protestant." What else could I be? I wasn't excused from school once a week for Religious Ed., so I wasn't Catholic. I didn't spend Sunday in the living room listening to blue-suited white-haired gentlemen, as the Perry boys did at Los Alamos, nor did my family and I socialize at the church across the street from our home in Berkeley, so I wasn't a Mormon or an Episcopalian. I couldn't see any connection with the "Israeleets" of the Bible stories my mother read me, nor did I wear a little skullcap (that reminded me of Brownie Girl Scout beanies) or pray in Hebrew. So I wasn't Jewish. "Protestant" was fine with me; my parents never told me otherwise, and it *seemed* to make sense.

How "Protestant" I really was did not emerge until after my father's death. Going through his papers, inside a plain white envelope, was a card that read, "This certifies that Claudio Giuseppe Giorgio Segrè, child of Emilio Gino Segrè and his wife Elfriede Hildegard Spiro, born on the 2 day of March 1937 at

Palermo Italy received CHRISTIAN BAPTISM on the 7 day of April 1943 at Berkeley, California." The seal on the certificate indicates that the minister was from the "Northbrae Community Church." Even today, the sight of the certificate with "CHRISTIAN BAPTISM" in large, florid Gothic type shocks me.

That certificate, I suspect, was largely my mother's work. Even in the land of the free, even with an ocean between her and the madness of Nazi rallies and Italian Fascist racial manifestos, my mother did not feel entirely secure. Nearly forty years later, I understood my mother's uncertainties. The occasion was a retirement dinner for a colleague of mine, a distinguished German-Jewish émigré historian. In reminiscing about what it had been like starting his academic career in the United States just after the war, he quoted from the letter of recommendation his professor—a well-known American scholar—had written for him: "Mr. X is a competent historian. He does not have the abrasive manners of the Jewish race."

"Claude Segrè, Protestant," was fine with me as a child. If anybody asked me about my religion, I had an answer. For the most part, however, nobody asked. My friends who went to church on Sundays envied my freedom. My parents seemed to regard religion with about as much interest as they paid to baseball.

Yet I wasn't entirely comfortable. From time to time, I heard my parents remark that someone they had just met, or perhaps someone they had passed on the street, was *ebreo* or *ebrea*. I thought I caught them exchanging knowing glances, as if they'd identified a member of a secret brotherhood. I tried to fix that man or woman in my mind. For the most part, I saw only the usual adult, dressed more or less as my parents did, and perhaps speaking with an accent—but so did nearly everyone else among my parents' friends. What set these *ebrei* apart? What were my parents talking about? Could it be that we had something in common with them after all?

———

My father was not much help. For him, I gradually understood, religion was like music: he didn't have much of an ear for it. As he noted in his memoirs, he "never had a religious crisis." In matters of faith, however, as on most other topics, he was a person of the book. He read about religion and he read religious works because he read everything. That was part of being an educated man. So he devoured Descartes, Galileo, Tolstoy, some of Plato's dialogues. He read the nineteenth-century French historian-philologist Ernest Renan's *Life of Jesus*. He plowed through explications of Buddhism and Judaism and other major religions. He read the Bible—the Old Testament, at least the parts he could get through. Some he found "sublime and rich with moral teachings; others seemed barbarous and cruel." The varying images of "Adonai" impressed him. In some cases he found them "so churlish and vindictive as can be conceived only in the mind of a priest."

Reading, however, did not lead him to faith. What religious feelings he had, he recognized as "childish." He cherished them, they comforted him, for "they remind me of people I once loved and of old times." On the rare occasions that he did attend religious services, he sometimes found them moving because of "the traditions they evoked, from family history and from feelings rooted in the subconscious." On an intellectual level, he wrote, he regarded religion much as Einstein did. As a scientist, Einstein believed that the laws of nature determined what took place in the natural world, and thus he could not accept that prayer, or some address to a Supreme Being, would influence events. Nevertheless, he recognized that believing in the laws of nature as an explanation for the world was in itself an act of faith—though one often justified by the successes of scientific research. And yet in doing scientific research, Einstein recognized the existence of some spirit in the universe vastly superior to that of man—a spirit "in the face of which we with our modest powers must feel humble." Thus, Einstein recognized, "the pursuit of science leads to a religious feeling of a special sort, which is indeed quite different from the religiosity of someone more naive." When I came across that passage, it struck a familiar chord. I thought of my father—aloof, apart, elitist. Whatever religious feelings he had were those of the *gente colta*.

Yet my father certainly considered himself Jewish, probably more in a cultural than a religious sense. His upbringing was almost entirely secular. He was not bar mitzvahed. He did not know Hebrew. His family did not generally observe the High Holidays. When he was doing his military service, he was not even aware that he had a right to a leave to celebrate Yom Kippur. "Being Jewish," however, did mean marrying within the faith, even though my mother was not at all religious.

In his education and his attitudes, my father was typical of his generation of middle-class Italian Jews. As my grandfather's story attested, emancipation for the Jews in nineteenth-century Italy came relatively easily and the trend toward secularization and assimilation was high. By the time of my father's generation, as the memoirs of contemporary Italian writers such as Primo Levi and Vittorio Dan Segre (no relative) illustrate, in Italy whatever it meant to be Jewish was fading rapidly. Without Mussolini's anti-Semitic legislation in 1938, without the experiences of the Holocaust, the Jewish tradition in Italy would have dimmed even more.

With such a secular father, my seeking faith, tracing the outlines of a religious identity, was like groping about in a cave. At times, as I grew up, I came across movies or novels with a Jewish background. I envied the son in the clichéd scene when the father thunders, "My son, have you forgotten the Sabbath?" or "If you marry her, you are no longer my son." My scenes with my father were far more nebulous, as if we were bumbling around in the dark. In my scenes, the son was uncertain whether to follow the father. Is the father leading? Or is he standing apart, his critical

eye on the son's fumblings? I often felt that my father, as the
English essayist Charles Lamb put it, was determined that "my
children shall be brought up in their father's religion if they can
find out what it is."

From time to time, as I groped about in the cave, my father
handed me a torch—usually in the form of a book. In 1950, for
my thirteenth birthday, for example, he gave me a Bible. Its tan
leather cover and gold lettering were neither elegant nor memorable; I think he ordered it from Sears Roebuck. By now the
pages are the color of a tobacco-stained finger. It was evidently
a wartime edition, for it included a letter from President Roosevelt "commending the reading of the Bible to all who serve in
the armed forces of the United States" and assuring me that
"Throughout the centuries men of many faiths and diverse origins have found in the Sacred Book words of wisdom, counsel
and inspiration." My father filled in the presentation line, which
reads, "A sacred token to —— from ——" with "Claudio Segrè"
from "Papà."

What was I to do with it? Was this in place of a bar mitzvah?
(At the time, I wasn't even sure what a bar mitzvah was.) Had
he chosen it *because* of President Roosevelt's words, "men of
many faiths and diverse origins" had found inspiration in the
Bible? I didn't know what to make of this torch, nor of my parents' silences. When I joined a Congregational Church youth
group in high school, they said nothing. I edited the organizational newspaper and wrote mildly Christian and pantheistic editorials praising Nature, peace, brotherhood. I celebrated the
richness of a busy life of schoolwork, dates, and sports, leavened
with Christian moments of prayer or devotion.

At home, at Christmas, we celebrated a kind of secular win-
terfest, more out of my mother's nostalgia for the snow and fir
trees and carols of her childhood than for any religious content.
I went to midnight services at Christian churches selected at random. On those cold, foggy Berkeley nights, I loved hearing the
joy and affirmation of the carols, the grand swelling of oratorio
choruses. I tried earnestly to absorb—and then to spread—the

message of "Peace on earth, goodwill toward men." Occasionally my mother came to the services with me. We spent one Christmas at a ski cabin in the mountains. My mother, my sisters and I sang carols. "It was worth it just to see the smile on Papà's face and the way the singing seemed to draw out many German carols that Mamma sang as a little girl," I noted in my journal. I liked being "Claude Segrè, Protestant." It was a nice, generic, American white-bread way to reach God. So far as I could tell, I was not in disharmony with my upbringing and family traditions.

In college, I discovered that I wasn't nearly as free to search for my own religious creed as I had imagined. I left for college with high hopes. Maybe I'd have an experience like Paul's vision on the road to Damascus, or Luther's fit in the choir, or Saint Francis's dream of Lady Poverty. That didn't seem likely in Portland, Oregon, among Douglas firs and spruce, azaleas and rhododendrons, in Tudor-style dormitories fronted by huge English-style lawns. I thought I might become Episcopalian; instead, I turned Jewish.

I wanted to come to my faith, that of the People of the Book, through books, as my father had come to his beliefs. That didn't happen. I read about Christianity and Stoicism and noted in my diaries that "they don't provide a very good outlet for pent up emotions [read 'sex']." Somerset Maugham's *The Razor's Edge* excited me about mysticism and the spiritual life for a while, but not enough to find a clear spiritual direction. Disappointed with books (combined with long freshman and sophomoric discussions of religion with roommates and friends), I decided to settle matters the American way. I went shopping.

Sporadically I sampled various Christian denominations and explored the limits of organized religion. My critiques read a bit like restaurant reviews. "Plain on the outside, plain on the inside." So much for a Methodist service I attended during a summer I spent at Woods Hole on Cape Cod. "Very unattractive and devoid of religious feeling. The people were there because they had to go, not because they were inspired. The altar had many flowers and was cluttered up with the instruments for the service, but everything was puritanical in comparison to European cathedrals." So much for Catholics. Episcopalians and New York City's Riverside Church rated more favorably. The Episcopalian minister quoted from Somerset Maugham's *The Summing Up*. I was pleased with his "nice bedside manner" and that he was "not a bigoted holy man." At Riverside Church, "the service went smoothly and beautifully, all except for the guest preacher who was pretty much of a dud and overly pedantic."

Initially, Judaism did not fare much better with me. As a small, nondenominational liberal arts college, with a reputation for radicalism, Reed attracted many Jewish students, especially from Los Angeles and New York. In the spring, I attended Reed "community" Passover seders in the college Commons, and in the fall, Yom Kippur services. My "reviews" continued ruthlessly.

> Service long and not very interesting. Operatic cantor. Responsive readings much like any Christian Church service. . . . Didn't like the tribal aspects of the service. No love expressed for *all* men as in Christianity. . . . Tradition seemed ego-centric, selfish. I like the Christian concept of a brotherhood of all men and a "love thy neighbor" attitude better. It is more mature, I think.

A girlfriend during my sophomore and junior years precipitated more of a spiritual revelation than my shopping expeditions. My family might be secular, even areligious; nevertheless, a web of implicit assumptions bound us. The girl's name was Esther. I proudly showed her picture to my parents, and to my relatives during a summer trip to Europe. I noted the nods, the smiles of approval. Suddenly the questions became more explicit. "Oh, what about her family? Orthodox? Ashkenazi?" I felt increasingly embarrassed at my answer: "No, she's a Unitarian from Oregon." After Esther and I broke up (not over any religious question), I continued going out with girls from a variety of religious backgrounds. Yet when I went out with Jewish girls, though I could not explain why, I began to feel that they were more "my crowd."

I stumbled onto another part of the family web—the Holocaust. I happened to see *Border Street*, a movie about the Warsaw ghetto, at Christmastime during my junior year. Afterward I attended an open house at a girl's dormitory. The candlelit rooms with the fir boughs on the mantel and bookshelves, the softness and good cheer of the girls, the sweetness of the punch and cookies, the joy of the carols shocked me. "I kept thinking that it [the Holocaust] had taken place just thirteen or fourteen years ago. . . . I could only sing as fervently as I could, 'Peace on Earth, Good Will to Men,' " I wrote in my diary.

My own family's story, I knew only dimly. Mainly through relatives, like my mother's sister, my Aunt Lilli, and through family friends, I learned something about it. Whenever I tried to broach the subject with my father, he shied away. "Nazi *und* murder," he usually muttered. The odd mix of German and English sounded like a sorcerer's spell, as if my father were talking about a vicious fairy tale. He claimed that stories of the Holocaust gave him nightmares. At other times, like a clever child, he recited a little doggerel from the comic strips of his boyhood in which a European lectures a black cannibal:

> *Questa lezione elementar,*
> *Che è cattiva educazione*
> *Carne uman divorar.*

> (This lesson is elementary,
> that it's bad manners
> to devour human flesh.)

It was a lesson, he claimed, that the Germans under Hitler had not learned.

Nearly half a century later, he brooded over the scars from the Holocaust. He imagined a conversation with his grandfather and told me about it. In the conversation, my father explained about Fascism and how "they kicked me out of Italy." Even worse, my father described "a great persecution of the Jews . . . In Germany, they have killed millions of them, and many also here [in Italy], including Mother." The grandfather protests in disbelief: "We are not in the Middle Ages. What kind of nonsense are you telling me?" "Unfortunately, what I told you is true," my father replies sadly.

At other times, I uncovered the depth of his feelings quite by accident. Movies or television programs about the war, especially the Italian partisan struggle against the Nazis, moved him deeply. In one movie, at the last moment, the SS officer refuses to give the order to shoot hostages, including Jews. So far and no more. It was one of those rare moments when tears welled up in my father's eyes and his voice broke. Even among the Nazis there were limits, he murmured, as if he needed the comfort of at least that bit of faith.

I pondered his unwillingness to probe the darkness of the Holocaust. For once, I thought, I had found a topic too enormous, too frightening for him to grapple with. For my part, I wanted more. I was not satisfied with the Holocaust as a story of "Nazi *und* murder," of monsters in a nightmare. Germans were real. My maternal grandparents had lived among them. Nazis were real, thugs, politicians, criminals who ate, slept, perhaps even loved, as I did. What had gone so terribly wrong with them? I was determined to find out. When I embarked on an academic career, I studied modern European history as my field, especially the story of Fascism and Nazism. Gradually, very slowly, I came to understand how the Holocaust came about, how, in the historian-philosopher Hannah Arendt's phrase, "the banality of evil" was possible, in perspective how easy (though in no way inevitable) it all was when men of goodwill abdicated their responsibilities or lost heart.

Israel served as another one of those periodic paternal flash points. During the summer of 1960 I visited the Jewish state for the first time. I felt the bite—and the tug—of Zionism, as I noted in my diary:

> On that ridiculous slice of swampland and desert . . . you can hold up your head and be proud of David and Saul, Maimonides and Hillel, as the Italians brag of Caesar and Columbus and Leonardo, the English of Shakespeare and Churchill, the Americans of Washington and Franklin. After 2,000 years, they've come back to hold up their heads, to build their nation on that bit of waste sand with a terrier-like defiance. There's something between the cute and the pathetic about it—until you feel like crying over it because it's a dream come true. "If you will it, it need not be a dream," Herzl said.

I had my doubts about contemporary Israeli society. The Promised Land, the dream of the Millennium looked suspiciously like American suburbia—except that people spoke Hebrew. For me, I decided, the Messiah was

> just a plain old healthy child in a T-shirt, shorts and sandals, looking for all the world like a product of American suburbia, without a mark on him, growing up in a clean, modern apartment with a Daddy who doesn't wear a tie. That's the meaning of Israel. That's what everyone has been working and praying for for these two millennia. The Messiah is that little kid playing in the park.

Perhaps Israel had fallen short of the Zionists' lofty visions,

> but better that they should worry about too many PTA meetings and too much leisure, as Jews under the star of David flag, than that they should worry about Bund meetings.

Each in his own way, my father and I became involved with Israel. Toward the end of his career, my father joined the board of governors of Tel Aviv University. He regularly attended board meetings and served on a prize committee. When I settled on an academic career, I went to Israel for conferences, spent part of a sabbatical there, collaborated with an Israeli scholar. Since my sister Amelia married an Israeli and made her home near Tel Aviv, the trips also became an opportunity for family visits.

On the rare occasions when we all met there, I listened to my father grumble and complain about Israel and Zionism. My father admired the bravery of the Zionist pioneers, as I did. They had the courage of their convictions. He admired, yet he also wavered, and he could even be snide. "Everybody knows that he [an Italian Zionist leader] ran off to Israel because he got a girl pregnant," he snorted. Naturally, he worried about the safety of my sister and her family, and the *cacadubbi* in him regularly generated gloom-and-doom scenarios about the future of the tiny Jewish state, surrounded by a sea of hostile Arab neighbors. Yet I also thought I noticed a peculiar gleam of satisfaction in his eye as he, like a proud Biblical patriarch, posed with us all—children, in-laws, grandchildren—for a family picture.

Identifying as a Jew, empathizing with Israel wasn't enough, I discovered. What kind of Jew was I? I had never gone to Sunday school. My mother had never joined Hadassah; my father had never spent a Sunday on the phone raising money for the UJA. If anything, he was dubious of those who congregated there. So where did I belong? How observant should I be?

I tried to use my father for soundings. The echoes came back confused, disorienting. When my sister Amelia considered marrying the son of a Russian Orthodox priest, my father objected strongly. Yet when my sister Fausta married an English Gentile, there was no protest. When I married a Jewish girl, I heard no comment, for or against. When I observed the Jewish holidays and told my father, he would sometimes reply, "Bravo!"—but little more. Later I would learn that he, too, had been to services or had attended a seder.

A book finally gave me my bearings, and it was my father who first told me about it. It was a novel about an Italian Jewish family. When I first read Giorgio Bassani's *The Garden of the Finzi-Contini*, shortly after it appeared in 1965, I seemed to have discovered a story that summed up the traditions and experiences I knew best. In the nostalgic and tragic tale of Giorgio and of Micòl Finzi-Contini, I found a Judaism that I could identify with: Italian, secular and patrician, a Judaism in which secular learning was more important than religious study. I also felt a personal tie to the story. Distant relatives—my father's second cousins— lived in the little Renaissance town of Ferrara, halfway between Bologna and Venice, where the novel is set.

Yet when I thought about the book more closely, I wondered if my yearning to identify with it wasn't forced. What did I really have in common with Giorgio and with Micòl Finzi-Contini? I'd lived in Los Alamos and Berkeley, never—despite my relatives —in a small town like Ferrara. I knew nothing, really, of the aristocratic ways of the Finzi-Contini family. I didn't even know many of the Hebrew expressions that they used. Why should I identify more with them than with German Jewry? After all, my mother was German.

Yet I did. Perhaps subconsciously I was hearing my father: "If you're going to be Jewish, my son, do it my way." I was the reflection of my father's dominance over my mother, her rejection of her homeland and culture. I also found that the traditions of Italian Jewry—as I understood them—presented a relatively painless path to Judaism. The Italian Jews I knew were largely secular. According to their model, I didn't have to discipline myself seriously and follow ritual and dietary laws. Without overlooking the shabby, vicious and cynical anti-Semitism of Mussolini's regime, I could still identify with the long tradition of religious tolerance in Italy. If I felt uncomfortable with Malamud, Roth, Bellow and the American Jewish literary and intellectual tradition, I felt at ease with contemporary Italian Jewish writers: Primo Levi, Natalia Ginzburg, Giorgio Bassani, Vittorio Dan Segre. They fit into my father's ideal of *gente colta*.

In identifying with Italian Jewry, I discovered an added bonus—especially in the United States. At *oneg shabbats*, the festive gatherings over cakes and punch or coffee after Friday-night services, I relished the furrowed brows and the quizzical expressions when I told fellow worshipers about my background. "An Italian Jew? I didn't know there were any." Or the reaction among the connoisseurs of the multiplicity of Jewish traditions, especially marriageable women or matchmakers: "Italian Jews? Oh, they're the best kind! Are you married?" The Italian tradition set me apart from most of my coreligionists in the United States. As in so many aspects of my life, I belonged—but not quite, I concluded.

But I did belong. The central historical factor in my life, I realized, was the Holocaust. Hitler, and to a lesser extent, Mussolini, had been determined to snuff out the Jews. The enormity, the audacity, the obscenity of their crimes took my breath away, then filled me with rage. My immediate family had been relatively fortunate; yet we bore our scars and our dead. Without the Holocaust, most likely I would be living in Italy. Without the Holocaust, I would have known grandparents; without the Holocaust, I would have mingled with aunts and uncles and cousins more than I did.

For a while, I felt helpless. My father's and mother's silences, the Holocaust as "Nazi *und* murder" left me uneasy, hungering for something more. I decided to fill in the voids and the silences. I did so with every service I attended, with every prayer I uttered, with every class I taught, with every lecture I gave, with every piece I published about the Holocaust. I was also honoring my dead, and the millions I didn't know, Jew and Gentile alike. Against the enormity of the evil, my efforts appeared minuscule; without them, I knew, men of goodwill would have no chance at all.

CHAPTER 7

Civil Warriors

My adolescence, I see now, was one long civil war. I was at war with my father; I was also at war with myself. It was an odd sort of struggle. There were few large-scale campaigns. Pitched battles were minimal. What impresses me most now is the lack of engagements. From time to time, my father might fire a few quick shots my way. "How's algebra?" "You really ought to learn to work more with your hands. Do you know how to fix an electric outlet or what to do when the wires are stripped?" "Are you going to college? Have you thought of where you might go?" "Why don't you speak up more?"

I would duck. "Algebra's okay," I would mutter. (I was passing; I might even make a B.) Chores around the house, like electrical wiring, were to be avoided at all costs, especially under my parents' critical eyes, so it was best to pretend not to have heard. Sometimes I would fire back. "Of course I'm thinking about college," I would lash out. (What else would I do with my life at the end of high school?)

The skirmish over, my father and I would both retreat to the security of silence and solitude. Victory, it seemed to me, was to be gained by showing how little we needed each other, how self-reliant we could both be. We saw each other on a daily basis, but it was as if we were invisible to each other.

I see this as I leaf through my father's autobiography for the years after we left Los Alamos. Pages chronicle his postwar negotiations to get a job. He did not want to stay at Los Alamos. A job offer to return to Palermo he dismissed as scientific suicide. Several universities courted him. He finally settled on Berkeley. Other pages go on about what direction his research took. For the first time in his career, he felt he didn't have to publish to survive. He continued with his research and he also paid his dues to the profession. He edited *Experimental Nuclear Physics*, a big three-volume compendium that synthesized developments in the field. For a quarter of a century, beginning in 1952, he edited an important journal, *Annual Reviews of Nuclear Physics*.

As I skim the pages of his book, I nod in recognition and empathy. Two decades of academic life have taught me about the pressures of publishing and perishing and paying your dues. Yet as I scan the pages, I also feel uneasy. As he says, this volume is primarily about his professional life. Still, I wonder. What will he say about his personal life? His family life? About me? Then I realize that he won't say anything. He'll barely mention me or my sisters.

How can that be? I was there. Between 1946 and 1953, between the time my family and I returned to Berkeley and my high school graduation, we lived under the same roof. For seven years we shared meals around the oilcloth-covered table in the kitchen at Spruce Street. We vacationed together in Canada and in Europe. My father sometimes helped us with homework. In his autobiography, he even articulates his philosophy of child rearing: "I believe parents should educate their children in a broad sense, but afterwards it is better to leave them their independence," he notes. That's what his mother and father had done with him and his brothers; "for better or for worse," that's what he did with me and my sisters, he asserts. "I have not written here about the life of my children. It belongs to them and they are entitled to their privacy," he declares, as if he had had nothing to do with forming our lives. "Some of their decisions left me perplexed, and although I am sure I followed my conscience and my best judgment, helped by my greater experience, and in their sole interest, I would prefer not to have influenced their decisions." The irony, I'm sure, is unconscious.

What did my father see when he looked at me during those years of adolescence? For one thing, he had to look up to me. During the winter of 1951, at almost fifteen, I was about half a head taller than he was. I was fulfilling my vow at Los Alamos: if I couldn't match his standards and expectations, at least I could grow taller than he. He was proud of my height. From time to time, he looked at the soles of my feet and teased, "I'll have to do a little filing or planing down there, to bring you down to size."

I also looked vulnerable. Photographs of me record large expanses of tender skin, an invitation to razor nicks. My clothes still looked skimpy. My sweater vest tended to creep up, revealing my belt; my wrists show at the cuffs of my cotton plaid shirt. My glasses hide my eyes, hide me from the world, hide me from me. I like myself better without my glasses, even though my nearsighted eyes appear slightly glazed, as if the world were a blur. Without glasses, it is. Nevertheless, I smile timidly at my father. My hands are linked nervously, and my shoulders hunch slightly—but I *am* smiling, as if things weren't that bad. My father, in a suit and tie, confronts the camera with his eyes. He stands straight, confident, substantial. From the photograph you would never know that my mother was always after him: "Emilio, stand up straight."

In other pictures, I evade the camera. I glance this way and that, I frown and grimace, I regard the lens suspiciously out of the corner of my eye. By then I have a crewcut, so that I look even more vulnerable, like a duckling, with his first feathers just growing in.

The photograph I prefer is of me in the mountains. I'm sitting on a rock. My long, strong, brown legs, encased in dusty hiking boots, are clearly visible. So is my rugged plaid shirt, hiking shorts with many cargo pockets, my rakish-looking cotton hat, my big backpack, which is resting against another rock. I look like the tall, strong man of Nature, rugged, taciturn, independent, unfathomable. What mysteries lie behind this man of the Wild? says the photograph—or so I imagined at the time.

But there's an ambivalence in the portrait—or so I hoped. The man of Nature may be in perfect harmony with rocks, trees, wind and God's creatures, but he's not in perfect harmony with himself. There's a hint of sadness, of mystery, perhaps of tragedy. Why is this man of Nature so alone? What dark experiences drove him to live by himself, away from civilization? (This is to be asked preferably by an attractive and empathic female.)

I look in vain for the dark experiences. They aren't there. No bizarre family life, no unhappy love affairs, no tragic experiments with alcohol or drugs, no crippling diseases or accidents. I was fortunate. I was also much too busy—and that, perhaps, was my dark experience. "Do, don't be" was the message, intended or not, from my parents. So I did.

What I did, however, I usually kept quiet about. "Why don't you speak up?" my father said. Because it was safer not to. That way, he couldn't ask too many questions, generate his computer list of objections. He couldn't turn that powerful mind, clear, brilliant, searching, logical, onto the foundations of my life—school, piano lessons, sports, school dances, ski trips—as if he were dealing with one of his experiments. I often wanted his guidance. What subjects should I take this semester? What kind of science project should I do? Should I write a report on India or Italy? But I also feared his input. If there was a problem to be resolved,

he, the great *cacadubbi*, knew how to raise spooks and phantoms
that I'd never even dreamed of. If he didn't know too much, I
wouldn't know too much. When I knew too much, when I
weighed alternatives as carefully and lucidly as he usually did,
I became the way I saw him: frightened, even paralyzed, by
indecision.

I preferred making decisions my way. As a ten-year-old, I
learned to dive off the twenty-foot-high diving platform at the
university's Men's Gym. Slowly I would climb up the ladder,
slither through the hole at the top onto the platform. I'd glance
around at the green turf of the practice fields, the oval of the
Edwards Field track, at San Francisco Bay and the web of the
Golden Gate Bridge. Then I'd face what I'd been avoiding:
The Decision. With my knees a bit wobbly, I'd creep up to the
edge of the platform and peek down. The blue-green water of
the pool, deep and inviting as a tropical lagoon, shimmered in
the sun.

I knew what my choices were. Climbing back down in shame
and humiliation as others sometimes did? That was out of the
question. Should I dive? Plunging headfirst, using my skull to
part the water, seemed like a misuse of my cranium. But I pondered neither the gravitational forces to which I was delivering
myself nor the aerodynamics of my skull, as my father might
have. I learned that all I needed was to wait for a little surge of
courage, a rush of adrenaline. If it came, I'd tip over the edge.
If it didn't come, I'd hold my nose, point my toes and simply
step off into space. For a few seconds, I'd hurtle, free-falling,
then slash into the water, like a saber, I imagined, safe and proud.
Whether I jumped or dove, for the benefit of those watching me,
I surfaced snorting and shaking my head.

I had my doubts about my methods. My father's ways appeared more intelligent, more carefully considered. Yet so often,
he reminded me of my friends who stood at the edge of the
platform, staring down at the water for too long. The wind from
the Bay raised gooseflesh on their bodies. They shivered and

trembled. At last they slunk back to the ladder and climbed down in ignominy. Not me. I waited for the little adrenaline rush. I tipped over into the void, manfully slashed the water.

I often had occasion to listen to my father and his friends. I was quiet and respectful when visitors came for dinner or a party that my mother had organized, or when my father went hiking with a colleague. When I was present, I usually felt like a piccolo player in an orchestra piece that has one small passage or a little chorus or line. As a child, even as a teenager, I could never provide the main theme or direction. At best, I could add a little background color. When I did try to join in the conversation, I was always aware of how little I knew, how little I'd thought through what I wanted to say, how unreasonable I sounded. With everyone listening, waiting to capture my words, to analyze them, to dissect their arrangement, their linkages, their logic, the weight of their meaning and appropriateness, I could only blurt out a few phrases. Was I saying what I meant? Did I mean what I said? How could I? How could I possibly have intended something so silly? Didn't I see that it didn't make sense? Even worse, I felt how trivial my spoken words were. They felt light and crumpled, like a hamburger's paper wrapping thrown away at the roadside and blown about by the rush of the passing cars.

So I began to write. As a child, I had used a diary to keep track of my activities, because I knew that I was accountable. A diary was irrefutable evidence, in case my parents asked, that I was spending my time usefully, productively. I was learning things, I was improving myself. By the time I was in high school, I wrote because I wanted to hear myself—and to be heard. I needed my special, protected habitat where I could be invisible, safe from my father. There, with paper and pen, I could figure things out, say things to myself, let my real voice, wobbly and unsure though it was, come out. Writing became a different kind of talking. It was also a way of declaring, insisting that I was there, I was someone, I was someone worthwhile, I had something to say.

Among those who helped me discover that I had something to say was one of my English teachers at Berkeley High, John S. Barnes. The first day I walked into his class, I was struck by his handwriting. Those large, bold, sprawling, confident, unself-conscious chalk strokes on the blackboard in yellow or white—like the strokes in a Jackson Pollock painting—shocked me. It was nothing like the calligraphy of my junior high teachers, which tended to be clear, precise, uniform—and a little dull, as if they had practiced many hours with a copybook. Nor was it like my father's—restrained, clear, precise. Those daring, bold strokes of Mr. Barnes impressed me as the marks of a man who ignored rules and regulations or made his own. At times those bold strokes and loops frightened and overwhelmed me, yet they also stirred and excited me. With Mr. Barnes I felt I was teetering on the edge of the diving tower, and he was down below, at the edge of the pool, beckoning.

I compared Mr. Barnes to my father. After all, they were both teachers; they both presided over classrooms or lecture halls; they both marked student papers. And yet, though I couldn't always pinpoint why, I sensed that they were very different. My father, I decided, was a professor; Mr. Barnes was a teacher. It was okay to reach out and touch him.

Like my father, Mr. Barnes—who in the 1950s was probably in his thirties—appeared imposing, authoritative. From the perspective of my desk, he appeared to tower over me. Yet when I went "up" to him after class—and it felt that way, though I knew the floor was level—I saw that my six feet matched his, that maybe he was even a shade shorter than I was. Mr. Barnes dressed informally and comfortably—always, it seemed to me, testing the edges of propriety for a teacher. He usually wore a light-colored dress shirt and a knit tie, and brown crepe-soled shoes. He was always in his shirtsleeves, and the sleeves were always rolled up, as if he were ready for business.

My father, too, sometimes dressed casually. His shirt collar might appear a little rumpled and his tie might be a bit askew as Mr. Barnes's sometimes was. But my father never wore those soft-looking crepe-soled shoes, as Mr. Barnes did. My father's shoes were usually English or Italian; the soles were leather— hard, compact. They were made to absorb all of life's shocks, as my father usually did. I wished that he, like Mr. Barnes, would wear crepe-soled shoes and bounce cheerfully over cracks and potholes.

In class, Mr. Barnes was always ready for business, though he didn't always appear to be. He wandered around the room. He leaned against his desk or sat on the edge of it as he spoke or as we carried on a discussion. His voice was low and calm, but there was also an understated, infectious energy and enthusiasm pulsing through it. In that class you would not even think of passing notes, whispering, chewing gum. There was simply no room, no time for nonsense: there were too many exciting things to do, to see, to learn. On the rare occasions that someone did disrupt class, Mr. Barnes simply banished the offender. Out into the hall or out to see the principal. Out and gone.

Nor would you think of handing in your homework late or skipping assignments. For one thing, Mr. Barnes wouldn't accept late papers. Besides, it wasn't a question of "homework." To him, assignments were "jobs." Already that sounded adult, responsible, the way things would be no matter what we did after graduation. Despite his low-key style, beads of sweat formed on Mr. Barnes's receding hairline during class. I watched his fingers—and his shirt or the tops of his trousers—gather chalk dust. Imparting English language and literature to half a dozen classes of adolescents a day could be physically demanding work, as hard and dusty as moving furniture or digging in the garden.

Sometimes I compared Mr. Barnes's classes to what I recalled of my father's. I seldom went to hear my father lecture, for I rarely grasped what he was saying. Introductory Quantum Mechanics was not high school English. So, naturally, I focused on his teaching style. Like Mr. Barnes, my father wandered around in front of the class. He, too, wrote things on the blackboard— almost always, formulas. But much of the time, I had the feeling that the class wasn't there. He was there; he was on display. The students had come to watch him reveal how his head worked, what was inside it. For once, I thought, I was really peering into his mind.

It was a strange experience, fascinating and exciting, tantalizing and frustrating. For the most part, at my father's lectures I understood only that I understood nothing. He would explain something. Then, with a spurt of energy, he would write a formula on the board. From time to time, he would stand back, like an artist surveying his canvas. "Are the signs right?" he would ask the students. Or "Isn't that pretty?" That was a part that I liked. I could hear his enthusiasm, like Mr. Barnes's. For me, it was a bit like being blind. I couldn't see; I could only imagine the simplicity, the beauty of a formula or equation—how much hard-won knowledge, how much understanding was packed into those few chalk marks on the board. Unlike Mr. Barnes, my father did not invite questions from students. He seemed to be speaking mostly to the best and the brightest, and a student's question would often turn into a professorial challenge. "Oh, that's obvious, isn't it?" my father would say. Then he would explain and clarify; the student would listen—often, I sensed, embarrassed, almost apologetic that he, a mere mortal, didn't have the clarity and quickness of mind to grasp the notion the first time.

In class, Mr. Barnes also did something that my father never had occasion to do. Mr. Barnes took on the Big Issues—love and death, the meaning of honor, courage and virtue, the meaning of life. In "Period IV, Advanced Writing, Fall, 1952," we read Keats's "The Eve of St. Agnes," Christopher Fry's *The Lady's*

Not for Burning. We studied passages from Thomas Wolfe, from Herman Wouk's *The Caine Mutiny*, from Hemingway's "Big Two-Hearted River." What did each writer have to say about the Big Issues? How did he or she say it? Mr. Barnes asked us. After school, we aspiring writers, with Mr. Barnes as our sponsor, banded together in the Manuscript Club. At our biweekly meetings, in our stories, poems, plays, essays, we delivered our deepest meditations on the Big Questions. We published a mimeographed literary magazine. *Barnes' Yard, A Collection of Rare Birds*, we cleverly called it. At times, when thought failed, when words could no longer adequately express our cosmic thoughts and emotions, we simply recorded the cosmic sounds. "Ecce aaaah," we wrote. On those occasions, Mr. Barnes never did more than lift an eyebrow. He then raised the possibility that perhaps language was not such an inadequate tool, that it had served human beings well for thousands of years and perhaps it might also serve us well if only we'd let it. Our most intense, important feelings, he said, were serious, but not so solemn that they couldn't be leavened with a little wit, a little humor. This was wisdom, I recognized; probably also self-protection against the endless stream of too eager, too earnest adolescents, I realized much later.

My father was not one to tackle the Big Issues—whether in class or out. When I tried to hint at them, he shrugged. He was a physicist, not a philosopher or a poet, he would say—and then perhaps would quote one. If I insisted, he would mutter, "These are complicated and difficult questions," and I understood that for him they were the equivalent of what quantum mechanics was for me.

When I talked about Mr. Barnes (I don't know that my father ever met him) at home, my father generally preferred to interrupt and ask what steely-eyed Mr. Holmgren was teaching us in trigonometry, or how genial Miss Powelson was imparting to us the proofs of plane geometry. Yet, at other times, when I brought Mr. Barnes up in conversation, I sensed that my father was listening. Or was he listening *for* something? I suspected what it was. When we were talking about poetry, he was reaching mentally (and sometimes physically) on the shelf of the library in the living room or the dining room for the navy-blue cloth-covered *Oxford Book of English Verse* with the markers in the section on the Romantics, especially Keats, Shelley and Byron. He nodded with approval that Mr. Barnes had us studying Keats's "The Eve of St. Agnes," or Eliot and Fry. At least they were English or strongly Anglophile. Better them than the likes of Longfellow, Whittier, Henry Van Dyke or William Cullen Bryant, all American, all, to his taste, on the level of peanut butter. I was confident, though my father never said so, that if Mr. Barnes had applied, my father would have supported his membership in the Club of the *gente colta*.

With Mr. Barnes I felt visible, I had something to say. I always knew that I could say it better. Mr. Barnes was a hard grader, especially for those of us to whom A's were routine. The occasional "plus" as in B+ was one of those little crosses that I learned to bear. Yet, in the margins of my papers, those bold, Jackson Pollock–like strokes told me someone was listening, hearing me, as if I had something to say, something worthwhile.

If I was at war with my father, I was also at war with myself. I was engaged in a great campaign of self-improvement. The diaries that I kept through high school reflect that. They read like war bulletins or battle statistics: "60/68 in physics. A in English. Report card: 1 A, 2 B+s, B, B–. Lousy geom. 100 yards, 1:30.3." I was on the offensive, but I never made dramatic breakthroughs—at least to my satisfaction. My grades were good, but never as high as I wanted them to be; never, I thought, in the realm of the "high standards" my father often talked about. Yes, I made the swimming team as a breaststroker, and with practice, my times improved dramatically, but rarely enough to win events.

Nothing was good enough for me, not even at those rare times when my father told me that I had done well. In senior physics class, for example, my semester's project was to build a Wilson cloud chamber, an ingenious device for studying the tracks of radioactive particles. Normally these tracks are invisible to the naked eye. In a supersaturated atmosphere, however, they become visible in the same way that high-flying aircraft, invisible to the naked eye, often leave "contrails" (condensation trails) in the sky when atmospheric moisture condenses on the hot engine exhaust gases.

I built my chamber out of simple bits of equipment that my father's colleagues at the Radiation Laboratory helped me with. Pie tins formed the top and bottom of the chamber; a large plastic ring provided the walls. I lined the chamber with felt that I soaked to provide the supersaturated solution. My father furnished a tiny radioactive source.

When the great day came for my class demonstration, my father, who had provided explanations, came to hear me. I carefully parroted my father's explication. I then asked for the classroom lights to be dimmed. I shone a bright light into the chamber. Against the dark background, the little particle tracks, like the thinnest wisps of cigarette smoke, were clearly visible. I heard the gasps of my classmates, my teacher's approving murmur.

Afterward, my father congratulated me, complimented me. He didn't even say, "Yes, but next time you'd better be careful to . . ." or "Yes, but you forgot to . . ." "Bravo," he said. I barely heard him. I was relieved that the demonstration worked, relieved that my perfect grade of 200 points out of a possible 200 would look good on my battle statistics.

My father, with his passion for high standards, undoubtedly fed my joyless drive to achieve. So did my temperament as an adolescent. Like most teenagers, I had no sense of limits; I was encouraged to have no sense of limits. In school and out, at home and at play, I was always being told how to improve, urged to try harder, shown how to do better. The potential for improvement seemed limitless. Perfection lay just on the horizon. I was young and strong, I told myself. It shouldn't take too much effort to get there. But then why was it taking so long?

"You ought to learn to handle tools and machinery," my father often said to me. Knowing how to run a lathe, to read blueprints, to wire a piece of equipment could be useful, he urged me, though I couldn't see how. I never liked working with machines. I was always afraid that I would chop off what I was supposed to trim, or bore a bigger hole than I was supposed to drill; then I'd have to start over again. I also sensed that in urging me to work with my hands, my father was compensating for one of his own shortcomings. As an experimental physicist, he was often called upon to design and build equipment. By his own admission, that was never his strong suit and he admired colleagues who could do it well.

Nevertheless, in the fall of 1952, at the beginning of my senior year in high school, I decided to take up my father's advice. I enrolled in General Shop. It was an unusual choice, and I wasn't sure that my father understood who my classmates were likely to be. I was a white, middle-class student, college-bound. I had completed all my college prerequisites. Shop courses were usually reserved for vocational students, mostly poor, mostly black, who were expected to find jobs immediately after graduation. They—not the lathes and metal tools, not the welding and soldering, the study of blueprints and electrical circuits—interested me about General Shop.

I envied the shop boys their air of indifference and detachment. I marveled at the way they shuffled about, their jeans defiantly sliding below their hips so that they showed a flash of underwear. I liked the way they hunched in their dark leather jackets or their fire-engine-red athletic letter sweaters with the yellow block "B" for Berkeley. I envied the defiant tilt of their caps, with the bill turned insolently to the side or to the back.

They moved to a different beat from the society that I was familiar with. They shuffled, bobbing their heads and shoulders, as if to show their insouciance, their independence of ways and rules made mostly by the whites, by the middle class, by my kind of people.

In class, I made timid efforts to get to know some of the shop boys. They were not hostile; they were simply indifferent. They had their own world; I had mine. I had my "lunch gang" of friends. We boys met nearly every day at a picnic bench in a quiet courtyard of the school. We were all white middle-class males, sons of college professors, doctors and businessmen. We were all aspiring intellectuals, future doctors or engineers. We clumped together because we despised being "popular," because we despised high school fraternities and sororities. We did not seek to become class officers and we did not covet leading roles in the senior play. We had our unofficial female counterparts, a group of like-minded girls who ate at a table a few feet from ours. We all knew we had a future.

I worried whether the shop boys did. They were supposed to be acquiring vocational skills that would set them on the path to responsible jobs. So far as I could tell, the skills they were perfecting were wasting time, damaging equipment and annoying the instructor. A few were huge and powerful or lithe and sinuous. As their letter sweaters attested, on the football field they had a talent for crashing through piles of helmeted and padded bodies—or dancing around and between them. Athletic scholarships assured their futures for a year or two. Then what? At best, would they wind up selling insurance or used cars? Or become janitors? At worst, would they become small-time car thieves or bank robbers and spend long stretches of their lives in jail? I knew these boys had female counterparts in the home economics classes. I knew there were girls, black and white, who already limped about tiredly, who were destined for secretarial schools, then early marriages, early families—maybe even early deaths. I barely knew their names.

I felt vaguely that something should be done for the shop

boys, and the home economics girls, but I had no idea what or who should do it. For English class, I wrote an essay that concluded lamely that shop boys and college-bound students ought to get to know each other better. I felt so strongly that I even mentioned the essay to my father.

I hesitated. I knew that what I learned in school about the values of democratic political theory and American political institutions and society seldom harmonized with his ideas. For him, even Lincoln was puzzling and a little suspect. From log cabin to the White House made a marvelous story, my father admitted, but the raw democracy of it, the triumph of a man of the people was freakish. Lincoln's "government of the people, by the people and for the people" was a bad political principle (as well as redundant rhetoric), according to my father. To base a government on the whims and desires of the great mass of the population led to idiots like Mussolini—or even worse, to a Hitler. At the ballot box, however, I knew that my father usually voted Democratic because he felt that the Democrats were the most liberal and tolerant party and they supported civil rights measures.

I didn't have an easy time sorting out the contradiction in his politics. When I tried to defend American democracy, he said that the United States wasn't really a democracy. Think of the Founding Fathers, most of them plantation owners, men of property, educated men of the Enlightenment, the equivalent of a landed aristocracy, an elite. Venice had done well for centuries on this same principle of elites and great ruling families, he said. In the United States the great danger was that the country would fall into the hands of great mediocrities, provincial and naive— the likes of a Warren G. Harding. My father never forgot his horror, when he first arrived in Berkeley in 1938, at popular political naiveté and indifference. People didn't understand what a man like Hitler was capable of. If there was an Anglo-Saxon political tradition that he admired, it was English Toryism, as personified by Winston Churchill. With his quart of whiskey a day and his cigars and his willpower, Churchill inspired and led the English people through World War II. Here, my father said, was *"un uomo di fegato"* (a man with guts).

When I told my father about my concerns for the future of the shop boys, he shrugged. "Blacks aren't ready for industrial civilization," he said. "It's not their fault. Look at the way blacks drive. They're just not used to machinery. It's a question of culture." I was stunned. At first I thought he was teasing, and the *enfant terrible* in him was taunting me. He and my mother had always taught me that prejudice was wrong, that I should accept a person for what he or she was, without reference to color or religion or ethnic background.

So how could my father—a victim of racism—make such comments about my classmates in shop? I comforted myself with the notion that he was no garden-variety racist. He certainly had no sympathy with those who hissed, "Ship 'em back to Africa." Hitler's policies, of course, appalled him. I once heard him debate an avowed neo-Nazi at Berkeley, to the delight of an audience of university students. His opponent, who was more stupid than vicious, bumbled into an argument about race, intelligence and comparative brain sizes. "Well, then," my father said, "maybe you'd be better off with a whale's brain in place of yours." I could still hear the howls of laughter in the audience. From time to time, blacks enrolled in my father's courses. He watched the progress of "my little blacks," as he called them, anxiously. He helped and encouraged them, rejoiced when they did well.

And yet I also heard the conviction in my father's voice when he declared, "Blacks aren't used to machinery," as if he were merely declaring a well-known fact, a physical principle. There was nothing to argue about. In those rare moments when I pressed him, he appeared surprised and retreated to a lofty evasiveness. All you had to do was look around you, to watch blacks at the wheel, he said. His apparent scientific certainty on this matter, I realized, was a question of faith. More and more I understood that his faith and mine were diverging and that my going to college was likely to increase our differences.

.

In the fall of 1952, at the beginning of my senior year in high school, I could no longer duck my father's questions: "Do you know if you're going to college? If so, where?" I knew the answer to the first, but not to the second. Many of my classmates applied to the university a few blocks from our high school: UC–Berkeley. At that time, "Cal," as we called it, did not yet enjoy the worldwide reputation that it has today. Nevertheless, throughout high school, Cal was the standard, the ultimate mecca. But not for me. The campus stirred rebellious, even vaguely incestuous feelings. I'd grown up there. I knew the buildings and grounds from the Campanile to the Hearst Amphitheater and Memorial Stadium, from the oak groves along Strawberry Creek to the grassy slopes in front of the old President's House, where in junior high I'd played ferocious touchfootball games. My blood—once, I took a bad fall near the old Radiation Laboratory—had soaked the very earth at Cal. Also, I'd overheard too much gossip from my father about his colleagues, I told myself. Not that I would be likely to study physics. I'd probably major in the humanities. But I'd heard about those colleagues, too: "These humanists with their learned arguments —all windy rhetoric."

If I didn't want to go to Berkeley, he didn't know how to advise me, my father said gloomily. He knew nothing about the American college system. He would "ask Owen [Chamberlain]." Owen would know; he was American. Owen, it turned out, was a graduate of Dartmouth. Dutifully, I found out where Dartmouth was and applied there. In the fall, however, when the college recruiters came around, I attended a session with the admissions officer from Reed College in Portland, Oregon.

I don't remember what he told us. What lingered were the impressions, the images. Reed had a reputation for being radical.

My father at Trinity Site near Alamogordo, New Mexico, at the time of the first test of the atomic bomb (July 1945). In the background, one of the balloons used to measure radioactivity. *(Los Alamos Historical Archive: Jack Aeby)*

BELOW: One of the apple-green fourplexes similar to T-170, where we lived. *(Los Alamos Historical Archive)*

ABOVE: Some of the company that made Sunday outings so boring for me. Back row: my father, Enrico Fermi, Hans Bethe, Hans Staub, Victor Weisskopf. Seated: Erica Staub (left) and my mother.

Fishing on the Rio Grande.

With my sister Amelia at Los Alamos.

LEFT: My father's Jeep in front of the cabin in Pajarito Canyon where he had his laboratory.

BELOW: Fermi (left) and my father celebrating the end of the war in Europe (VE-Day) in the Valle Grande (May 8, 1945).

My father, dressed as an Indian, during a summer visit with his cousins at Forte dei Marmi, Italy (July 1919).

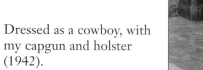

Dressed as a cowboy, with my capgun and holster (1942).

Engrossed in nature study in second grade at Los Alamos Elementary School (1943).
(Los Alamos Historical Archive)

LEFT: My parents, my sister Amelia, and I at Los Alamos (August 1945).

With my grandparents on the terrace in Tivoli, Italy (October 1937).

My mother in Rome, shortly
after she left Germany and met
my father (December 1933).

My father at the time he met
my mother.

ABOVE: Surrounded by my family: my mother with Fausta, my father with Amelia (1946).

My mother in the 1960s.

On my father's shoulders.

At fifteen, with my father
(1952).

My father and I in pith
helmets when I was about
four.

ABOVE: Zio Claudio,
my great-uncle and my
father's mentor.

LEFT: Zio Claudio and a
Japanese friend (1920).

ABOVE: My grandfather (center, wearing a hat), Uncle Angelo (far left) and Uncle Marco (standing just behind my grandfather, at his right), on the fiftieth anniversary of the founding of the paper mills in Tivoli.

My father in his Italian Army uniform (1927).

My father (front row, far left) at the beach near Rome where he first met Fermi (front row, far right). Enrico Persico sits between them. Standing behind Fermi is his future wife, Laura Capon.

BELOW: One of the photographs my father kept on the wall in his study at home: "the Pope" (Enrico Fermi, center), "the Cardinal" (Franco Rasetti, left) and "the Basilisk" (my father, right), in academic regalia (Rome, 1931).

OPPOSITE: My father receiving the Nobel Prize in Stockholm from the King of Sweden (December 10, 1959).

LEFT: With my father in Rome at the time of the Nobel Prize.

BELOW: With my parents and my sisters (Fausta, far left, and Amelia, far right) at the Nobel Festival.

BELOW: My mother (center) and my sister Amelia (left) chat with the Queen of Sweden at the Nobel Festival.

My mother on the King's arm, going into the Nobel Festival banquet.

My sisters, Fausta (far left) and Amelia, and I, meeting the King.

ABOVE: In Berkeley, with my bicycle (1946).

In high school: the strong, silent man of the mountains.

With my wife, Elisabeth (Zaza), and children (from left to right):
Francesca, Joel and Gino (March 1995).

Reed had no fraternities or sororities. The students didn't care about football. The school didn't even have a real team; anyone could play on it. The students read the Great Books, Plato and Aristotle and Saint Thomas Aquinas; they discussed T. S. Eliot and Shakespeare. In place of water fights and panty raids, we heard, they stood on street corners on Saturday nights, reading Shelley. When the Portland police came by and inquired what they were doing, the students replied, as if it were the most natural occupation in the world, "I'm reading Shelley." When the police asked them to move on, or, at least, if they had to read Shelley by streetlight, then to do it on campus, the students, of course, protested indignantly about violations of their constitutional rights. I also heard about the college seal. The official one said only "Reed College" but everyone knew what its motto should be, what the school really stood for: "Communism, Atheism, Free Love."

I found these stories about Reed clever and amusing, the sign of a mature and sophisticated student body. My father did not. He failed to see how the college's reputation for being "Red" was an advantage—not in 1953 with McCarthyism in its heyday. The House Un-American Activities Committee had been conducting hearings throughout the country. They had accused a Reed faculty member of being a Communist because he had taken the Fifth Amendment, and the college eventually fired him. Nevertheless, Reed fit my mood at fifteen-going-on-sixteen: intellectual, antiestablishment, a serious place for a serious education. I declared that I wanted to go there.

One night, my parents and I sat down to discuss the matter. It was serious enough to warrant gathering around the dining-room table and not the one in the kitchen. I remember how odd it felt. My parents and I were doing just what the advice for teenagers column, "Tips for Teens"—which I read avidly—in the local daily, the *Berkeley Gazette*, suggested. From that column, I understood that troubled teenagers could and should sit down with understanding, sympathetic parents, teachers, school counselors, football coaches, or pastors, ministers or rabbis, to discuss their personal problems.

I wanted to believe in that world. It was one in which all the participants managed to be white Protestants. Their English flowed smoothly and naturally, and their homes all had television sets and wall-to-wall carpeting. The adults were kind, gentle and sympathetic, with a heart-to-heart understanding of the teenager's growing pains. In that world, fortified by the wisdom and support of the adults, the teenagers marched forward, heads high, toward a bright future—or so I wanted to imagine.

I wasn't sure if anyone lived in a world quite like that. Certainly I didn't. That evening, when my parents and I discussed my college choices at the dining-room table, we perched on the hard, upholstered chairs with the wooden backs, the ones that to my mind always encouraged guests to sit up straight and properly at dinner parties. We had no television set to turn off. In lieu of wall-to-wall carpeting, I rested my feet on the Persian rug. My father's English did not flow smoothly and effortlessly; he spoke Italian. That night the rounded singing vowels sounded blunt and cutting. He had looked into the matter of colleges, he informed me grimly. Not many people had heard of Reed. Why did I want to go there?

Did I know what Portland, Oregon, was like? He made "Oh-re-gone" sound as close and attractive as Siberia. What was Portland's population? Did the city have any economic base other than lumber? Where did the other students come from? What were their family backgrounds? Were they timber barons of the Northwest? Or the loggers' sons and daughters? Was any of the faculty famous? Why not go to Dartmouth, to the Ivy League? That was where the American ruling classes went, that was the place to make contacts for any future career, my father said. A forefinger jabbing in my direction punctuated his questions and declarations.

My mother, too, had her questions. Portland was seven hundred miles to the north. Why did I have to go so far away? Maybe

I should try Berkeley. "Because he wants to get away from us," my father said. To me, he sounded as if he were smashing in a door with an ax. He turned to me. "It's the truth, isn't it?"

I shook my head. I protested. I also squirmed guiltily on that chair that encouraged its occupant to sit up straight. Maybe my father was right, I sensed. Maybe I did want to get away from my parents. They meant well, I knew. Concern and love prompted all those questions, I told myself. But if this was love, I didn't like it much. Parental love, I had gathered, mostly from "Tips for Teens," was supposed to be gentle, warm, soothing, healing. This variety was more like medicine, probably good for me; but like medicine, it stung and smarted.

Why *did* I want to go to Reed? I didn't really know. All I had were impressions: what the admissions director had actually said, what my classmates who had also heard him thought he'd said. The color photographs of Tudor-style dorms fronted by huge green lawns looked classically collegiate and inviting. The dorm rooms looked cozy and intimate, the way a student body of six hundred students sounded.

I didn't know what to say. I liked traveling, I told my parents. I liked seeing new places, living in a different part of the country. In the conversation, that was my piccolo passage, I thought, and I waited to be drowned out.

That wasn't much of an argument, my father snorted. At least, if I wanted to live in a different part of the country, I could have picked a more significant part of the cultural landscape, like a college on the East Coast, like Dartmouth.

Reed was a serious place, a place of culture, perhaps even a cultural center, I ventured a little more boldly. The students read the Great Books. There weren't any fraternities or sororities. Even *I* could play football on the Reed team. (My mother paled visibly and implored me not to.) Portland was supposed to be a beautiful city. Mount Hood, with plenty of opportunities for skiing and mountain climbing, was not far away. (My father seemed to like that.)

This was the blind leading the blind. I had no idea what I was saying; but then, again, neither did my parents. After a while, my father gave up. I never really answered their questions and the solemn decision, with its mule train's weight of guilt and anxiety, became all mine. They would be peering over my shoulder, I knew. If I failed, they would be there to say "I told you so." Would Reed be good for me? At fifteen-going-on-sixteen, I hadn't the faintest idea. Would I fail? Would I become homesick? Would I hate the rainy weather in Portland? I didn't even think about it. I was at the edge of the diving platform at the Men's Gym. I felt a little rush of adrenaline; I plunged, headfirst.

In my memory, I plunged bravely, confidently. In memory, I was tough and hard. Without hesitation, without sentimental farewells, I simply got in a car with two friends and future classmates one afternoon in early September 1953 and drove away, north to Portland.

A fragment of a diary entry shows otherwise. Tough and hard, steely and independent as I was (or imagined myself to be) I was also sensible enough to acknowledge certain debts:

Wednesday, September 10, 1953. Tomorrow, I leave for college. . . . Tonight is the last night that I sleep in the nest. Tomorrow, when I leave, I shall be trying my wings in earnest. . . . The problems, decisions, heartaches and joys will be mine. All successes and failures will be my own doing. I have had sixteen years of experience to help me meet the world. I have gone through many trials with the help of my parents and friends. I have learned from my mistakes. Tomorrow I shall seek new teachers and friends to help me with new challenges.

With a flourish of teen-column rhetoric—or had I been listening to too many high school graduation speeches?—I concluded: "I will be looking at a new world and with God's help, and head lifted high, I shall go to meet it."

CHAPTER 8

European Conflicts

Regularly, faithfully, dutifully I wrote home from college. I described the beautiful, bucolic Reed campus—the green lawns, the Tudor dorms, the Douglas fir, the walks in "the Canyon" behind the college, the explosion of rhododendrons and daffodils in East Moreland in the spring. I rhapsodized about skiing at Mount Hood, hiking in the Columbia River Gorge during the fall, wandering along the rugged Pacific beaches near Astoria. I described how, during spring vacations, with a group of classmates, I drove to Sun Valley. There we skied and drank. At night, the walls of our motel echoed with our serenades of each other, mostly in the form of mock operatic arias and recitatives, most of them improvised, all of them off-key. In my letters home, I recounted bits about the campus dances, the plays, the dinners, the concerts I attended. I hinted at my first love affairs. I mailed my parents copies of the college newspaper, which I edited in my junior year, and the literary magazine, which I edited in my senior year. I reported what I was studying, who my friends were, the politics of the college.

In perspective, my letters read like offerings, propitiations, maybe even corporate quarterly reports. I'm worthy, they say;

the tuition money spent on me is a good investment, much, I see now, as the young Emilio Segrè was eager to assure his own father, Commendatore Giuseppe Segrè, that his investment in his son—for example, financing a study trip to Pieter Zeeman's laboratory in Holland—was a good one. I was eager to show my father that Reed was a serious place. Few of my classmates planned to become anything so ordinary as lawyers or business-men. If my friends didn't get a Rhodes Scholarship, the least they aspired to was graduate school in philosophy or history or the sciences, or medical school. Those who didn't study hard, dropped out—and the attrition rate was high. Those who claimed their degrees at the end of four years, as I did, often felt like survivors. I didn't complain. So far as I knew, based on my father's example, that was the way things *should* be. Hard work was the best cure for whatever problems life presented.

My father's replies to my letters are, for the most part, cryptic, filled with practical issues, with warnings and admonitions. Do not buy a car unless you have secured automobile insurance. It is time to think of your financial future. In your economics courses, try to learn about personal finances and the stock mar-ket. If you must major in English or literature, learn the practical side, such as how to write for a newspaper.

At times, it occurred to me that he didn't know what else to write. He was a professor at Berkeley, so he knew something about student life at an American university. Yet, to him, my college experiences must have been the antithesis of his own. At the University of Rome, he had lived at home, surrounded by his parents and uncles. He attended lectures and then studied with his friends, sometimes in the rustic surroundings of the villa at Tivoli, where the maid prepared soup for the hardworking students. He dressed like a gentleman, for a while presenting himself as a dandy, complete with a cane.

I lived seven hundred miles away from home in a residential college. I visited only for brief periods during Christmas and summer vacations. In the best tradition of small American liberal arts colleges, my classes were often seminars instead of lectures. In democratic fashion, I sat at a table with my classmates and my professor and discussed the day's portion of Plato, Aristotle, Locke or Marx. Except when I went out on weekends, my sartorial aspirations extended to gray and navy-blue sweatshirts and blue jeans. Beards—or at least several days' growth of beard— were *de rigueur* among Reed men. I also rolled my own cigarettes—something my father, who generally smoked pipes and cigars, never did. Rolling my own had several advantages. It was cheap; it harmonized with my self-image as the silent, homespun outdoorsman. Finally, I found that rolling my own improved my social and love life. With my handcrafted smokes, the paper stuck better to the corner of my mouth; the cigarette bobbed up and down provocatively while I impressed girls with my deep understanding of Platonic reality.

I wanted more from my father than admonitions about car insurance. What did he think about God, Judaism, Love, the Cold War—something beyond his generic Chicken Little prediction that at any moment the sky might fall in, that atomic bombs might rain down on us? He worked very hard, and had his own worries, I knew. By this time, in the early 1950s, in addition to his research, he was fretting over whether he had a chance at the Nobel Prize. His quarrels with his brothers over family property in Italy often consumed him. He probably also concluded that once I was in college, I was well on my way to being on my own. I still wanted to know what he, my father, thought about love and marriage, God and death. Most of all, I wanted to hear from him that all my studying was worthwhile, that he was proud of me.

At moments, I had hints that perhaps he was. Freshman year, for example, I wrote home about studying the concept of *hubris* (overweening pride) in Greek tragedy and about the theories of the Austrian economist and Harvard professor Joseph A. Schumpeter. Back came a note from my father. What was *hubris*? And who was Schumpeter? "As you know, your mother is German and she's never heard of him. Evidently Reed is giving you quite a refined education." I savored my moment of triumph. Perhaps, I decided, I was making progress. Perhaps, eventually, I might apply for membership in the club of the *gente colta.*

I sometimes wrote my letters home in Italian or in French. Perhaps I did it in part to show off; perhaps I did it because I was a dutiful son and my parents had told me that practicing a foreign language was a good thing. Mostly, however, I did it because voices in those languages were there inside me, voices clamoring to be heard. If I ignored or repressed them too long, I felt uneasy, even physically uncomfortable, as if I were suffocating a part of me, as if, instead of using the full range of my vocabulary, I was restricting myself to baby talk. When I wrote in Italian or in French, I felt a kind of lift, a buoyancy. Mentally and spiritually I stood up a little straighter; my chest seemed to fill out. I was more than a struggling American college student in a small liberal arts college amid the forests of Oregon; or, several years later, an underpaid, overworked reporter lost in the urban jungles of Los Angeles; or, still later, a young academic teaching and publishing to avoid perishing on the fringes of the Texas Hill Country. I was polite and well educated; I was from the *buona borghesia,* middle class—even *upper* middle class.

The voices inside me, the letters home—all served to remind me of all that I was. So did the girls I went out with. They liked it when I deciphered Italian or French menus as naturally as if I were picking out items at an American steak house. They loved to hear me say "cappuccino" or "espresso" with no hesitation, no self-consciousness. Professors and prospective employers, too, noticed the "languages" and "travel" sections of my admissions or job applications. When I read Goethe or Montaigne or Dante, they spoke directly to me in a way that perhaps they didn't to Americans, I thought. For me to read these classics, sometimes in the original, was more than higher education, something you did in college. These people, their ideas, reminded me of home, of that "European culture" that I'd heard so much about as a child.

Like my parents, I dreamed of Europe, the never-never land of culture. From summer trips to Italy, from visits with relatives and friends, I knew how Europeans, especially Italians, lived, how I might aspire to live: cars were driven by chauffeurs; maids served sumptuous meals around one o'clock, the normal Roman hour for a midday meal. During the winter, the people I knew skied at Cortina d'Ampezzo or Gstaad. During the summer, you went to the beach for a month, perhaps to Rapallo, perhaps to Ancona or Rimini or Amalfi, depending on the changing fashions. After the beach came a month at Cortina again or the Dolomites to take "a little mountain air." At lunch, sprinkled with cousins or uncles, brothers-in-law or sisters, people talked about their personal affairs, but also about the politics and the future of Europe or the latest French movie. For them, Europe was not some exotic once-in-a-lifetime two-week whirlwind tour. For them, Paris and Florence, Madrid and London were places they went to as part of their lives, places where they had relatives and friends. When they talked about Europe and Europeans, they were talking about themselves.

I also dreamed about Europe because I needed to make sense of my life, to give it a certain logic. I was the son of Emilio Segrè from Tivoli and Elfriede Spiro from Ostrovo; the grandson of Giuseppe Segrè from Bozzolo and Amelia Treves Segrè from Florence; the grandson of Max Spiro and Gertrude Aschert Spiro from Ostrovo. With such roots, what was I doing moving furniture or mowing a lawn or fumbling among the frozen-juice cans in a supermarket in Portland, Oregon?

At times, I felt mildly schizophrenic, or as if I suffered from some multiple personality disorder. I spent the vast majority of my time studying and then working in the United States. I knew how to talk baseball or Cub Scouts, how to answer the "How you doin' today?" of grocery store cashiers and bank clerks with a countergrunt, "Fine. You?" I knew how to drawl slightly when I spoke to garage mechanics, so that I felt we were almost speaking the same language. I knew the mascot and what the victory sign was for the local football team. I knew that in the United

States you never knew whether to shake hands with men or whether to hug or kiss a woman friend who was not a lover.

I was lucky, I told myself. I never experienced the wrenching culture shocks that my parents did in Berkeley and Los Alamos. I was safe, secure. I could feel it in a parking lot on a Saturday night. After a good movie or perhaps a satisfying meal at a restaurant with a shade too much wine, I would scan the rows and rows of cars, take in the bright lights of surrounding stores and buildings, blinking all those familiar, comforting brand names. Where was I? Portland? Berkeley? San Francisco? Los Angeles? Philadelphia? Washington? Did it matter? This was America. Wherever I went, for thousands of miles in any direction, I could repeat the same experience: the huge asphalt squares, the rows and rows of cars, the blaze of lights that would burn all night. I felt cradled in the arms of the wealthiest, most powerful society on earth.

I was safe. I also felt only half alive. There was that other side of me, stiff, cramped, eager to get out. I needed to shape my mouth into big, rounded vowels. I longed to ask for an espresso or a cappuccino where they were not exotic brews, misspelled on the menu and purveyed at exotic prices. My eyes hungered for the curves of church cupolas and the outrageous, irregular forms of certain piazzas. I wanted to loiter around fountains and statues that were not monuments to Founding Fathers, heroic pioneers, or Confederate war heroes. I wanted to sit by fountains that looked like more than a major leak in a water main or the mental lapse of a city engineer. Europe, I decided, would make me whole again. Or would it?

I graduated from Reed in 1957. For a year and a half, I pursued a graduate degree in English at Stanford. In 1958–59 my father had a sabbatical leave in Rome. This might be a time to explore the European in me, to find out where I belonged, I decided. Perhaps, too, in Italy, I might find more common ground that I could share with my father.

He had his doubts. "All in all you're American," he wrote me around the time I left for Europe. I had gone to school in the United States; I spoke the language well, he reminded me. My grandfather, too, referred nostalgically to his birthplace in Bozzolo, my father noted, "but he never went there even to visit and the people he knew in Tivoli or in Rome were different from those his parents knew." My father added, "I don't want you to worry about traditions and historical antecedents of limited validity." So far as he was concerned, I had "no duties or obligations as in families where there has always been a son who was a general or a judge or a cardinal."

I settled in Rome in a tiny third-floor walk-up studio apartment on Piazza Scanderbeg in the heart of downtown Rome. Two blocks down the narrow, winding, cobblestoned streets the Trevi Fountain sparkled and flashed on sunny days. Just up the hill lay the Quirinale, the Presidential Palace, once the home of popes, now that of the President of the Republic. There wasn't much to my apartment. One room contained a bed, a small couch, a couple of chairs. A small closet in the wall contained my books and clothes. Adjoining the main room was a small bath. I was pleased with my frugality, and I knew my father would be pleased, too. Yet the apartment was light and airy, and I padded around on hardwood floors. When I settled down to write, it was not at a rickety, wine bottle–covered table. I sat at a bright red imitation-Chinese armoire that opened out as a desk. If this was an artist's garret, it was certainly an upscale one, I decided—and imagined that my father would be pleased at that, too.

I felt free. I could do as I pleased. I wasn't sure what I pleased, and that frightened me. At Stanford, I had completed my course work in the Creative Writing Program under Wallace Stegner; so I wanted to be a writer. Or should I continue with graduate work, pursue an academic career?

I enrolled at the University of Rome. My father, too, had studied there. I settled on a vague plan of getting a degree in Italian literature. Since I already had my B.A., the Italian degree wouldn't take much effort, I thought. I had not reckoned with the Italian university system. Lectures occurred sporadically; libraries were places where students went to learn that books could not be found; paperwork depended on the favors of eccentric and whimsical old *bidelli*, the beadles or porters who dispensed precious forms and certificates. These papers enabled the student to seek other precious pieces of paper at office windows that were generally closed. These papers in turn yielded other forms that might or might not then allow the bearer to take a class or an examination. I very quickly gave up on the system.

Instead, I hung around with artists. For a while, before I found the apartment on Piazza Scanderbeg, I roomed with a painter. I spent evenings with musicians, listened to them discuss their craft and attended their concerts. I met actors, went to their plays. After the show, I went backstage and congratulated them; we had drinks together or supper and talked theater. I met writers and editors. I felt my father's eyes on me, sensed his uneasiness. What I was doing was all very well, but what, if anything, would these forays into the arts lead to? "What I'm sorry about is that you're firing all your bullets one after another without bringing down a nice boar," he remarked in a note to me at the time.

I often visited Tivoli during that period. Bits and pieces of my childhood memories, of my father's childhood memories, came alive. I remembered how, as a child, during summer visits in 1949 and 1951, I ran up and down the gravel paths and hid in the grottoes at Villa d'Este. I loved the play of light and shadow, the shade of the cypresses, the breezes from the grottoes, the spray from the fountains. I stood in the shadows of Villa Adriana's looming walls, marveled at bits of frescoes and mosaics; ahead of my parents and sisters, I raced along the dusty roads that wound through the silvery olive groves and climbed an old tree barefooted. In my diary, I noted the age of the olive trees and how gnarled they looked, yet they were not as old as the California redwoods, I remarked chauvinistically. With my family, I often went swimming in the sulfur baths at the Acque Albule, my father's favorite pool.

We visited the little villa where my father was born and spent his childhood. The garden behind the house appeared small and cramped. There wasn't much for me to do there except try to catch the goldfish and read Italian comic books. There was no place to play, no big playgrounds or grassy fields as in Berkeley. No one played baseball or football here.

Tivoli was not the little village I had imagined. Even during my father's childhood it was a small town with a substantial industrial base thanks to entrepreneurs like my grandfather. Beginning in the late nineteenth century, they had harnessed the waterpower of the Aniene River and built small factories. Now I could see that the city of Rome was seeping across the *campagna*, the countryside, toward Tivoli, blotting out the sheep pastures, engulfing the Acque Albule. Big blocks of apartments, as graceful as penitentiaries, sprouted up on the edges of town. Developers turned the hillsides of Monte Ripoli into mazes of walks and constricted streets, clogged with cars. Tivoli was becoming a bedroom community for the Romans. "They've ruined everything," my father always complained.

I wasn't so sure. The villa where he was born, for example, was still there. Until the 1980s, it remained in the family. For about a month during the summer of 1959 I lived in the house, reading, writing, exploring the town, trying to see it as my father had. During that month, cousins, seeking relief from the Roman heat, lived in the ground-floor apartment. I camped alone on the second floor. The furniture was covered with heavy brown wrapping paper, thick with dust. I curled up in my sleeping bag on a lumpy woollen mattress that probably dated back to my father's childhood. I smelled the dust; I padded around on the cold stone floors. At lunch, I ate my *pagnotta*—the equivalent of a submarine sandwich—of mortadella, salamis and cheeses in the dining room overlooking the overgrown garden where my father had played as a boy. I listened to the water dripping from the little fountain in the goldfish pond.

I prowled around among the residues of my father's childhood. The oak and walnut furniture, the armoire mirror before which my grandmother straightened her hat, the massive desk at which my grandfather probably sat, the heavy, carved chairs around the dining-room table reminded me of the weight, the stability the sense of roots that my father often talked about. "People could settle down and accumulate enough over the years to fill all those drawers and closets," I noted in my diary. I anguished over the corollary, as my father did: how much he had to leave behind when he emigrated.

At night, just before I drifted off to sleep, I listened to the crickets chirping and the wind in the elms. It was easy to remember that when my father was a child, the house stood on the edge of town. Beyond it, the road wandered through fields and olive groves to little villages. I sensed how Tivoli, in my father's day, might have been "rustic" and "countrified," as one of my father's cousins described it in a family memoir. Her phrase was "rustic, countrified, and at the same time refined." That puzzled me. I remembered how often my father insisted that he was surrounded by *gente colta*, people of culture. I recalled my own doubts about the "primitive diet" on which I was raised in Berkeley. Had Tivoli been a center of culture? I looked for the traces. When I strolled around the Roman ruins and Villa d'Este, I imagined Liszt and D'Annunzio doing the same. In the apartment, I browsed through cases of old books left from my grandfather's day: German grammars, Darwin's *Origin of Species*, Ernest Renan's *Life of Saint Paul*, works by the German socialist Karl Kautsky. I pictured my grandfather and my great-uncles, in their stiff collars, sitting around at night, gravely discussing the inroads that socialist ideas were making among the working class, even among the employees at the paper mill. I leafed through old Baedeker guides that belonged to my Great-uncle Claudio, with titles like *From Paris to Constantinople* and, simply, *Berlin*. I found old souvenir catalogs and guides to art exhibits and expositions in Rome, Paris, London, dating from the turn of the century.

Whenever I went out on the terrace and glanced down at the passersby along the broad street below, the Viale Arnaldi, I imagined my grandparents strolling there with their friends. From listening to my father and talking to relatives, I knew something about the doctors and the lawyers, the businessmen and the teachers who made up my grandparents' circle. They formed part of that middle-class elite that governed Tivoli—and liberal Italy—before World War I. My grandparents' best friends were Count Luigi Pusterla and his wife, Emilia. Pusterla was a member of the nobility who had fallen on hard times. He supplemented his income by selling lottery tickets. He was a typical product of the late nineteenth century, anticlerical, a believer in science and progress. Garibaldi was his great hero, and the walls and ceilings of the Pusterla home were painted with scenes of Garibaldi's exploits. The Count had a fondness for the classics and a white beard; to my father, as a child, he appeared as old as a Roman. I pictured the Segrès and the Pusterlas strolling up and down nearly every afternoon from two to four, gossiping and telling each other the latest news in the town, shaking their heads about the corruption and ineptness of Parliament or sharing memories from a recent trip to Florence or even London.

Yet the more I explored Tivoli that summer of 1959, the more I wondered about my father's memories of it as a center of culture. Was Tivoli more "refined" than the Berkeley I knew? I pondered this when I went out walking at night. I had the streets to myself. Through half-open shutters, I could see the flicker of television screens, hear the fanfare of television news and the melodramatic tones of the announcers. During the day, I watched the housewives gossiping at the butcher's, or haggling in the market. At the cafés, in the afternoons, the men seemed content to smoke cigarettes, read the pink sports papers and argue about the latest soccer match. When I went to the movies,

I watched flickering prints of old American Westerns or World War II John Wayne sagas. So far as I could tell, the "refined" and "cultured" people of my father's day were in short supply.

The best I could turn up was a charming and somewhat theatrical Marxist factory worker and his friends with whom I spent an evening in an *osteria* over a couple of liters of white wine. My friend played the guitar and, in a rousing tenor, belted out current Italian popular songs and American classics like "Polvere di Stelle" ("Star Dust"). In between numbers, we debated Marx, capitalism (especially the wicked American variety), the plight of blacks in the United States. His arguments generated more heat—which we both enjoyed—than light. When reason failed, he resorted to empathy. Ah, when he thought of the sufferings of American blacks and of the working class, tears came to his eyes! he declared. I looked and saw none. His empathy, I suspected, was in inverse proportion to his rapidly improving income. If this was the level of culture in contemporary Tivoli, I wondered, what had happened in the generation since my father's childhood? Or had my father's nostalgia and fertile imagination built Tivoli into something it never was?

"Rustic, countrified, and yet refined." I turned the cousin's phrase over and over in my mind. Couldn't it also sum up my childhood? Like Tivoli, the Berkeley I knew as a child was a small, provincial town a continent away from the great centers of American culture. Yet, regardless of my father's convictions, Berkeley was an unlikely place to grow up "barbarian" or "primitive." Berkeley was a university community. As a child, I had access to endless lectures, exhibits, plays and concerts. San Francisco, with its Chinatown, its North Beach, its opera company and museums, lay just across the Bay. Most of the visitors to our house when I was a child came not from Rome or Florence but from all corners of the globe. They often appeared more at home in Italian, French, German or even Hungarian or Chinese than in English.

Children often idealize the childhoods of their parents—or is it the other way around? As I tell my own children about my Berkeley childhood, I see their brows furrow first with wonder and delight, then with perplexity and uncertainty. Their early years are rooted in a medium-size provincial capital, among the pecans, the magnolias, the red oaks and cedars of a Southwestern university town. Will they view their Austin childhood as somehow a lesser one than mine in fabulous Berkeley by the Bay?

As a child, I rarely heard about my grandfather, my Nonno Giuseppe. When my father talked about him, he usually began: "Papà loved to read aloud, Shakespeare and Tolstoy, as well as Carducci, Pascoli, D'Annunzio and the other contemporary Italian poets of the day." There was a peculiar brassy quality to my father's voice, like fanfare, as if he were announcing to the world: "My father may have been a businessman, but he was no ordinary ignoramus." My father also liked to say, "When I needed a scholarship to go to Holland to study with [Pieter] Zeeman, Commendatore Giuseppe Segrè came up with it." I noticed the full title, "Commendatore Giuseppe Segrè," as if my father were saying, "Here's a man of substance, a man of importance. He was shrewd enough to recognize a good investment—me." Could that investment have had any doubts about himself? I wondered about the bravado in my father's voice when he talked about his Papà. I wondered if my father was hiding something.

During that summer in Tivoli, during that year abroad, I began to hear more and more about my grandfather. I felt his looming presence everywhere. "Il Commendatore," old business associates, even relatives, generally said respectfully; few called him casually, familiarly, "Zio Beppo."

Among those who did was my distant cousin, Bindo Rimini. "Zio Beppo" was a shrewd businessman, Bindo claimed in considerably saltier language. My grandfather had charm. He knew how to get the best of the deal and yet leave partners or clients smiling, satisfied, eager to do business with him again. He was a

generous man, always ready to lend a spendthrift "nephew" like
Bindo a few lire to go out and have a good time with the girls.
And sometimes the old man went along himself, even when he
was in his seventies.

A niece, in a family memoir, painted quite a different portrait
of my grandfather. Like my father, Silvia Treves Levi Vidale
recalled her Zio Beppo's taste for literature, the "warmth and
passion" in his voice when he read aloud. He had a way of evok-
ing historical personalities "until then . . . closed up in my text-
books" so that they became "alive and present," she added. But
she also recalled that Zio Beppo was "so big and gruff and rough
that I always felt a great subjection, almost a fear." Did "Pippi,"
as my father liked to call himself as a child, feel that way about
his Papà? If he did, he never said so. I wondered if perhaps he
didn't dare.

I studied photographs of me with my grandfather when I was
a baby. There's one when I'm seven months old. We are on the
terrace of the villa in Tivoli. My grandfather is not holding me;
my grandmother is. In fact, though I'm between the two of them,
he seems oblivious to my being there. He stands with his hands
behind his back, as if off in his own world—one that doesn't
include children. He wears a three-piece gray suit and tie.
Though he is only half a head taller than my grandmother, he
has the air of being a big man, ample and robust, at least by the
Italian standards of the day. He stares directly at the camera, as
if no one else were near him. With his white hair and his thick
mustache, his expression, though not glowering or aggressive,
challenges. I'm reminded of photographs of my own father
nearly two decades later. I prefer the images of my grandfather
as a young man, newly married. His face looks softer and
rounder, as if he is well fed. He appears less dignified and authoritative, as if that mustache occasionally dipped into his wine.

Intelligence, determination, hard work and a good marriage
—that was the essence of my grandfather's success, I learned
from the bits and pieces my father told me in that brassy, bravado

voice. From my grandfather's modest beginnings in the village of Bozzolo, near Mantua, in the Po Valley of northern Italy, he worked his way into a position of wealth and ease. Although he did not have a university education, as his two brothers did, he became a successful captain of industry in the paper business. For his achievements, the Italian state honored him with the title of *commendatore*, the equivalent of a knighthood. Early in his career, while he was working near Florence in a ceramics factory, one of his business associates introduced him to my grandmother, Amelia Treves, the daughter of a prominent architect whose works included the synagogue in Florence. For Giuseppe to marry into such a wealthy professional family was a step up the Italian social and financial ladder, and several rungs up within the tiny Italian Jewish social hierarchy.

Papà was busy with his business, the paper mills, my father said. He made it sound as if this were the way fathers normally behaved. In place of his real father, he had a "deputy father," his Uncle Claudio, my father used to say. During his adolescence, Pippi actually lived with his Zio Claudio one floor below my grandparents' apartment in Rome. The reason—an apocryphal one, according to my father—was that his snoring at night disturbed his much older brother, Marco. In the extended family of those days, however, such a living arrangement did not mean any great separation between my father and his parents. The family shared meals and my father retained a study table in his parents' apartment.

Zio Claudio, my father's "deputy father," was short—under five feet—and peppery. His photographs suggest a stocky, round-faced little man with simian restlessness and energy. For thirty-seven years he worked as a geologist with the Italian State Railways. His great contribution was to found research laboratories to investigate the various geological problems associated with laying out railway lines. His research led him to publish more than forty papers, and he was the first member of the "railroad family" to be elected to the Lincei Academy (the Italian equivalent of the Royal Society), according to his obituary. In family photo albums he is always impeccably dressed, even on field trips. Other photographs show him—always in a suit, with a derby, wing collar and watch chain—on some of his many voyages, for example, in 1901, through the Balkans to Constantinople. As he grew older, he became deaf and spoke in a loud voice, my father used to say; to the horror of polite society, he swore aloud.

"Incomparable teacher, disinterested friend, tireless animator," who knew how to instill in his collaborators "enthusiasm for work, zeal and faithfulness in carrying out their duties" for the "benefit of the Railroad Administration and the greatness of the Patria," his obituary reads. A grateful nephew benefited from these qualities, too, I sensed. I thought of my own name, Claudio Giuseppe. In it, my father honored first his bachelor uncle and second his own father, thus memorializing the hierarchy of fathers in his life.

My father's tone when he talked about his Papà resonated in my head. What lay behind that voice? The clues finally came during his last years, when he shared with me a letter that he had written to his own father in November 1937. The occasion was the fiftieth anniversary of the founding of the paper mills. My father could not be present for the festivities and thus congratulated my grandfather in the letter. My father, then thirty-two, went on to compare his own future fifty years down the road with what his father had achieved. "If one is a Rutherford, that's one thing," my father wrote, but a "good, but not extraordinary scientist" like himself could easily be replaced. At the end of half a century, my father hazarded, his own scientific work would probably be summed up in a few tables or in three notes in a great German compendium on physics. My grandfather, on the other hand, had only to look out from his terrace to view his life's work. There, below him, he could see the plant; he could savor knowing that hundreds of people—"and not just the parasite sons and grandsons"—enjoyed fruitful lives thanks to the jobs he provided. "With this, I've written you more than I would have said to you face to face," my father concluded, and added, "despite our great and tender affection for each other, you evoke in me a certain reserve and timidity."

Another clue came during my father's years of retirement. In the conversation that my father had imagined having with his own grandfather, the old man says,

> "Your father [Giuseppe] seemed to me much more human than you; he loved women, he knew how to deal with people, he liked fun and even played practical jokes, sometimes pushed rather far. He liked human relations and was good at them and I believe he was more generous than you."

He himself was more of a Treves, my father concluded, more like his mother's people—"rather difficult and inhibited persons, although very smart."

During that summer in Tivoli, and in the years that have followed, I came to know my grandfather better and better, and I began to understand what lay behind my father's bravado voice. I don't remember my grandfather; yet when I was in my forties, long after he was dead (he died of natural causes in 1944), I'm certain I heard his voice.

At the time, well launched on an academic career, I was spending a sabbatical year in the San Francisco Bay Area. Living in California, I succumbed to some of the charms of its pop psychology and had been infected with a mild case of "letting it all hang out," of getting to know my father, man to man. I was "doing lunch" with my friends. Why not lunch with my father? I thought. We would talk to each other, really talk to each other, I imagined, not just father to son, son to father, but also man to man, friend to friend. It was a radical departure. I would never have dared initiate such a meeting when I was younger, but I was a grown man, I had my own life. Why not? Perhaps he, too, would see me in a new light. I made a date to meet him in San

Francisco. He was amenable, but our schedules conflicted. He might have to wait for me at the restaurant. To my surprise, this perturbed him. He grumbled and complained, even more than he usually did. Finally he saw that there was no way around it. "Don't do this to me," he warned, his voice suddenly loud and gruff. "*Me lo lego al dito* [I'll keep it tied like a string around my finger]." Stunned, disappointed, I already sensed how things would go (as in fact, they did)—the lunch would take place, nothing would change. I also felt the power of that gruff, brusque voice, my subjection, my fear before it.

"But why?" I protested. "What's wrong?"

"My father would never have allowed that with me," came the reply. "It's a question of respect."

In his voice, in that peculiar brassiness, in that brusqueness that left no room for dissent or contradiction, I knew whom I was hearing. It was the voice of Il Commendatore Giuseppe Segrè.

In Rome, at the Chinese armoire-desk in my little apartment overlooking Piazza Scanderbeg, or at the long table overlooking the garden in Tivoli, I wrote. I did stories and journalistic pieces. I kept notebooks. I published small newspaper articles. Writing didn't come easily. Plays, novels, stories did not pour out as I thought they should—as my father thought they should, if I was going to be serious about writing. Was it because I wasn't writing the right things? Because I wasn't sending them to the right places? Was I working enough? Of one thing I was sure—and so was my father: I certainly wasn't getting paid enough, not even to live on.

Worst of all, I wasn't feeling the way I wanted to feel. Around my artist friends, I acted stiff, awkward. I wanted to be like them, but when I looked at myself, I appeared too polite, too conventional, too much like a *figlio di Papà* (Daddy's little boy). They had thrown themselves into their art, heart and soul. I seemed to be dancing on the fringes, as if I didn't quite belong. I felt frustrated and a little frightened, as if I were not developing normally, as if my growth had been stunted. I also felt resentful, as if I had been cheated out of a great experience, like being in love.

I wished I'd come from a family of writers like the Manns or the Brontë sisters, where writing was the family trade. In Italy I was surrounded either by academics, like my father and my Uncle Angelo (who had, however, retired to devote himself to painting), or businessmen, like my grandfather and my Uncle Marco. In my frustration, I decided to be practical. If, for the moment, I was not developing as a writer, then I should learn something about the family business, the paper mills in Tivoli, perhaps consider making a career out of them.

When I was a child, the paper mills, the Cartiere Tiburtine, as the company was known, struck me as ludicrous. First, there was the word association. For no particular reason, except a childish confusion between the English word "cart" and the Italian for paper mill, "*cartiera*," I conjured up a creaky wooden Sicilian donkey cart. Anyway, whoever heard of making paper? I couldn't imagine how it was done. And mills? They were for grinding wheat into flour. None of my friends' fathers who were businessmen made paper. Besides, in my family, we didn't do business. We worked at the university.

Yet, as I learned over the years, the paper mills were crucial to my family's history. Thanks to the Cartiere Tiburtine, my grandfather had leaped from his modest origins to middle-class wealth, ease and respectability. Thanks to the mills, my father enjoyed private tutors as a child, money to travel and to study abroad, money to ease his early years as an immigrant in the United States. In turn, the mills allowed me to enjoy many of the same privileges that my father did. I, too, was free to attend the college of my choice, to travel, to study abroad. I could afford to choose an academic career without forgoing material comforts.

As a child, I had often visited the factories. There were two of them, both named after old Roman ruins: Ponte Lucano and Mecenate. Ponte Lucano was the modern one that my Uncle Marco built after World War II. It was located near an old Roman bridge, not far from Hadrian's Villa, just before the road began to twist and wind up the hillside to Tivoli. It was a modern gray structure, straight and flat, an elongated box. Its centerpiece was the big papermaking machine. At one end, the wet pulp, gray and viscous, like a cake batter, or paper-mâché, fed in. A long series of wheels and belts transformed the thin liquid stream into a thin but substantial solid that you could write on or wrap things in. That magic transformation from batter to paper was something I never tired of watching.

Otherwise, like most modern factories, Ponte Lucano offered little except to the technical expert fascinated by the machine. The employees seemed to be an intrusion. There wasn't much for them to do except watch the machine, make minor adjustments and look forward to their lunch break. That was when they could sink their teeth into their *pagnotta*. After that, they looked forward to quitting time, to the moment when they could go to their lockers, shed their blue smocks and drive off up the hill on their bicycles, motor scooters or motorcycles.

Mecenate, the original factory, was located in Tivoli. Going there was like stepping back to the days when my grandfather ran the business. To get to Mecenate, you had to wind down from the main piazza through the twisting streets of the town's medieval quarter. I caught scents of what was cooking for the noon meal, heard snatches of popular songs on the radio. Women, gossiping, paused to look at me. A moment later I imagined that I'd been transformed into a snippet of local news. "That boy. *L'americano.* A Segrè."

The factory itself perched on the edge of the gorge that the Aniene had worn through the hills. The view from the director's office was magnificent. You peered down into the ravine and the winding stream meandering among thickets of bamboo of an

Asiatic green. On both sides of the stream, you could see small plots of land with little bamboo structures. These were the arbors where the *pizzutello*, the grape peculiar to Tivoli, hung lush and thick in August. Vegetable gardens sprouted around the arbors. Many of the employees, I knew, owned or shared those plots, where they grew string beans and zucchini and tomatoes. Then, as the sides of the gorge rose, the landscape became drier. The Asiatic green gave way to the Mediterranean green and silver of the olive groves. The little church of the Madonna del Quintiliolo stood out like the centerpiece at a banquet table. The factory at Meccnate was ingenious. Gaius Cilnius Maecenas (70?–8 B.C.), the Roman statesman and patron of literature, had built a villa on the site. On its ruins, my grandfather had built his factory. Integrated with the Roman columns and arches were the vats and pulpers, the creaky paper machines that transformed bundles of old scrap paper, straw and pulp into rolls of butcher paper. In the giant cement vats, big rotating millstones ground up the pulp. I thought of Indian women, grinding corn for cornmeal.

Unlike the employees at Ponte Lucano, who wore clean, antiseptic smocks that suggested they were technicians, the ones at Mecenate, mostly men, still appeared to be craftsmen. Their work clothes consisted of old trousers, held up by bits of string, and tank-top undershirts that many washings had turned to an uncertain yellow. Bits of dried pulp flecked their hands and faces. To protect their hair, they often wore little triangular hats, like Napoleonic cocked hats, made of folded newspapers. Like cooks deciding when the soup was done, they determined when the batch of pulp was ready for the machine by running their hands through the vat, letting the viscous liquid slip between their fingers.

The women workers, in blue smocks, shuffled around in old slippers or sandals. Usually they were hired to clean up. When they saw me coming, they gave a couple of unusually vigorous sweeps with their brooms, then leaned comfortably against them and flashed big gold-toothed smiles. *"È bella l'America, vero?* [America's beautiful, right?]," they began. Or they launched into stories about my grandparents, about the saintliness of my grandmother and the gruff justice of Il Commendatore. I learned not to bother questioning the authenticity of the stories. The storyteller either swore that he or she had witnessed the episode in person or knew for a fact that it was true because that's what had always been said in the family, in the factory, in the town. The women often spoke of their own families, of their pride that "my son (or my daughter) is studying," or perhaps they told a hard-luck story about a disabled (or dead) husband, or an inadequate pension or welfare check. "So I work hard," they would say with a sigh, and demonstrate their dedication and energy with a few more vigorous sweeps. Even I understood that though Mecenate was a charming, colorful, humane place to work, it probably wasn't good business.

When I went to Tivoli, I often stood at the edge of the main piazza, looked at the roof of the old plant at Mecenate and pondered its story. My grandfather was one of a group of entrepreneurs attracted to Tivoli in the 1880s by the potential of electricity from the Aniene River. Cheap power, combined with the town's centuries-old craft tradition, including papermaking, promised to transform Tivoli into a thriving industrial center. At first my grandfather worked as an assistant to the director of the power company. Eventually he succeeded his boss, and then, in 1887, founded the Società Cartiere Tiburtine.

Under my grandfather's direction the company prospered. Like most industrialists of his day, he ran the Tiburtine like a fiefdom. His word was law. Even when my father was in his twenties and my grandfather appointed him to the company's board of directors, it was purely a formality. For example, the first time my father was asked to sign the minutes of the board of directors' meeting, my grandfather handed him a blank sheet of paper. When my father nervously asked to see the actual minutes, my grandfather lost his temper, so like "a member of the Comintern" presented with one of Stalin's decisions, my father signed, he recalled.

Miraculously, the factories survived World War II, including an Allied bombing raid on Tivoli. My grandfather's death in 1944, however, proved to be disastrous in the long run. My Uncle Marco, who had worked in the business for many years, took over direction of the company. My father and my Uncle Angelo assumed at first that this arrangement was in keeping with my grandfather's wishes. In the 1930s, my grandfather had indicated orally that he planned to leave the company to my Uncle Marco and to compensate the other sons with properties and securities. My father and my Uncle Angelo also presumed that my grandfather did not leave a will, for in 1938, Mussolini passed racial laws that restricted Jewish ownership of property. To evade the laws, as my grandfather did, Jews often nominally transferred titles to their assets to Gentile friends and associates. To leave a will under these conditions was difficult and dangerous.

Accordingly, in 1947, the brothers divided my grandfather's estate as they understood his wishes. Under this division, my Uncle Marco gained a controlling interest in the paper mills. Six years later, however, my father and my Uncle Angelo discovered that my grandfather had indeed left a will—one that most likely my Uncle Marco knew about. The will provided that all property, including the mills, was to be divided evenly. Outraged at what they considered their brother's deceit, my father and my Uncle Angelo unseated my Uncle Marco as chairman of the board. The brothers, however, never found an effective replacement. By 1959, when I came upon the scene, the company, which had floundered under my uncle's direction, had declined even further.

I realized that my involvement in the paper mills would mean far more than simply making a living or forging a career. If I could somehow contribute to untangling the financial and emotional morass of the Tiburtine, I would also earn my father's gratitude and respect in a way that few other endeavors of mine could. For him, the paper mills were an unending source of grief, rage, frustration. I saw my father at his worst, frightened, anguished, paralyzed with fear and dread, when he had to deal with them in any way. From time to time, he sank into a depression and he developed an ulcer. For him, the mills were not simply a business, a source of material comfort and security; they were his father's creation, his handiwork, his monument. They deserved honor and respect. Moreover, I sensed that, despite his achievements as a scientist, my father felt a twinge of guilt that he'd never matched his father's financial successes. The least he could do, my father vowed, was to preserve and pass on my grandfather's patrimony to another generation. Given my father's relationship with his brothers, that proved impossible.

I couldn't understand the hostility between my father and my uncles. The sibling relationship I knew best was with my own sisters, and that one was close and warm. I thought about my uncles. Toward me, they were always pleasant enough. My Uncle Angelo could be gruff, impatient, prickly at times, but I often enjoyed his cutting wit. My Uncle Marco sometimes appeared too eager to impress me with his accomplishments as a businessman, too eager to remind me that as a teenager he had once taught his younger brother some principles of physics. But my uncle could also be gracious, witty and charming. Good manners seemed to come naturally to him. Where had the fraternal bitterness, the hatred come from? When I asked discreetly about their relations as children, neither my father nor my uncles provided many clues. Anyway, I told myself, we are all family, aren't we? So why can't my father and his brothers simply shake hands like brothers and gentlemen?

Experience taught me why. During that year, 1959, I attended meeting after meeting between the brothers or their representatives. I came to know each brother's retinue of lawyers, consultants, *uomini di fiducia*, trusted friends who, I decided, could be relied upon mainly to increase divisions and suspicions. I listened to conversations and phone calls. Most of them, so far as I could see, were pointless. When I said so, trusted friends, consultants and lawyers looked at me in pity. Of course I was too young, too naive, too American to appreciate how these maneuvers were actually part of a complex and tricky strategy that would finally get us what we wanted. As I watched and listened, I felt at moments as if I were in Plato's cave. In the foreground was the nominal world of business, the contracts that had to be signed, the new orders that had to be secured, the loans that had to be arranged. But that surface world was illusion. In the background were the brothers, still playing out their childhood conflicts, their rivalries, vanities and jealousies. Who was really more clever, more intelligent? Who was more savvy? Who had really accomplished more?

One meeting finally disabused me of any hopes that my father and my uncles would reconcile and that the Tiburtine would survive. The sole purpose of the meeting was to get the brothers to shake hands. The old white-haired lawyer who presided was courtly and correct. He was my cousin's father-in-law. He had an old-fashioned sense of honor and courtesy and he meant well.

When we were all assembled in his office, he said simply to my father, to my uncles, "You're all brothers. You're all gentlemen. Now shake hands like gentlemen." Nobody moved.

"You?" the lawyer said, turning to my Uncle Marco. My uncle shook his head.

"You?" He turned to my Uncle Angelo. My uncle didn't move.

"You?" he said to my father. My father sat there motionless, stony-faced.

There was nothing to be done. It was another morning wasted, another series of phone calls, coordinated appointments, complicated conversations, anticipating the various options, mapping intricate strategies; another occasion for lawyers and consultants and trusted friends to whisper urgently to their patrons, "If he (they) agrees, then you do this; if he (they) doesn't, then you do that. But under no circumstances must we do this."

In that world of intrigues and plots, schemes and conspiracies, my father seemed totally out of place. Sullen, grumbling, protesting, he appeared at the meetings, his face dark, angry, pouting. Like a little boy throwing a tantrum, he refused endless cups of espresso. On the one hand, he probably wanted to bite back as his brothers were doing to him, but he didn't know how. At the same time, his mind desperately groped for clear, firm, rational solutions, as if he were observing an experiment, collating the data, coming to some neat conclusions. He wanted numbers, statistics, not promises, not impressions, not the *chiacchiere* (chatter) that according to him made up so much of the business world. The market for paper products was picking up in Italy? How much? How soon? What was the per capita consumption of paper in Italy? What was the projected figure during the next decade? He mistrusted plans and promises, no matter how well intentioned. If a deal was to be made, he wanted everything in writing, every clause for every contingency, no matter how unlikely or remote, spelled out to the point of exasperation.

I felt embarrassed, ashamed, powerless at the spectacle of my father and his brothers quarreling. I resented being one of those trying to clean up their messes while they whined and complained and felt sorry for themselves. I hated seeing my father at his worst: hyperanxious, selfish, petty, spoiled, tyrannizing over those whom he had no reason to fear—like me. I resented helping my father wipe his nose when I desperately wanted him to help me with mine. Most of all, I was horrified, as my father was, at the decline of the business. Observing these meetings, it seemed to me, was like watching a pack of jackals feed on a carcass.

One particular session stands out in my mind, a board of directors meeting to approve the 1957–58 balance sheet. We gathered in a notary public's office in downtown Rome, a big, old-fashioned room with high ceilings, a mahogany table surrounded by a dozen leather-backed chairs, bookcases filled with leather-bound law books. A chandelier with yellowish-orange lightbulbs shaped like candle flames shed a shadowy light over the room. Since the meeting was purely routine, neither my father nor my Uncle Angelo was present. They sent their representatives. My Uncle Marco attended the meeting. In his dark blue suit, he looked like a dignified business executive posing for a formal portrait. He appeared grave and pensive as he listened to the interplay of his lawyers, the accountant, his brothers' representatives. From time to time he jerked his head up at certain words and phrases. He looked as if he'd caught some intricate point that must be carefully weighed, its possible value and meaning minutely examined. Meanwhile, his brothers, through their surrogates, appeared to enjoy dancing circles around him. My Uncle Angelo's representative was a small, chubby, smiling Sicilian, a professor of business, the patriarch of a clan, rich, respected, powerful. He sat doodling nervously all the time: squares, then annexes to them, always geometrical figures. When my Uncle Marco asked about certain items or expenses on the balance sheet, the man often replied that he "didn't remember"—and appeared to relish his memory lapses. My father's representative was a cheerful, energetic lawyer, an upbeat, courageous man, scrupulously honest. Yet he, too, appeared to amuse himself with darts and jabs at my Uncle Marco and his entourage.

The president of the company was a man in his fifties with silvery hair. Like his name, Marchesi, he had the haughty air of a marquess about him. Periodically he fished a Turkish cigarette out of his silver case and wedged it between his upper lip and front teeth. He looked as if he had sprouted a miniature tusk. Occasionally he took his thick, metal-framed glasses off, revealing large, nearsighted eyes. I fancied that they reflected the cruelty of a cat playing with a trapped bird. He did nothing to stop the stonewalling, the grandstanding, the verbal fencing. Indeed, it seemed to amuse him. His coldness and indifference enraged and horrified me. Surely what was going on was not in the company's best interests, I told myself, and if he didn't have the company's best interests at heart, why did he take the job as president?

I felt I had to do something. The day after the meeting, I sat alone in the little apartment that I was sharing temporarily with my parents and pondered the folly of the situation: the time and energy wasted, the desecration of my grandfather's work. Maybe this was the moment for me to act, to do something to turn this situation around, to show that I could make a difference. Maybe I should call the president, appeal to his sense of humanity, plead with him to do what he could to bring the brothers together, to save the business, to put an end to this senseless playacting.

In my head, I rehearsed the conversation dozens of times. I mouthed the words. They appeared to be at once reasoned, passionate, eloquent, an irresistible appeal from the heart. When I actually tried saying them aloud, I heard only disjointed phrases that sounded naive, puerile. I could easily imagine the president at the other end of the table, his voice polite, courteous, but raising an eyebrow, making mocking faces, wondering what possessed me. Perhaps he understood my naive goodwill and my desperation, but my intentions could do nothing to resolve the situation.

Even worse, I imagined my father's dismay. I could hear him yelling at me, shaking his head in exasperation: What did I think I was doing? Didn't I understand whom I was dealing with? It was all very well to be young and idealistic, but this was business. I was dealing with crooks and hitmen, with hyenas and vultures. I had my answer ready to fling back at him: this was his wonderful Europe, the land of *gente colta*; this was the close-knit family he liked to fantasize about.

I had my hand on the telephone receiver; I never lifted it.

So the endless round of meetings in company rooms, in lawyers' and accountants' offices, in hotel lobbies continued. So did the early-morning and late-night phone calls, the demands, based on the latest developments, real and imagined, for immediate meetings. Dutifully, I attended when it was appropriate.

And yet I didn't want to give up. I desperately wanted to find myself, to settle on a career. The company appeared to promise financial security and a respectable position. I felt the warmth of family loyalty, a duty to the memory of my grandfather. I thought of my conversations with the machine tenders in the factories and the women leaning on their brooms. They were glad to see me. To them I symbolized continuity, structure, a secure future—as the company had for nearly three generations. With them I felt important, worthwhile.

I fantasized about what my lifestyle might be like if I went into the business. I knew how academics lived, and I thought I knew about writers' lifestyles, but I didn't know much about being a gentleman businessman. I pictured myself ten years down the road. I'm driving a silvery-gray Jaguar XK 120, with long, loping lines, red leather seats, shining spoked wheels. My voice is always low and calm. I wear gray suits with vests and striped ties—but also an occasional paisley or Liberty print, just to show that though I'm correct, I'm also me, a man of taste and spirit. I'm always neat and pleasant and generally well tanned from long weekends on the Riviera or skiing at Cortina. My pens and pencils are silver or gold-plated. Business means presiding over a lot of meetings, sitting at the head of a long mahogany or teak table in the conference room. My style tends to be agreeable, elegant, but firm. If things aren't getting done, I reprimand, I even fire people—with generous severance pay, of course. People like me; they say that though I'm a good businessman, I was really cut out to be a gentleman, a scholar, an artist. I spend too much time thinking about the welfare of my employees and providing for them. I do too much charity work.

In another scene, I imagine that I'm loading up the Jaguar in front of a hotel in Gstaad or Saint Moritz, waiting for my wife, who is beautiful and sophisticated, from an Anglo-French background with a Rothschild branch somewhere among her cousins.

French is her first language, but we usually speak Italian or English. We've been skiing. I'm still a very good skier. Our three children are trilingual cosmopolitans. The older boy and the girl go to Swiss boarding schools. They wear navy-blue blazers with gold or silver buttons and coats of arms on the breast pocket.

These were fantasies, of course, and yet that year I found someone who, in his way, shared them with me. He believed in the business, he was family, he was devoted to my father. In an odd sort of way, though they were polar opposites in personality and interests, my father was devoted to him as well. His name was Bindo Rimini. He was a distant cousin; the blood tie was almost nonexistent. His mother, Ada, sweet, sad, long-suffering Ada, was my father's second cousin. She was a small, white-haired woman who always wore black and a mournful expression—except when she saw me. Then she seemed to light up for a moment, as if in me she were seeing some hope for the future after all. She might have been my grandmother, I decided. Her husband had died long before, leaving her to raise two young sons, Bindo and Riccardo.

My father was attached to both boys, but closer in personality to Riccardo, a physician who emigrated to South America at the outbreak of World War II. My grandfather apparently favored Bindo and acted as his surrogate father. In turn, Bindo watched over me. If my own father had his Zio Claudio, I had Bindo.

Bindo was short and stocky—like Napoleon, too short, the malicious tongues said. Perhaps to compensate, he walked around with his chin high, so that no matter how much you towered over him, he appeared to be looking down on you. That tilt of his chin gave him an air of defiance, pugnaciousness. Unfortunately, when he tipped his chin back, his neck seemed to retract between his shoulders. He was balding, and his round eyes bulged a bit behind his round metal-framed glasses. The unkind made comparisons with toads and frogs. Although he was in his early fifties, pudgy, and smoked too much, he loved to demonstrate that he was still quite *sportivo*: he could do a back flip off the diving board, and, with the grace of a tap dancer, he could run down a flight of stairs backward.

My father snickered at the way Bindo camouflaged his stocky frame in custom-made clothes, at his habit of tugging at the shoulders of his jackets, pulling at the cuffs of his shirts, complaining that he would have to return this one and that one because it was always crinkling and creasing. Was it his fault that nothing ready-made fit him properly? Bindo complained, as if tailored clothes were one of his afflictions. "Bindo's lazy," my father would sniff. "He's an ignoramus. He's full of hot air. He tells stories. He never read a book in his life. He barely reads the paper. He has a degree in chemistry, but he doesn't know the first thing about it. Nothing. Nothing." (On this last point, Bindo agreed completely. He often marveled that he had actually gotten his degree. He found it most useful in impressing future clients and bullying secretaries overprotective of their bosses: "This is *Dottore* Rimini speaking.") I would listen to my father's outbursts. Bindo was family, and yet where was the educated European, the distinguished member of the *gente colta* I had been taught to respect as a child?

And then, inexplicably, my father would begin to mutter, almost as a counterpoint: "*Bindo ha tanti numeri* [literally, 'Bindo has so many numbers,' meaning so many talents]," as if Bindo were a safe and if you just got the combination right, you were into a treasure. Bindo was honest, my father would say; he was straight. Bindo was no fool when it came to business, my father would hint. Like his brother, Bindo spent the war in South America. There he had probably made fortunes and then lost them again, my father speculated. Lazy, ignoramus, windbag Bindo might be, but my father believed in his "numbers" and entrusted him with many of his business affairs.

I didn't know what to make of this energetic little man with the manners of a drill sergeant and the stories of a traveling salesman. Bindo sized me up. I was careful, fragile, serious— maybe too serious. "*Giovanotto, fai dello sport* [Young man, do some sports]," he advised me, and then declared dramatically, as if this were the opportunity of a lifetime, that I had to make up my mind. If I wanted to go into the paper business, he had to know. Then he would open doors for me—doors that no one else could open. I would have to go on trips with him, so that he could introduce me to his clients, learn how to make deals. He took me to his tailor and got me fitted for a gray suit—but no shirts. It was time I learned something about Life, he proclaimed.

From time to time, I went with him on business trips. I learned to wear gray suits and navy ones, with dark ties. I listened to him shout at waiters (I could never bring myself to shout) and then leave them big tips so that they remembered him. I gulped espressos or sipped beers in hotel bars and dawdled over lunch in dining rooms. I watched Bindo make deals.

"So what about it?" he says, beginning his sales pitch. The client has just been treated to a detailed review of where Bindo plans to go on vacation, or why he is thinking of buying a new Alfa Romeo, or why he prefers to have his daughter learn English at an Oxford summer program rather than one at Cambridge. "I'll get you that shipment of Kraft liner [a type of paper] at a very special price. The technical people really have it together these days. It's top-quality stuff."

"I'm glad to hear that, because the last shipment wasn't fit to wrap fish with," the client replies.

"I know, I know, but they were having trouble with the machines," Bindo says sorrowfully. "Now they really have it together." He leans forward, perhaps takes the customer's hand confidentially in his. "You know, I'll be taking a beating on my commission, but I'll give you a special price." And Bindo names the price.

"That's not a beating—that's robbery," the customer protests, pulling his hand away and shaking his head in outrage, like a dog getting out of a river. "How many times have I bought from you. Am I a good customer? A steady customer? Am I?" And with the air of someone still traumatized by the last deal, he stares straight into Bindo's eyes.

"You're not just a customer. You're one of my oldest friends," Bindo protests. "Remember when we were students and we used to go to that whorehouse together? Oh, that blond one—what was her name? Ingrid?—was really something. No Scandinavian ice water in her veins."

"She wasn't blond. That was peroxide. I think her name was Maria, and she was from Naples."

A little digression about the charms of Scandinavian versus Mediterranean women ensues before the talk drifts back to business. Or perhaps Bindo points to me. "What do you think of this young man?" he says, as if I were a fine specimen of beef. "You know who his father is?" Bindo pauses dramatically. "This is the son of Emilio Segrè. Emilio's my cousin. They say he's going to win the Nobel Prize. I'm betting on it. My cousin, the Nobel Prize winner. What do you think of that? I'm twenty times smarter than Emilio. I just don't know any physics." And Bindo laughs before steering the conversation back to the deal.

"You know, I've heard that we may be raising prices soon," Bindo says. "Maybe next month. I'll make you a deal. Order now—at the old price. I shouldn't do this. It's going to cost me. I don't care. We're old friends, aren't we? My wife got her diamond. She won't need another one for at least a year."

"This is a holdup," the customer protests. "You know it. I could get the same thing at half the price from—" And the customer names the competition. "But I need the stuff. Can you get it to me next week? I'm doing it just because we're friends, you know."

"Of course," Bindo says. "It's just because we're friends." A handshake. Another drink. The deal is done. Bindo winks at me. If the customer's back is turned, Bindo winks again and wipes his forehead with the back of his hand, as if to say, "That was a close one." Afterward he mutters to me, "I didn't know if I was going to make it. He knew that at that price I was taking him

to the cleaners. Our rivals have cut their prices by twenty per-
cent. But he likes working with me. See, it pays to be nice to
people. You just have to know how to deal with them."

On weekends at his beach house at Fregene, near Rome, I
learned Bindo's version of social skills—though I didn't neces-
sarily model myself on him. At the beach, Bindo wore a small
linen cap to protect his head from the sun, and prescription dark
glasses. His belly bulged comfortably over his skimpy "sleep"
(slip), as the Italians call men's bathing trunks. He shuffled
around in expensive sandals, holding himself a bit like a gorilla,
shoulders back, chin high, greeting everyone, inspecting everyone and everything.

"Buon giorno, signora," he would sing out. "How are you?"
When the polite response came back, "Fine. How are *you?*"
Bindo took the question quite literally and often gave an update
on the state of his health. "Not too bad. The usual. I talked to
my doctor the other day. He's very good. First-rate. Very expensive first-rate. He said I ought to be more careful about my
liver. A little less wine. A little less bread. My blood pressure's a
little high. I really ought to exercise more." Or, always restless,
Bindo would roam about among his friends, who were sunning
themselves on deck chairs or sleeping on a towel. He was ar-
ranging his evening poker game, planning the snack menu. "I
was thinking of making those little spaghettini. You know the
ones I mean?" When it came to spaghetti, Bindo could be very
precise. "Not the thick ones. The little ones. I'll make them with
just a little tomato sauce, and maybe a little cheese, a little Pecorino. *Poco, poco.* Do you like Pecorino?" And he would be dem-
onstrating, with his thumb and forefinger almost touching,
precisely how much Pecorino he would include.

His inspections, of course, included pretty girls. When one
walked by, he leered shamelessly: *"Buon giorno, signorina.* What
a beautiful day." And then he stuck his chin out to better examine
her breasts. As soon as she had passed, he would nod to me.
"Did you see those tits? They're for you. Ah, if only I were your
age again." And he would tug at his "sleep."

Bindo's sorrows extended beyond ill-fitting clothes and no longer being my age. One of the major disappointments of his life, I sensed, was that he was never made president or chairman of the Cartiere Tiburtine. He knew the business; he revered my grandfather, declared that he loved my father "like a brother." But when it came to giving Bindo the responsibility, my father and my uncles were too bitterly divided and suspicious. They claimed either that Bindo wasn't up to the job or that he was too much my father's man. So, with two associates, Bindo continued in his business as a representative of British and American pulp manufacturers in Italy.

He went on as he always had, even after he finally married and fathered two children, breezing along on the surface of life, making everything appear so easy. "It's so simple. If you people would only listen," he used to say, and he would turn to me. Did I want a Mercedes sports car with butterfly doors—something right for a young man like me? That car would go two hundred kilometers an hour with no problems. He could swing a deal. It would take "a few grand." That wasn't so much, and the way he said it, it didn't *seem* like much. What was unthinkable, outrageous, out of reach for most people wasn't so at all for Bindo.

Yet I also learned not to take him too literally. I never shopped for the Mercedes; I never would have driven it at two hundred kilometers an hour, anyway. What I liked best was imagining that I could. All I had to do, I told myself, was make up my mind, will it. Experience told me that things weren't as simple as Bindo made them out to be; but neither were they as difficult as my father viewed them.

Unlike my father, Bindo never seemed to agonize over things. For him, the world wasn't so fraught with guilt, burdens and complexities. You didn't have to be well read, deeply educated, thoughtful and profound. You just had to know how to get along with people and occasionally do a little work—not even a lot. Life wasn't so hard; it was fun. I loved Bindo, I loved his faith in the simplicity of things, and I was stunned at the twist of fate that killed him in 1983. During a routine operation, a simple one, a perfectly ordinary one, one that was "nothing at all," I can hear him saying, he died quite unexpectedly from an overdose of anesthesia.

Neither my hopes and fantasies, nor my goodwill, nor that of Bindo and the other employees loyal to the Tiburtine were enough to save the company. In 1959, the Cartiere Tiburtine were sold to a large Finnish paper company. The Finns arrived, a little too stiff and formal in their dark suits, but with goodwill and plenty of money. They had sound business reasons for buying the Tiburtine; they wanted access to the Common Market. Like most Scandinavians, they also fell in love with Italy, with its light and color, its charms and mirages. I got to know many of the Finns well. Often I served as an interpreter for them, translating back and forth between English and Italian. Late in the spring of 1959, I visited Finland briefly as a get-acquainted and goodwill gesture while the negotiations for the sale continued. I admired the Finns' modern, American-style factories, their obvious care for their workers. I often compared their huge, powerful, efficient machines and the creaky, antiquated arrangements at Mecenate, and I realized that translating Italian into English or English into Italian was really a metaphor. I needed to explain two cultures to each other. I wondered how the Finns would fare in Italy. Even though the managers were successful and experienced, I worried that the Italians would take advantage of them.

In fact, the Italian deal did not turn out well for the Finns. They did what they had to do: they tried to modernize and streamline and make the factories more competitive. They closed Mecenate, with the loss of many jobs. The result was a long strike. Finally the Finns gave up in frustration. They sold out to another Italian company and retreated to a less baffling and Byzantine way of doing business.

The sale of the paper mills did nothing to reconcile my father and his brothers. It simply removed the chief and most immediate source of conflict. There were plenty of others left. Afterward, each brother simply drifted off to his corner of the globe: Uncle Angelo to Florence to paint many pleasing Impressionist-style landscapes, still lifes and figure studies; Uncle Marco to pursue his other business interests from his top-floor apartment in the Parioli District in Rome; my father to do physics at Berkeley and enjoy the splendor of his house on Crest Road. For the rest of their lives, there was little communication among the brothers and no heartfelt mourning as each died. Curiously enough, however, after my Uncle Angelo died, my father did inquire from time to time about the fate of his canvases (they remain in storage) and a new edition of a work he had done on the economic history of the ancient world (never completed). The fraternal hatred extended generally to the spouses, though there was some timid reconciliation between my father and his niece and nephews. The cousins, especially after the fathers died, have reached out to each other. We are scattered, our lives are different, but we have managed to reestablish family ties.

By the time the mills were sold, I had already made up my mind about my own future plans. I gave up my fantasies of my gray Jaguar, my expensive wife, my blazer-clad, trilingual children. The paper business—business in general—was certainly a trade that ran in the family, but it wasn't one that I knew. I felt more comfortable pursuing the academic life and my dreams of being a writer. By December 1959, the arrangements to sell the paper mills were in their final stages. Ironically, the nightmare that had haunted my father for more than fifteen years was coming to an end just at the moment when a dream he had seldom dared to dream was about to be fulfilled—he was to receive the Nobel Prize for physics.

CHAPTER 9

Royalty

On a Sunday night late in October 1959, my ex-landlady called me. She had heard rumors on the radio that my father and his colleague (and former student) Owen Chamberlain would share the Nobel Prize for physics. The next morning, October 26, friends telephoned to confirm the news, and on the front page of the Roman daily *Il Messaggero* there it was: "To Emilio Segrè and to Chamberlain, the Nobel Prize for physics." In smaller type: "Segrè was born in Tivoli and studied under Enrico Fermi. In 1938 he emigrated to the United States." I didn't care for the accompanying photograph. My father's shoulders seemed to obscure his neck. My mother would have slapped him on the back and told him not to slouch like an old man. Beside him, Chamberlain, all nose, chin, cheekbones, looked too serious. Meanwhile, like it or not, I'd become Son of Nobel Prize Winner.

That morning, as I often did, I walked by the Trevi Fountain on my way to my favorite corner *caffè*. As usual, no one was there except a couple of street sweepers in blue smocks. With a few desultory strokes, they pushed around the cigarette butts, crumpled napkins, candy and film wrappers left from the previous night's tourist orgy. I wondered what it would be like to clean up after the Nobel Festival. I wondered if I'd be invited to contribute to the royal mess.

Did I look any different with my new status? Evidently the street sweepers didn't think so, for when I passed by, they didn't look up. At the *caffè*, Roberto, who usually served me, appeared gray and tired. To my *"Buon giorno"* he merely grunted, *"Dottore,* what're you taking? The usual?" I considered letting him in on the great news. Then I decided that neither he nor I was ready to confront our new relationship this early in the morning. I drank my customary cappuccino, but indulged myself in my two favorite sweet rolls, first a *cornetto,* like a croissant, topped with almonds and filled with almond paste, then a *bomba,* a deep-fried ball-like "bomb," dipped in sugar and filled with custard. I wondered what Swedes ate for breakfast. On my way to the bus stop, I passed by a newspaper kiosk and checked the headlines again. They hadn't changed. My impulse was to do an Indian dance while waving the paper and shouting, "Lookee here, everybody, that's my Papà!" I didn't.

At the office of the Cartiere Tiburtine, though, my father's cousin Bindo just about did. He saw it as much his day as my father's. Boisterous, boyish—some said boorish—as ever, Bindo danced about restlessly, waving the newspaper like a banner. "This one [pointing to me] is the son of this one," he said, indicating the front-page picture. "How much money does Emilio have in the bank?" he called to no one in particular, and boasted that he had bet my father a thousand dollars that he would win the Prize before 1960. To those who grumbled at his excitement, Bindo said, with the expression of a spanked puppy, "Wouldn't you be happy, too, if someone dear to you received an honor like that?" His telegram to my father was pure Bindo: "Congratulations. They gave you the Prize because you discovered me. On your way to Stockholm, stop in Rome to get some decent clothes."

I wished I were at home in Berkeley to share the excitement with my family. Perhaps, I fantasized, I might even, in some way, share the moment with my father alone. That would have been difficult. As I read later, my father met his undergraduate class on Monday morning at eight o'clock as usual. When the students stood up and cheered, he seemed genuinely surprised. At the Lawrence Radiation Laboratory someone had scribbled on the blackboard under the date, October 24, 1959, "Assoc'd Press Unconfirmed E.S. & O.C. have Nobel Prize" and then to the right, with an arrow pointing to the names, "Confirmed." At a press conference later that morning, my father appeared "quiet, thoughtful, calm"—or so a Berkeley paper commented. In my imagination, when I peeled away four decades from my father's fifty-four years, stripped off the bow tie and pin-striped suit, I could see the bright boy, the "first in the class." In another photograph in the suburban Lafayette paper, my mother is at the piano, my sisters are looking on, and my father appears to be turning the pages of the music. Apparently the Prize had miraculously cured him of his tone deafness.

Over and over, I wondered what the reactions of friends and relatives would be—and if any of them would call me. I imagined our neighbors or my friends reading the news. "Oh, he lives just up the road." "I know his son. Claudio was in my class. We used to go skiing together." I wondered if in their minds I would take on a new aura, if I would radiate celebrity. Would people regard me with a new curiosity, accord me special status, like royalty, like the King's son, as I dubbed myself with a trace of self-mockery?

As the day wore on, I found myself glancing in the mirror, at my reflection in shop windows. I saw a tall, slim, twenty-two-year-old who wore heavy, navy-blue rimmed glasses and moved with a certain military stiffness, as if to give himself more gravity and substance. I tugged at my sleeves to see if a little cuff was showing, glanced at my shoes to see if they were well enough polished. I spoke to shop clerks, to employees of the paper mills, with what I thought sounded like polite authority. I was looking and acting more and more like my image of a European gentleman, perhaps a very junior member of the *gente colta*. Now, as Son of Nobel Prize Winner, I had become a member of the intellectual royalty. By evening, though, I had given up on all the poses. They were too much trouble. I was back to being me—whoever that was.

That day and for several days afterward, journalists descended on me. They liked writing about my apartment and its location, as if they were unearthing another of Rome's hidden treasures. They described the parquet floor, the green spread on the sofa bed, the closet, the view from my window over the red tiled roofs, the geraniums across the way, the cats sunning themselves, the chime of the Quirinale clock tower.

During the next few days, I enjoyed reading the interviews (including concocted quotes) with me in the Italian papers—or were they with my double, perhaps, a mysterious clone from the world of antimatter that my father and his colleagues had discovered and for which they had become Nobel laureates? In the newspaper stories, I recognized my "lively eyes," which "showed intelligence," and my "slim figure," which "moved with catlike steps." However, my glasses had dark, heavy rims whereas my clone apparently wore tortoiseshell frames. I was also certain that my Italian was perfect, and so it had to be my clone who, according to the papers, spoke with "barely noticeable foreign inflections." He was the one who pronounced such banalities as "Classical studies are more developed in Italy than in the United States." Yet I envied him his father, who, according to the stories, was "not a professor, not a scientist, only 'Papà,' gentle, quiet, affectionate." I wished my walks with my father were like my clone's with his:

It was the season for mushrooms, I remember, and we had gone to hunt them in the shady woods near Tivoli. That was one of the rare times when my father spoke to me about the developments in physics. He spoke to me as he would to a layman, but his words were so fascinating that at that moment I was sorry that I hadn't followed his path. Physics, through his words, and in that surrounding, no longer seemed to me an abstract study, but more like poetry and philosophy.

My interviews left me nervous. The journalists departed "with a hurried, sidelong glance, a quick mechanical parting, with the expression of a cat who had just swallowed the canary" of my real thoughts, I remarked in my diary. But the journalists hadn't really gotten the canary. There was none to get. I wasn't sure what I thought. "His last great wish in his scientific career has been fulfilled. I'm glad for the man, proud of the father," I wrote. I was even more acutely aware that "my father is a man apart . . . an idiot, but a genius," as Bindo was fond of saying. I compared my status to that of Prince Charles, the heir to the British throne, "a prince through no particular merit or fault of his own." In my new role, "I'm one of those admiring, watching; perhaps I have a special pass for the front row, yet I'm always forming the circle, not the center of it, and I'm glad. Glad, too, that I don't have his long shadow before me in my field," I concluded.

During those heady days, I wrestled with how my father had become "king"—and why. If a psychologist had asked me to check the boxes for a personality profile of my father, I would not have checked "ambitious." Certainly he was not ambitious in the conventional sense of hungering for power or control over men or organizations. He cared nothing for running laboratories or departments. Nor did he aspire to whispering in the ear of the powerful, for example as a science adviser to the President. When he served in some executive position, such as a brief term as chairman of the Physics Department at Berkeley, or on the board of trustees of Tel Aviv University, or when he edited a journal, he did so largely out of duty.

Then why did he eye the Prize? He was already Superman,

wasn't he? His work—the pleasure and excitement of his research—spurred my father on more than any potential honor, I decided. I was sure of that, and I admired him for it. Yet even supermen hunger to be recognized by their peers. With him, that was certainly the case. His work, increasingly important, mounted up. In the late 1940s, as he looked back, he began to think that his research on the new chemical elements and on radiochemistry might bring him a Nobel Prize. As an informal confirmation, a referendum among nuclear chemists at that time ranked him among the top ten in the United States. To aspire is one thing, to realize that aspiration is another. The Nobel Committee, like God, helps those who help themselves. My father's hopes rested on his work on the transuranic elements, those having an atomic number greater than uranium's. Yet in 1951 the prize for that research went to his colleagues at Berkeley, Edwin McMillan and Glenn T. Seaborg. For my father, the news was a terrible disappointment. He had assumed that somehow the Nobel Committee would divide the Prize.

For eight years, between 1951 and 1959, my father wrestled with frustrations, bitterness and fear that the Prize would elude him. I knew something of his fears and frustrations because, in bits and pieces, I heard about them. In May 1958, for example, as we took one of his favorite Sunday walks in the hills around Lafayette, he recalled with nostalgia his days in Rome, when the institutions and equipment of nuclear physics were simpler and more intimate. Between "spasms of self pity, the old familiar, self-deprecating 'I'm an old senile idiot' lament, he assessed himself clearly," I noted in my diary. He was in his late forties, past the age when scientists usually have done their best work, he said. I admired his calm, realistic acceptance that his best work lay behind him. I saw in him, I thought, an "ability to grow old gracefully that so many people lack. It is the stamp of quality." Inside the man, I heard the boy still struggling fiercely to be "first in the class," still crowing, "Look how bright I am! Look how clever I am!"

Despite his disappointment, despite his feelings of ineptitude when it came to maneuvering and lobbying for the Prize, my father persisted. As he later told the story at the Nobel Festival, he was the frog in the Aesop's fable who fell in the pitcher of cream—and kept on jumping until he was saved. To have a chance at the Prize, he knew he needed support. A Swedish colleague who was privy to the workings of the Nobel Committee advised my father that he needed Fermi's nomination. Other friends and colleagues suggested that my father enlist the help of Ernest O. Lawrence, the 1939 laureate. Directly and indirectly, my father solicited the support of both men, but he was skeptical that anything would happen. Fermi could never be persuaded to do something unless he truly believed in it, my father claimed. He had no more faith in Lawrence, with whom he had never felt comfortable. Even Superman, I noted, had his self-doubts.

As matters turned out, he needn't have worried. He found out afterward that both Fermi and Lawrence had repeatedly supported my father or proposed him for the Prize. Fermi's support in particular—the approbation of his great teacher, his model, perhaps the greatest all-around physicist of his generation—meant almost as much as winning the Prize itself, my father said later. Most important of all, my father kept on working. He was wrong when he dubbed himself an "old senile idiot." One of the remarkable aspects of his scientific career was that his best research was not quite over—not yet. In September 1955, together with his ex-students Owen Chamberlain and coworkers Clyde Wiegand and Thomas Ypsilantis, my father discovered the antiproton—a negatively charged proton.

The notion that every particle of matter would have its antiparticle had been argued for a long time. Paul A. M. Dirac, mathematician and physicist, had posited this notion in 1928. In 1932 Carl D. Anderson discovered the positron—a positively charged electron. Photographs of cosmic ray impacts showed tracks of rare particles that seemed to be antiprotons. What my father and his colleagues did, with the aid of an extremely powerful atom-smasher, the bevatron, was to create the antiprotons artificially. In a highly complicated and sophisticated experiment, they bombarded a copper target with protons. Out of that collision came protons and the elusive antiprotons. The discovery raises the question of whether an entire world of antimatter exists. Perhaps somewhere in a far-off corner of the universe there is a world built of material of "reverse" atoms. On the surface, such a world would look like ours. However, as a Swedish science writer commented, "Don't fall in love with a girl from Antiprotonia. If you try to kiss her, the explosion would make a hydrogen bomb detonation look like a cap pistol."

By 1958, my father's chance for the Prize had revived. In May, when I called him at home, he mentioned that he had seen Lawrence's letter of nomination for the Prize for 1959. Undoubtedly it was some *"imbroglio,"* my father grumbled, and yet his skepticism did not quite mask his excitement. "He said to keep it under my hat, of course, but from the way he hung up so abruptly . . . it was obvious how the great news radiated in his mind," I remarked in my diary.

In July I noted, "More invitations are piling up for him to speak this Fall besides Germany: Uppsala and Stockholm— Mecca. . . ." The latter invitation had not come just so he could appreciate the beauty of the Scandinavian winter, my father later remarked. Even in Wyoming, where I'd spent the summer vacation from college as a ranch hand, everyone had heard of him through an article in *Time* and was asking me about antimatter.

As the October date for the announcement of the prizes approached, my father was on pins and needles. For some reason, that year, the Nobel Committee, contrary to all precedent, leaked names of candidates before the final choice. Since my father was high on the list of nominees, Swedish journalists called him in Berkeley for biographical data. On October 26, the announcement came over the radio, and shortly afterward, the official telegram. For me and for my teenage sisters, I learned, that meant an invitation to a party to end all parties—the Nobel Festival.

For an aspiring European gentleman, a king's son, I chose a decidedly proletarian means of transportation to Stockholm for the Nobel Prize ceremonies. The "Scandinavian Express" train took me from Rome to Stockholm in exactly forty-eight hours. In a big suitcase I packed new clothes such as my tuxedo, my tailor-made three-piece gray suit (ordered under Bindo's watchful eye), my shiny black shoes, as pointed as a mosquito's stinger and, indeed, dubbed "mosquito killers." In keeping with my high-minded literary aspirations, I followed Somerset Maugham's advice, which I'd read somewhere: I packed a variety of books to suit various moods, from Dante's *Inferno* to the Italian literary critic Francesco De Sanctis's *History of Italian Literature*.

As Son of Nobel Prize Winner, on his way to Stockholm, I tried to appear civilized and well-dressed. I also relished playing the Prince and the Pauper. With a borrowed coat as a blanket, I curled up in my second-class train compartment. I shared it with Italian emigrants returning to Germany from a visit home. I made friends with a bearded and sandaled Swedish medical student who had taken a year off from school to explore sunny North Africa.

Why was I going to Stockholm at this time of year? he asked. "To attend the Nobel ceremonies," I said.

"Oh?" he said dubiously. There would be a lot of people. Did I have an invitation? He hoped I could get in.

"I have a good chance," I told him. What did the Swedes think of the festival? I asked him.

He shrugged. December was pretty dark and gloomy in Stockholm—a good time to have a party.

The Nobel Festival, I discovered, combines a solemn, cosmopolitan ceremony celebrating the world's greatest scientific, intellectual and artistic achievements with a jolly Swedish national winter festival. Every year, during the period around December 10, the day of the awards ceremony, Stockholm comes alive with lights, for the Nobel Festival also coincides with the feast of Santa Lucia, the patron saint of lights. The gala dinners, parties and balls are like scenes out of a nineteenth-century Russian novel. The men don tuxedos or tails, complete with medals and decorations; women rustle about in ball gowns and extend gloved hands to their guests or escorts.

When I first glimpsed my parents and my sisters on their arrival at the Stockholm airport, I was already heady from a couple of official lunches and dinners. My parents, especially, looked tired, crumpled and drab after the long trip from California. My father was buried in his big overcoat, his head covered with a big green velvet hat that his dear friend, Dr. Giacomo Ancona, had lent him. He looked as if he had no neck. He peered at me through a pair of severe clear-rimmed bifocals. When he took off his coat, I could see that his suit was not too well pressed and—in those pre–pocket calculator days—mechanical pencils and a slide rule bulged out of his pocket. Why did the great and famous so often look so rumpled, so modest, almost meek? I pondered.

My mother wore one of her tailored suits and an Italian silk blouse (which to me looked austere and Germanic); she also sported a modest gray hat. My sister Fausta, then fourteen, tall and thin as a bamboo shoot, had outgrown Amelia, then seventeen. Nobody looked ready for a gala. Amelia, especially, appeared a bit fidgety; a few days before, she had developed a case of poison oak.

To get them into the party spirit, I rhapsodized about our rooms at Stockholm's Grand Hotel. I loved the thick carpets, the sleek, modern design of the furniture, the beautiful wall hangings. I also reveled in the exquisite plumbing. The bathtub could be filled with hot water in less than four minutes. Most of all, I enjoyed perching cozily on the windowsill late at night to study the fine web of streetlights along the river and watch the falling snow soften the city's gray and austere outlines.

My parents' room quickly assumed an air of cheerful chaos. I was surprised at how many personal papers my father had brought with him—all of them necessary, he claimed. In addition, cameras, rolls of film, mailers soon mixed with layers of morning papers, travel books, pamphlets, calendars, reproductions and photographs from tourist and travel organizations. Flowers and baskets of fruit, compliments of the Nobel Foundation, lay scattered about.

The comfortable disorder of the room sometimes contrasted with my father's mood. On the surface, he appeared to be at ease. He would wander around dressed except for his coat and tie, patting the hairnet that he sometimes used to control his hair. Inwardly, however, he was churning over his worries. From time to time, he lashed out like a little boy threatening to pick up his marbles and go home. In addition to his usual gloomy ruminations about the Cold War and taxes, he brooded about the final sale of the paper mills to the Finnish company. Indeed, as he often recalled afterward, he was just pulling on his dress trousers, getting ready to go to the Nobel Awards ceremony, when Bindo called. Always restless and excitable, Bindo demanded that my father return to Rome to sign the papers for the sale. Naturally my father didn't go, but it was the sort of incident that he later claimed poisoned this high point in his life, and my mother never forgave Bindo for it. When my father's eruptions became too much for me, my sisters were there to ease the tension. "With them, I seem to enjoy the loose, joking horseplay that I so seldom achieve with anyone else. I'm very fond of them both," I wrote.

In private, my father might be tense, irritable, gloomy, explosive. In public, he often glittered with wit and cleverness. At an otherwise dull and sluggish news conference with the rest of the science laureates that year—Jaroslav Heyrovsky, of the Academy of Science in Prague, winner of the Prize in chemistry, Arthur Kornberg of Stanford University and Severo Ochoa of New York University, cowinners of the Prize in medicine, and Owen Chamberlain, cowinner in physics with my father—he provided much of the spark. To a question about what would happen if our world and an antiworld met, my father quipped, to the laughter of the audience of journalists, "Well, that would be bad." I was surprised at how well he pulled it off, affably, full of good humor. Yet what I naively considered the most interesting, thought-provoking questions met with silence. One journalist, for example, commented that the science prizes were often divided among collaborators; what was the role of teamwork in contemporary science? Owen Chamberlain finally broke the silence with a comment about the complicated nature of research these days. He made a point of mentioning the important contribution of another collaborator on my father's antiproton project, Clyde Wiegand. Then silence again, lest, I realized, the replies reflect on the Nobel Committee's choices or the sensitivities of various colleagues.

As the news conference reflected, the Nobel Festival was often a family affair. My father and his colleagues sat at a long table facing the journalists. The wives sat beside the husbands. My sisters and I and two of the Kornberg boys, looking bright and shiny and American in their suits with snappy bow ties and bristly crew cuts, balanced the opposite ends of the table. My mother's role, and that of the other wives, impressed me as ritualistic. The wives had to be mentioned; the only thing that was asked of them was whether they were going shopping for Christmas presents. From the way the women reporters (and there were a surprising number of them) put the question, I was sure that the paragraph about the wife had already been written; it was the same as last year's and could be repeated next year. I remembered Laura Fermi's modesty about herself in her autobiographical *Atoms in the Family:* "But I only launder my husband's shirts." How could this apparent disparity in status and achievements ever harmonize into a marriage? I mused. And yet it does.

The round of embassy parties and Nobel Foundation receptions and dinners developed my European-gentleman social graces, I thought. I asked hall porters to press my suits; I spoke French to the tailor (his English wasn't too strong) when I went to rent tails for the Nobel Banquet. In my imagination, I relished the expressions that would appear on my friends' faces when I mentioned ever so casually: "When I went to fit my tails for the Nobel Banquet, I had to speak French to the tailor." I learned to lift glasses of champagne from waiters' and butlers' trays as they scurried by; I quickly got accustomed to the noise of medals and decorations on men's evening dress, jingling like loose change in the pocket. I summoned up the courage to approach other Nobel laureates who particularly interested me, like that year's winner of the literature prize, the Italian poet Salvatore Quasimodo. Perhaps I was only my father's son, an accessory to his presence, but I was gaining confidence. I was sure I would know how to behave on the Big Day.

The Big Day was December 10: the day of the awards ceremonies and the banquet. At four-thirty, the ceremony was scheduled to begin; at three-thirty the caravan of big, black, official-looking limousines idled in front of the hotel; at two-thirty, we were wiggling and squirming into our clothes. For my father, it was the first time in fifty-four years that he'd worn tails; for me, the first time in twenty-two.

Major technical problems loomed. I hadn't worn suspenders since the first grade, and I had trouble getting the tension right. Next I had to adjust the shoulder straps on that cousin to the corset, the white waistcoat. My father's was a hand-me-down. Past Berkeley Nobel Prize winners offered it to each new laureate when he made his trip to Stockholm. The mystery of the white tie remained. Should it rest against or below the little wings of the collar? Though I had my doubts, my father and I elected for below. A quick check of other laureates and festival participants in the lobby, and a more leisurely one during slow moments in the ceremony revealed that the choice was probably optional.

When we were dressed, we inspected each other. My mother, magnificent in her long, pale-green satin dress, looked like the gracious epitome of a Frau Professor or a Nobel Prize winner's consort, I thought. My father was resplendent in tails. On a green-and-white ribbon around his neck dangled his decoration from the Italian government. Like his father before him, he, too, was a *commendatore*, paradoxically a "knight of the Italian Republic." Amelia, in her long, white formal, making superhuman efforts not to touch her poison oak, and Fausta in a party dress cinched with a red sash, looked most familiar—perhaps because I'd seen lots of girls at high school or college formals. As for me, I joked that in my white tie and tails, I looked as solemn as a constipated penguin. To my secret satisfaction, the outfit gave me more seriousness and maturity than my two decades could generate alone.

At three-thirty, hotel doormen ushered us into the waiting limousines. At mid-afternoon, a gray twilight was already stealing over the city, as we drove to the Town Hall for the ceremonies. From our front-row seats, my mother, my sisters and I had plenty of opportunity to study the auditorium and the audience. On the stage, decorated with yellow chrysanthemums, empty chairs were arranged in rows. At the front, however, they formed a semicircle. That was where Swedish Academy members and Nobel laureates from previous years sat. A podium occupied center stage. All around us were the recipients, a bit nervous and stammering. Their proud families and relatives gossiped and fidgeted. Mentally I stripped away the tails and the medals, the Nobel laureates, the academy members and the King of Sweden. This ceremony was no different from a junior chamber of commerce meeting to honor the model boosters of the year, I sneered to myself.

Promptly at four-thirty, the King and the royal family made

their entrance and settled in their reserved front-row center seats. Everyone stood up to clap. In their gowns and tiaras, the Queen and the princesses moved majestically. For me, the King was most striking. Gustav Adolf VI was a tall, white-haired man, slightly bent with age. Before he sat down, he bowed slightly to the audience. His air of dignity, humility, modesty and utter simplicity was unforgettable. He was a king who needed no title. I felt tears in my eyes. This was decidedly no ordinary awards ceremony.

The orchestra played the Swedish national anthem. The Nobel laureates, with my father leading the way, entered from the rear to occupy the six seats along our side of the podium; opposite them sat the members of the academies who were to make the presentation. My father, I'm sure, intended to appear as solemn and dignified as the King. Yet a pompous scowl—one that reminded me dimly of old newsreel images of Mussolini— clouded his face. He appeared shy and ill at ease; he tried to cover up his discomfort by pretending that he was bored. He seemed to ignore the speakers. Instead, he looked around, from time to time caught my mother's eye. In his memoirs, he recalled that chief among his thoughts were regrets about those who were not there to see him: his Uncle Claudio, his parents, Fermi (who died in 1954), and Senator Orso Mario Corbino, his political and administrative mentor when he was a student at the University of Rome.

The ceremony followed the same pattern for each laureate. First a member of the Swedish Academy explained why the laureate was being honored. Then, to the accompaniment of a fanfare, a footman brought the awards (a gold medal and a diploma) to the King, who made the actual presentation. He handed the award to the laureate, shook hands with him, in good English congratulated him on his achievements and wished him an equally fruitful future. The laureate acknowledged the crowd's applause for a moment and then returned to his seat.

According to tradition, the presentation of the prizes began with physics, and my father was the first to be honored. After the Swedish Academy's representative had made his brief speech, my father slowly, deliberately, descended the steps from the stage to the platform where the King stood. My father paused at the foot of the stairs, glanced at me. I knew he was deliberately taking his time. Before he claimed his seat onstage, he had entrusted me with the task of taking pictures. At first, I balked. I didn't like being a photographer in a penguin's costume. Nevertheless, as my father walked over to the King, I fumbled desperately, trying to get them both into focus. At the climactic moment, as my father was reaching out to accept the diploma and the medal from the King, I pressed the shutter button. Nothing. I'd forgotten to wind the film after the last shot. By the time I'd wound it, it was too late. To my relief, I realized the Nobel Committee had long experience with such contingencies. They arranged for teams of photographers who provided the laureates with dozens of shots of festival highlights.

I studied the other laureates. As the rest of the audience did, I felt a particular empathy for the chemistry prize winner, Jaroslav Heyrovsky from the Czechoslovakian Academy of Sciences, Prague. He was a timid old man, sad, drab and somehow broken. Whether this was from hard work or from living under an East European Communist regime, I couldn't tell, but, as many in the audience did, I sensed his triumph against enormous material and psychological obstacles. He got a particularly warm round of applause. With my literary aspirations, my special interest was the Sicilian poet Salvatore Quasimodo. Small, dark, sleek, with a Daliesque air about him, he appeared to relish the pomp and circumstance. When the King wished him well at the presentation ceremony, for example, the poet appeared ready with a lyrical acceptance speech.

The Nobel Banquet at the Stockholm Town Hall followed the ceremony. While the other guests filed directly into the hall and found their seats, the Nobel winners and their families waited in an antechamber to meet the royal family. As we waited, we, the intellectual royals, confronted the issue of how to deal with real royals. How did one bow? *Did* one bow? In shaking hands with the King, did one do so with gloves on or gloves off? For the women, who were all wearing gloves, this was a major issue. On or off? On or off? Nobody seemed to know.

Suddenly His Majesty came through the door, and there was no more time to ponder. The King worked his way down the line, shaking hands. Plans to bow or curtsy vanished. In the narrow room there was no space, anyway. Nevertheless, I found myself trying to bend my knees and saying, "How do you do?" as I shook hands. The Queen and one of the court ladies put us all at ease by simply asking us whether we were having a pleasant time and whether we were enjoying Stockholm. When the King reached the end of the line, he said gallantly, "I believe that I have the pleasure of escorting Mrs. Segrè." My mother thus made a grand entrance into the banquet hall on the arm of none other than His Majesty.

My parents, of course, sat at the head table—set for 125— with the royal family and the other honored guests. I threaded my way along the edge until I reached number 381 at table nine (out of a total of nineteen). Opposite me sat Amelia, and second down to the right, Fausta. Each had her student escort, who wore a blue-and-yellow sash (the Swedish national colors) that extended over one shoulder and down across his chest.

I discovered that I, too, had an escort. Cecilia Stahle, the daughter of the Nobel Foundation's business manager, was a pleasant brunette with a peaches-and-cream complexion. As a good mother should, hers had made discreet inquiries about me the night before. My date was lovely, charmingly correct. She was also a veteran of these affairs; this was her third or fourth banquet. Pomp and etiquette might be amusing for the laureates and their families, for old people and for tourists, but Cecilia Stahle was none of the above. She listened to my gallant efforts at talk, small and big, and responded with heroic efforts of her own. Yet I couldn't help noticing the way her eyes appeared to glaze over, though she barely touched her wineglass.

The banquet began with a rousing toast to His Majesty. Then came the food: first, a fish course (Suprême de Turbot à la fine Champagne), followed by rice and cold chicken (Poularde Froide à la Gelée) and a Waldorf salad. The dessert featured brandied pears (Poires Flambées). Glasses were kept filled with vintage French wine and champagne. The orchestra played; we "skaled" (toasted) each other Swedish-style. The custom was that you couldn't drink without catching someone else's eye and toasting. The young men, of course, "helped" each other when they looked thirsty.

Like many formal banquets, this one concluded with speeches over coffee, liqueurs and huge cigars. For the most part, the Nobel laureates acknowledged their hosts for their lavish hospitality, then thanked those who had supported and encouraged them, especially their wives. Quasimodo, the poet, always going against the grain, launched into a complex and hermetic discourse about the marvels of Sweden as a civilized country. For a while I thought I might thank—and perhaps impress—my attractive hostess by translating for her, but I quickly lost the thread of Quasimodo's speech and she didn't seem to care whether I found it again or not. My father spoke last. Since I'd worked hard at editing it, I knew it nearly by heart. In a few well-chosen words, he talked about how the common language and understanding among scientists approached Nobel's ideals of a world of international understanding.

Once the speeches had ended, we flowed down a grand staircase to meet representative university students from all over Sweden, who had been eating in the hall below us. They greeted us with cheers, shouts and banners flying. The girls looked radiant in their evening dresses; the men, in tails and perky white student caps, burst into enthusiastic cheers, songs and welcoming speeches. It was a spirited and moving encounter.

According to Nobel ceremonies tradition, a physics laureate replied to the student welcome, and the honor went to my father. As his colleagues and fellow Nobel laureates T. D. Lee and C. N. Yang had done two years earlier on the same occasion, my father chose to tell a story. It was an Aesop's fable that he had once heard from an old Quaker woman during the darkest days of World War II: the tale of the frogs in the pail of cream. Like scientists, my father said, these particular frogs were curious, so they jumped into the pail to investigate the cream. When it came time to get out, one jumped a few times, gave up, drowned. The other, "perhaps a little less intelligent, but far more persistent and stubborn," continued jumping. Gradually, an island of butter formed and he was saved. He always liked that story, my father said, because again and again throughout his life, the spirit of the jumping frog had saved him. The students promptly bestowed another honor on him: the "Order of the Always Smiling and Jumping Little Frog."

Then the band struck up the "Blue Danube." Couples quickly paired off, whirling and swaying to the music. Down the marvelous staircase, making their grand entrance into the ballroom, came the other banquet guests. This wasn't an ordinary dance; this was a ball, the Nobel Ball. An invitation to it is probably one of the greatest compliments that you can pay your girlfriend or your boyfriend in Sweden. So grand was the occasion that even my father was persuaded to dance briefly with my mother.

As I listened to my father, I stood stiff and tall, looking down the steps into the student crowd, imagining that many of the girls were eyeing me with interest. After all, wasn't I the son of a Nobel laureate? For this magical evening, at least, I imagined I had the aura of a prince. My hostess quickly disabused me of that fantasy. She did her duty. She danced with me once. Then she disappeared with her boyfriend. If I wanted to waltz to the "Blue Danube" or "Tales from the Vienna Woods" or two-step to a popular show tune, I had to do so primarily with my sisters. I was learning that my exalted status had its limits.

Nevertheless, my rank and the occasion of the ball still offered privileges. I could aspire to talking literature with a Nobel laureate. During one of the intermissions, from a book jacket photograph, I recognized Pär Lagerkvist, Nobel laureate for literature in 1951. Screwing up my courage, I introduced myself. I found myself with a gentle, timid, kindly old man who didn't seem to follow what I was saying. Either I was making a fool of myself or he was hard of hearing. Speaking French, I discovered, improved his comprehension immeasurably. I told him how much I admired his novel *Barabbas*, and for a while we talked about how he came to write it. At this point, my father arrived. Perhaps bored and always curious, in his steamroller French he crashed into the conversation. Lagerkvist essentially repeated what he'd told me; my father, still oblivious to what he might have interrupted, wandered away. By then, the thread of my discussion with Lagerkvist was broken. Clearly, the Prize had done little to improve my father's social graces.

The following afternoon, the laureates gave their lectures. Faced with the choice of my father or the enigmatic Quasimodo, I never really debated the matter: I chose Quasimodo. I would have done better to listen to my father. What I opted for was a literary tea crowded with ogling old Swedish ladies and gentlemen, nostalgic, especially in the middle of December, for the sun and color of the Mediterranean. The poet delivered his text in such a splendid, mellifluous, rolling voice that I couldn't follow what he was saying. "Long is the night that never finds day," from *Macbeth*, was his theme. In Quasimodo's mind, the phrase summed up the poet's struggle with his art and with society. Afterward, Quasimodo took me aside and asked if I'd been shocked, if perhaps his words had been too much for me to digest. In my best hermetic style, I grunted and nodded.

My father's lecture, entitled "Properties of Antinucleons," dealt with the results and implications of his work on antimatter. Naturally, the technical parts meant little to me. Most interesting were his opening acknowledgments. After thanking the Nobel Foundation, he paid tribute to Fermi, his master. He did so by quoting the lines in the *Divine Comedy* in which Dante describes his own master, Virgil:

Thou art my master and my author
Thou alone art he from whom I took
The good style that hath done me honor.

From Fermi, my father concluded, he had learned "not only a good part of the physics I know, but above all an attitude towards science that has affected all my work." My father also paid tribute to Lawrence. They belonged to quite different scientific traditions and outlooks, my father noted; yet Lawrence's leadership and instigation had "created the instruments on which most of my work was done," my father concluded.

The last round of parties and receptions wound down that evening. The Nobel Festival faded into a grand and dreamy memory. But when I woke up the next morning, and on all subsequent mornings, I was still Son of Nobel Prize Winner.

Since that October morning in 1959, the phrase has followed me, defined me, set me apart, will continue to set me apart, for the rest of my life. My wife and my three children, Gino, Francesca and Joel, will continue to bask in its reflected glow. How bright is the glow? How much did the Prize affect me? How much did it affect my father? How much did it affect our relationship?

The first effect—or noneffect—on me was that it transformed me into a minor celebrity, more in Italy than in the United States. Americans who encounter the name for the first time are usually so busy wondering how to pronounce it ("Seh-*gray*" is my best hope) that they don't consider whether it is famous. If a mangled surname qualified as a disability, I could always be assured of parking in a space reserved for the handicapped.

My trips to Italy present other complications. Passport control, bank officials, hotel clerks, postal employees often seize on my documents, usually my passport, as a golden opportunity for a diversion from the routine at hand. The official leafs through the document slowly, glances at the picture, matches it with my face, and the name registers:

"Segre?"

"Segrè."

"Right. There's the accent. Are you by any chance related to the writer? You know, the one who goes by 'Pittigrilli' [a popular novelist known for his mildly pornographic works]?"

"No."

"Well . . ." The official, now stimulated by the challenge, scratches his head. "But Segrè is a well-known name. I've heard it somewhere. Many years ago there was this Communist party leader. Umberto, I think."

"Segre," I say. "Not related. I'm Segrè."

"Right. But I've heard the name. My literary friends tell me there's a famous critic—I've never read him."

"Cesare. Not related."

"Well, there's another one, I know. He's an Israeli journalist."

"Vittorio Dan. Friendship unites us, but accent divides us."

"But I know your name. I just know it. I've read about it."

"Are you thinking of my cousin? Claudio Segrè? He's a banker."

"No. No. There's a scientist. A physicist. The one who worked with Fermi. The Nobel Prize winner."

"He's my father."

"Ah!" A big smile of relief. The itch has been scratched. *"Complimenti!"* A more careful inspection of the fine piece of horseflesh follows: "So you're the son. What do you do? Physicist like your papà?"

"No. Writer—college professor."

"Oh, what do you write?"

"A little of everything: history, biography, essays, stories."

My interlocutor, disappointed that I haven't written some blockbuster novel or murder mystery, sees *my* disappointment that he's never heard of my work. With a gallant envoi—and an eye to the seething line behind me—he concludes: "Well, *complimenti* again. Best wishes. I hope you'll get the Nobel Prize, too."

Italy produces other pleasant surprises. At a party one evening in Rome, I was introduced to a beautiful black woman, with a Caribbean lilt to her English. "Segre? Really? Oh, that was my maiden name. My great-grandfather was a French planter. Perhaps, way back, we're cousins." Regretfully I had to point out that, once again, accent sundered us.

By definition, titles set people apart, often accentuate their accomplishments or those of their family. "Son of Nobel Prize Winner" affected me that way. As the son of immigrants, I already felt set apart both in the United States and in Italy. Son of Nobel Prize Winner separated me even more from the "ordinary world," I noted to myself at the time of the Nobel Festival. At home I was used to "the extraordinary man as ordinary company. I just didn't know any better," I wrote in my diary. Son of Nobel Prize Winner sharpened my already acute sense of duty, responsibility, my desire, my *obligation* to achieve. Like it or not, I was born into the "Big Leagues," I noted. Thomas Mann had written *Buddenbrooks*, the novel that won him the Nobel Prize, by the time he was twenty-six. I still had four years in which to do the same.

My father probably sensed my mad aspirations while we were in Stockholm. It might have been nice if we had gone off together to talk about them at one of the bars in the Grand Hotel for half an hour. I would not have dared suggest it. The festivities, the speeches he had to give, his usual round of worries— the paper mills, taxes, the Cold War—took precedence. Moreover, we had never had father-son talks of the sort I fantasized. They were not my father's style. And yet, why not? My father believed in high standards. Why should they not apply to fatherhood, to him as a father?

And yet he surprised me. A couple of weeks after we returned to Italy from Stockholm, we did have that talk. From time to time, when he was in Rome that year, he and I frequented a restaurant in the center of town on Via San Nicola da Tolentino. It was the kind of place where the menu was handwritten and dog-eared and hard to read under the naked bulbs; where the tablecloths were linen, but frayed and mended; where the wood and rattan chairs scraped across the stone floor like fingers across a blackboard. My father liked the place for its *ossobuco* (bone marrow) and its *bollito di manzo* (stew), dishes that reminded him of his childhood in Tivoli.

When we met for dinner one night, he must have noticed how burdened and frustrated I looked, how my shoulders sagged and my head drooped, must have heard the ponderous gravity of my voice, seen the solemnity of my eyes behind the heavy rims. Perhaps I hinted at Thomas Mann, *Buddenbrooks*, and the herculean task that lay ahead of me. He did not seem to hear me. We talked about everything else—world politics, family feuds, the paper mills. Then, while I was reaching for my coat to leave, and thinking that I needed to get on to another appointment, he started in. He meant to sound paternal and reassuring; he reminded me of an old-fashioned schoolmaster delivering a lesson. From time to time he glanced at me to see if I was listening, but most of the time his eyes wandered or fixed on a spot on the wall, as if he could thereby better concentrate on his lines.

Whatever my aspirations, he said, I should keep in mind that his road to Stockholm had consisted mostly of hard work. He didn't have Fermi's or Rasetti's supreme intelligence. He couldn't grasp things as quickly as they. Hard work had to compensate for talent; competence for true genius, like Fermi's. His words cut my swollen aspirations down to size. In a diary fragment, dated January 4, 1960, I wrote: "I can't remember his exact words, but I remember the stance," and I was grateful. Competence—whatever that meant—was a tangible goal, one that I could manage. "At least, if I can't become a star, I can become as competent, I can go as far as hard work and discipline will carry me." I could still *do*—and that seemed to be the essence of being.

For my father, naturally the Prize was enormously gratifying. He had received all the recognition he could hope for. Yet, external applause was one thing; his personal standards were another. He was keenly aware that there were those laureates in physics, like Einstein, Planck, Rutherford and Bohr, who gave prestige to the Prize. If they hadn't received it, it would have been a loss for the Prize, not for them, he remarked. Then there were mediocrities, who through good luck got the Prize and got prestige from it. Most of the laureates—and that was probably where he ranked himself—were more or less even. He was world class, all right. Yet he also knew his place. Sometimes he was reminded of it. Fermi, my father recalled in his memoirs, once said to him, "Emilio, you could take all your work and exchange it for one paper of Dirac's and you would gain substantially in the trade." Not to be outdone, my father said, "Agreed, but you could trade your work for one of Einstein's and come out ahead." Nevertheless, before those whom he considered truly great, the Galileos, the Newtons, the Maxwells and the Faradays, the Einsteins, the Bohrs, the Rutherfords, and even his own master, Fermi, my father remained in awe. He had the grace, the good sense, to understand where he really ranked among the giants. I admired him for it.

The Prize brought us together in an odd sort of way. My father became a kind of family "dog-and-pony show" or a "show-and-tell" session. People were curious to meet me because I was the "son of." I could reward my friends by bringing them home to meet my father. He was usually patient about it, even enjoyed it, as long as I wasn't cutting into his work. In a curious and detached way, we both enjoyed his fame. As I noted in my diary, "I get an odd image of us all standing around the base of a statue entitled *Fame*. We all enjoyed walking around it, seeing the resemblance to my father, 'this guy we know.' " He walks around it, too, sees the resemblance and is pleased, just the way you would be pleased if somone told you you looked like Gary Cooper or some other movie star. . . . You don't mind being mistaken for him once in a while as long as you don't have to be him—as long as you can be yourself.

Everyone looks, I remarked, and then everyone, including my father, "wanders back to his own affairs which we all know are not those of the famous."

At other moments, however, the Prize distanced us. We forgot or failed to distinguish between public roles and private life. More and more, the aura of the Prize permeated my father's life. He received invitations; he traveled; he consulted here and there. Everywhere he went, he was received with the honors and trappings that were appropriate to his status. Inevitably some of that rubbed off in his private world. His house filled with honors, memorabilia and souvenirs from his trips: engraved silver dishes and trays, medals, trophies, books, certificates, diplomas. To me, the house no longer felt like home.

In subtle ways I sensed that he was taking on a role: the distinguished and eminent scientist had now also become "Nobel Laureate." So many honors, so much glory suggested the pomp and glitter of an imperial viceroy's parade. In my imagination, as I watched him driving by in his car or in his carriage, in his cocked hat, his epaulettes and feathers, his medals, waving to the crowds, I had a hard time recognizing him. Or I recognized him all too well and wondered what he was doing wearing such a funny costume.

The reflections from the Prize never fade away. Yet time does dim them. Decades have passed since 1959. "Oh. Your father won the Nobel Prize? When?" I now hear. Moreover, laureates, especially in physics, tend to come in bunches. From one year to the next, it's hard to remember who won. Over the decades, the dazzling radiance of 1959 has faded into a comfortable glow.

CHAPTER 10

Family Trades

"My compliments on your illustrious father," well-meaning Italians—rarely Americans—said to me, still say to me, in the wake of his winning the Nobel Prize. When they find out that I'm a writer, they add, "I hope you'll win the Prize for literature." The compliments and best wishes remind me of the interiors of Baroque churches in Rome—all grand ruffles and flourishes. Americans are usually more subdued. Many smile sympathetically and then touch on what they imagine are my burdens. "It must be tough to be the son of such a famous man" or "It must be hard to live up to such a famous name," they murmur.

Now I shrug off the ruffles and flourishes, or I make light of the burdens of my legacy. But when I was in my twenties, I only pretended to shrug—then quietly set a timetable. If I couldn't, like Thomas Mann, have completed a Nobel Prize–winning novel by my mid-twenties, then perhaps I could switch to Hemingway's or Faulkner's or even Quasimodo's Prize-winning timetable, whatever it might be. Nothing less would do.

My father, despite his talk of high standards, certainly never imposed such goals on me directly. In choosing a career, I had no obligations, he said. I owed our family nothing, and I had no particular standards I had to meet. Yet, as he, with his love for biological metaphors for human behavior also said, I was "imprinted" on his career pattern. Like a little duckling, I followed the parent's example. It wasn't the only one, but it certainly was the most prominent and obvious one.

And yet his model, I realized, was a difficult if not impossible one to duplicate. I tried to make allowances for the differences between us. My interests and talents were not his. As my father often said, humanists and artists matured later than scientists and mathematicians. Moreover, scientists often worked in teams and groups; scholars and artists were usually more solitary. Then there was the small matter of talent. It was unlikely that I would have the same gifts for my field that he had for his. Finally, I pondered the sheer romance of his story. From Tivoli to Rome, from Rome to Berkeley, from Berkeley to Los Alamos and back to Berkeley; from slow neutrons and technetium to the atomic bomb and the antiproton. Finally, the Nobel Prize. How did he do it?

I marveled at his story; I brooded over it. I still do today. How could he be so certain he wanted to be a physicist? Did science run in the family? How did he find such a great teacher as Enrico Fermi? How did he come upon such extraordinary colleagues as the "boys of the Via Panisperna," the school of physicists who developed around Fermi at the University of Rome in the early 1930s? How could he be so lucky? More than three decades after the fact, I asked him. He shrugged. "A remarkable series of circumstances . . . had been given to him," he replied. "Had been given to him . . ."—the passive mode indicated how fortunate he felt at the set of gifts: his talent, his passion for physics, his good fortune in finding kindred spirits. Such miracles were wonderful to contemplate. Could I make them happen to me?

I began by looking for at least the comfort of a genetic expla-

nation for my father's scientific talents. The generation succeed-
ing him has produced two nephews and a grandson who turned
to physics, and a zoologist daughter, my sister Amelia. Before
my father, however, there is no such family tradition, with the
exception of my Great-uncle Claudio, the geologist-engineer.
There are no stories to tell about how my grandfather took his
son to the laboratory, where he touched the apparatus and asked
precocious questions. If anything, my father's choice of a career
caused my grandfather considerable anxiety.

My father came to physics in the most natural way possible,
I realized: as a result of his native curiosity and wonder. For
example, as a child, he observed the diffraction of light through
a pitcher of water. The colors delighted him. Decades later, at
the breakfast table in Lafayette, when the morning sun was right,
he would point to a pitcher and the rainbow of colors and say
to my sisters and me, "Isn't that pretty?" Before my father could
read, he fingered a mechanic's tools. He examined his older
brother Marco's camera and wondered how it worked. As soon
as he could read, he devoured popular scientific books and magazines. When he was about six, he studied the workings of an
internal combustion engine and the liquefaction of helium. At
the age of seven, in 1912, he kept a notebook entitled "Physics."
In his clumsy, childish hand, he wrote—with plenty of spelling
errors, he recalled—about simple experiments that he had done
based on a popular science book, G. Tissandier's *Le ricreazioni
scientifiche*. Both his mother and his Zio Claudio encouraged him
and nurtured his sense of wonder. His mother helped him with
the diagrams in his physics notebook. In place of his father's
support, he had that of his Zio Claudio. Together, uncle and
nephew visited the uncle's testing laboratory for the Italian State
Railways. Zio Claudio also gave my father some old treatises on
physics. One included the dedication: "To my dearest nephew
with the hope that soon physics will serve the arts of peace."

That sense of wonder about the natural world, that curiosity
to explain it, attracted my father constantly. For him, physics was

fun, just as writing was fun for me. Neither field suggested a promising career. To be safe, my father enrolled as an engineering student at the University of Rome in 1922. His matriculation happened to coincide with the period when the Fascists marched on Rome and Mussolini came to power. Initially, politics had little to do with his career opportunities. In those days, a future in physics was dismal, especially in Italy. Positions in industry or government work were practically nonexistent. University jobs were scarce. In all of Italy, there were no more than twenty such positions, and each one was occupied. Retirement or death created a single opening each year. That left my father with the most likely option—unacceptable to him—of teaching in a secondary school. Not only were career opportunities limited, but Italy was very backward in "modern physics," the atomic physics and quantum mechanics that my father wanted to study.

Yet my father could not have chosen a better moment in its development to enter the field. In the 1920s and 1930s, modern physics as it was then understood—the physics of the atom, the physics that ushered in the nuclear age, was primarily the work of his generation. In 1927, my father attended the now-famous International Physics Conference at the north Italian lake resort of Como. There he glimpsed the giants and the future giants in his field. They were all his age: Wolfgang Pauli was twenty-seven; Werner Heisenberg, twenty-six; Paul Dirac, twenty-five. Niels Bohr, the "old man" in the field, was forty-two. My father and his colleagues who studied with Fermi at the University of Rome's Physics Institute were not at a great disadvantage. Since the field was new, brainpower counted more than elaborate institutions or equipment. Moreover, exchanges and communications between laboratories and institutes throughout Europe and the United States were common. For an aspiring nuclear physicist, it was an extraordinary time.

Nevertheless, for his first two years at the university, my father followed the prudent path, the one that his family favored: he studied engineering. By the third year, he had became increasingly dissatisfied both with the professors and with the curriculum. Then he had a remarkable bit of luck. In the spring of 1927 he came upon Enrico Fermi, a phenomenal teacher, who eventually became his colleague and lifelong friend.

Fermi, at twenty-six, was a graduate of the elite Scuola Normale at Pisa. He was newly appointed to a chair in theoretical physics at Rome, and he was recruiting students. He did so in part through his assistant, Franco Rasetti, who had also studied at Pisa. Rasetti, tall, gawky, eccentric, often accompanied my father on mountain-climbing expeditions. On these outings Rasetti gave lectures on physics while simultaneously hunting wild orchids or trapping insects to add to his collection. He had a reputation not only as a physicist but also as a paleontologist. In Italy he and Fermi had no peers when it came to knowing modern physics. They were supermen. So Rasetti assured potential students.

The summer of 1927 proved to be a particularly memorable one for my father. First, he was officially introduced to Fermi. The occasion was a Sunday outing with a group of friends to the beach at Ostia, near Rome. Outwardly, the party appeared to be an ordinary one—young men and women seeking sun and sand. Undoubtedly the group hummed popular songs and perhaps speculated caustically about Mussolini's latest "triumphs." But the main sport, especially for the men, was flaunting their brilliance and encyclopedic knowledge.

As Laura Capon, Fermi's future wife, recalled in a memoir, Rasetti could rattle off the monastic rules of lamas in Tibet; the times of departure of major European express trains; the death dates of all the kings of England; the rate of exchange of the Brazilian cruzeiro. If Fermi and Rasetti came upon an anthill, they posed such questions as "How many cerebral cells work at building this mound? Would you say that ant brains yield more or less work than human brains per unit of cerebral matter?" And Fermi would take out the pocket slide rule that he always carried and begin to calculate. Then there were geography quizzes for the young women. "Fantastic," Rasetti would say in mock horror to Laura. "You don't know the capital of Afghanistan? A country of 270,000 square miles?" My father's contribution was to recite poetry in three languages, discuss medieval history and speculate about quantum mechanics. Thirty-five years later, my father was still putting on such displays at family dinner parties. While my mother carved the roast and I poured the wine, my father, like a child prodigy, mesmerized his guest, a faculty colleague. "My, that's unusual for a physicist," the man exclaimed over and over again as my father recited bits of Italian or French poetry, or discussed the biochemistry of mushrooms, or argued about the origins of Fascism.

Fermi, as my father always recalled, was in a class by himself. That was clear from his childhood in Rome. He was the son of a civil service employee, an inspector on the Italian State Railways. When he was fourteen, young Enrico was devastated by the sudden death of his older brother; he withdrew into physics. At a used-book stall in Rome's Campo dei Fiori, famous as the site where Giordano Bruno was burned at the stake for defending Copernicus, the teenaged Fermi picked up a two-volume treatise, *Elementorum physicae mathematicae*, published in 1840 by a Jesuit physicist. Fermi read through the two volumes, apparently unperturbed that they were in Latin. A family friend, an engineer, lent him books on trigonometry, algebra, analytical geometry, calculus; he also suggested that Fermi study at the prestigious Scuola Normale in Pisa. Fermi's entrance examination essay on "The Characteristics of Sound" stunned the school's admissions committee. Its brilliance and mathematical sophistication were on the level of a doctoral candidate, not that of a seventeen-year-old high school graduate. Fermi soon outgrew his professors at Pisa, and in 1926 won the chair in theoretical physics at the University of Rome.

Short and stocky, Fermi possessed a boundless energy that matched the quickness of his mind. Outwardly, he was cordial,

direct, polite, but personally, he was very reserved, even detached, as if he were "above the transient noise and excitement
of current events. He was mindful of eternity," my father wrote.
If the conversation was not about physics, he was more likely to
listen than to speak. Fermi's "natural reserve" meant that "he
seldom commented on persons and activities he disliked." My
father's relationship with Fermi extended over nearly three decades, until the latter's death in 1954. Time mitigated the age
difference and even the scientific gap between them. Yet, in my
father's eyes, colleagues and friends though they were, he and
Fermi never became really close. "Even knowing him well and
seeing him frequently, I never learned some of his opinions on
important political events and persons," my father observed.
Time only seemed to increase Fermi's reserve. The awe and obedience with which my father regarded him did not diminish. It
was a dynamic that suggested my father's relationship with his
own father.

The summer of 1927 proved memorable for my father in another way. In September he attended the International Physics
Conference at Como. He had no invitation; he was not even a
student of physics, but he figured that by trailing after Rasetti,
who in turn followed Fermi, he would be admitted. My father
gazed in awe at the assembled giants in the field, including Rutherford, Planck, Lorentz, Compton, Millikan, von Laue, Som-
merfeld, Pauli, Heisenberg. Only Einstein was not present,
because he refused to enter Fascist Italy. So far as my father
could see, the only Italian whom the delegates recognized and
respected was Fermi. The age spread also encouraged my father.
Although Rutherford, Planck and Millikan represented an older
generation, Pauli and Heisenberg were my father's contem-
poraries.

My father returned to Rome in the fall of 1927, determined
to work with Fermi and Rasetti. The head of the Physics Institute was an energetic Sicilian, Orso Mario Corbino, who was
politically active and a member of the Italian Senate. His goal

was to elevate Italian physics to become the avant-garde in the field. His first move had been the appointment of Fermi to a chair in Rome. Corbino followed up by recruiting the best and brightest young students he could find, including my father. Over the next three or four years, Corbino assembled the famous "boys of the Via Panisperna." In addition to my father, the group included Rasetti, Edoardo Amaldi, Bruno Rossi, Ettore Majorana, Oscar D'Agostino and Bruno Pontecorvo.

In the fall of 1927, at Via Panisperna 89A, my father began one of the most exciting periods in his scientific career. The laboratory perched on a hill in a small park near the center of Rome. Every day my father worked there from eight in the morning to one in the afternoon; a two-hour lunch followed, then back to the laboratory again from three to about eight o'clock at night, and on Saturday mornings, but never after dinner and rarely on Sundays. The experience of working at the laboratory was a kind of ecstasy for him, comparable to "being in love," he once commented to me. Fermi's teaching and his personal example inspired "immense enthusiasm," so that his students were "completely absorbed in physics, and in saying 'completely,' I am not exaggerating," my father wrote. On Sundays, the group took the day off, went on outings with other young people—nonphysicists—but the conversation often drifted back to physics, anyway.

Given the dim career opportunities that he faced, my father's talk of changing his field from engineering to physics received a frosty reception at home. At least with an engineering degree he could always find a job, his parents and his Uncle Claudio argued. My father hesitated, tried to compromise by continuing with engineering and physics at the same time. Finally, he chose. With Corbino smoothing the administrative details, my father became a physics major. His background was such that he was a formal student of physics for only one year, from the fall of 1927 to June 1928, when he got his university degree.

Graduate school in physics for my father in the early 1930s

was much as it is today: an international affair. Young physicists migrated to work at the leading research centers throughout Europe and the United States: Niels Bohr's laboratory in Copenhagen, Pieter Zeeman's in Holland, Otto Stern's in Germany, Lord Rutherford's at Cambridge. In the United States, students pursued postgraduate training at schools like Caltech, Columbia or Berkeley. My father was typical. In the summer of 1931 he worked with Zeeman in Holland and returned there for several weeks in 1932. Then to Hamburg to work with Otto Stern during the winter and spring of 1931–32. In 1934, he went to the Cavendish in Cambridge. During the summers, beginning in 1933, he made trips to the United States, to Ann Arbor, to Columbia University, to Berkeley.

In the meantime, during 1934–35, under Fermi's direction, my father and his colleagues completed the work on slow neutrons. In 1937, in Palermo, with Carlo Perrier, came the discovery of technetium. Then there was the dramatic period at Los Alamos. Finally, during the postwar period, came the crown of his life's work, the antiproton work and the Nobel Prize.

I couldn't duplicate my father's career pattern, but I did know how I wanted to feel, how I *ought* to feel, about my life's work. I wanted to be as devoted to it as my father was to physics; I wanted to feel the "immense enthusiasm . . . like being in love" that he experienced when he worked with Fermi and Rasetti at the laboratory on the Via Panisperna. I, too, wanted to study with great masters and work with great colleagues. But how?

Neither the life of a freelance writer nor the mirage of a business executive in Rome appeared to be the right path for me. The one occupation I knew well was that of student. I could use my languages, I told myself; I could launch an academic career and at the same time continue writing. So, in the fall of 1960, I returned from Europe. For a semester I attended Columbia University as a graduate student in comparative literature. I was twenty-three; I didn't know what else to do.

Daunting obstacles like learning Latin, writing long seminar papers about medieval English ballads, and mentally processing dozens of articles in scholarly journals marked the path to academic success, I discovered. Scholarship impressed me as divorced from "real life." In my head, I often heard echoes of my father's contempt for humanistic scholarship. After a semester, I withdrew. The safe, nebulous years of graduate school, the year abroad of seasoning, were over. I was up against it: I had to find a job.

I remembered my mother timidly asking me, when I was about ten, what I planned to do when I grew up. I would be a writer, I said. What kind? she asked. At the time, in the throes of my passion for baseball, I said, "A sportswriter. Then I could get into the Oakland Oaks games for free." "A sportswriter?" she said dubiously. "Not a journalist?" I wasn't sure what journalists, as opposed to newspapermen or sportswriters, did, but I gathered that journalists didn't write about things that interested me, like sports or murders. Thousands of people read their articles on politics every day, my mother said. If the academic world wasn't for me, then perhaps I could aspire to becoming a political columnist, a pundit.

I didn't know how to become a Walter Lippmann or a Joseph Alsop or a James Reston. I knew, however, that the first thing to do in looking for a job was to pull together the scrapbook I had compiled of my articles. I was pleasantly surprised at how quickly the pages filled up. There were stories that I wrote during a summer job as a college student with the weekly *Canby Herald* in Oregon; stories and editorials from my year as editor of the student newspaper, the Reed College *Quest*; freelance pieces from my college days, from my year and a half (between graduating from college and when I left for Europe) as a graduate student in the Creative Writing Program at Stanford; from my time in Italy. Over the years, without thinking much about it, I had been learning the craft of journalism.

Since I happened to be in New York, the next logical thing to do was to knock on doors: everything from *The Christian Sci-*

ence Monitor to *The Atlantic Monthly*, from *The Nation* and *Midstream* to *Scientific American* and *Consumer's Reports*. I discovered the world of trade magazines: *Heavy Truck Salesman* and *Auto Laundry News*, *American Glass Review* and *The Concrete Trader*. I was willing to start at the bottom, I told myself enthusiastically. In the hallway of a grimy New York office building, waiting for an interview, I realized what the bottom really was—and that there was no guarantee that I would rise above it. I found myself sitting next to a potential rival, a kind, balding, middle-aged man from Cleveland, who had made his career in trade magazines. He was polite and cheerful in a dogged sort of way, but he looked frayed and used. Too many years of publications like *Chain Saw Age* and *Walls and Ceilings* had rounded his shoulders and curved his back. I went in for my interview. At the end the editor said he doubted that he had anything for me. I was relieved. Then, unexpectedly, three days later, I found a job with a news service, United Press International, in its Los Angeles bureau. It wasn't really a permanent position; I was to substitute for staff when they went on vacation; yet the job might extend indefinitely. It was a beginning.

When I first saw the UPI office, near Hollywood and Vine, my heart sank. What I found was a modest storefront buried among small shops and second-rate coffee shops just off Hollywood Boulevard. I had the feeling that the company had rented some space, and the movers, while driving by, had dropped off a few teletypes, chairs, desks and filing cabinets on the sidewalk near the front door. Somebody, probably the staff, had shoved the furniture inside and, without bothering to arrange it, had gone to work. Maybe it was too soon for me to aspire to the airy lofts at the top of tall office buildings, where, in my imagination, political reporters and pundits working for *The New York Times* or *The Wall Street Journal* or *The Washington Post* had their brilliant insights. Yet this looked positively ratty. Was this the physical equivalent of the modest laboratory on the Via Panisperna—by today's standards—where my father had started out? I was sure that this was several cuts below.

Nor was the entrance to the office promising to a serious, high-minded, aspiring journalist. The first person to greet me was a stunning Finnish blonde with perfectly regular features, a complexion that reminded me of peaches and satin, and a temperament that matched. Ansa Mikonnen was friendly with everybody, even some small-time gangsters, it was said. When she was out with them she carried their guns in her purse, the story went. Like the rest of the staffers who were single—and some who were not—I fell a little in love with Ansa. Her heart, I soon discovered, belonged to a mysterious "John," whom nobody seemed to know. Like the others who worked in the office, for a while I moped and pined and made eyes at Ansa; I ate lunch with her and invited her to dinner, and finally got over my infatuation.

Beyond Ansa's desk came the horseshoe-shaped table with the day manager sitting on the inside, orchestrating our assignments, collecting our finished copy. From time to time, when nothing much seemed to be happening, he would sing out, "Faster, men, faster." This seemed to have nothing to do with the serious, high-minded discussions my father had with his colleagues—or that I hoped to have with mine.

Yet, around that desk, I did learn. I mastered the discipline of writing faster and faster, regardless of ringing phones, managerial eruptions, collegial chatter, clacking teletypes, fawning public relations men, neighborhood winos and my pining heart. I learned that there was no time to wait for inspiration. Nor was what I wrote inspired. I learned to "freshen leads"—rewriting opening paragraphs so that they would sound more current for our afternoon client papers. I learned to generate copy, UPI prose, on demand. Producing it was "like building a brick wall," as I jotted in my diary. "The mortar of verbs is fairly uniform and ready-mixed. You slap in a few clauses, add a common verb and keep any complicated relative clauses out."

I was also called upon to master "radio style," the copy that disc jockeys read at the end of the hour after spinning the top forty. It was the easiest style of all, my manager admonished me in a memo, yet mine was "at best . . . horrible," perhaps because I hated doing it. I imagined—and sometimes I heard—the disc jockeys fill the airways for fifty-five minutes with the mental equivalent of cotton candy and popcorn. Then, for five minutes, their voices became sober. Then, like little boys who have been admonished to straighten up, they read the news, *our* news, *my* news. On the radio, it sounded ideal for anyone who happened to be vacuuming the living room or trying to sleep off the previous evening's binge—but not for the audience I had in mind (that my parents had in mind, I realized) for my future astute political observations.

Nor were the stories we covered at UPI the weighty, substantive stories I aspired to. I was not asked for analyses of foreign policy, of domestic social problems, of current cultural trends. At UPI, I covered such standard fare as fires, robberies, political press conferences, murder trials, public utility board hearings. In addition, I worked on "human interest" features. The more bizarre the story, the better our bureau manager liked it. When a poor black elementary school janitor literally found a fortune in the middle of the street—a bag of money that had fallen out of a Brink's truck—I was there for his press conference. When a tiny Amazonian jungle Indian, with her missionary guardian, proclaimed that she'd been saved by the Word of God, I was there, taking notes. Hollywood was a major beat. I was considered too green to be entrusted with interviewing stars (we had two veteran reporters assigned to that), but occasionally I ate lunch in the studio cafeterias—and on rare occasions at the Brown Derby—with some pretty young thing and her "flack," as we called the publicity agent. In my notebook, I scribbled down her inane answers to my inane questions. The profile I wrote reminded me of the ones I used to read about my classmates in my high school paper.

When reality wasn't bizarre enough, I learned to improve

upon it. For two days I covered an international bathing-beauty pageant in Long Beach. Interviews with the girls and the pageant officials yielded only smiles and platitudes. My editor was growing increasingly impatient with the material I was phoning in. I was supposed to be working, he barked, not just ogling the girls. His growls jogged my memory. Miss Panama, I suddenly recalled, had been so homesick that at midnight she had sneaked out of her room and gone for a moonlight ocean skinny-dip, as she used to do at home. An unimpeachable source, who spoke only on condition that he remain anonymous, revealed to me that Miss France and Miss Germany had insulted each other's national honor. The incident took place in the women's bathroom. Amid the screams of the girls, a male pageant official had invaded the bathroom and pulled them apart. He emerged, witnesses said, looking as if "a couple of tigresses had raked his cheek." My editor particularly liked the last quote and did not ask me, as he usually did, whether I was sure about it.

For a few months, I liked the excitement and variety of my work. I enjoyed the bizarre stories I covered, the thrill of racing to a breaking story, the authority of my press pass when I had to cross a police line, the oddball characters I came across— including my colleagues in the office.

Our manager, Hank Rieger, was a kind man devoted to his job, but not my idea of a great mentor. Hank was short, pudgy, balding; he sat in solitary splendor behind a makeshift partition. There he filled out time schedules, signed paychecks and, he said, "protected us" from New York (the main office)—whatever that meant. From time to time he emerged—or, rather, erupted— from his cubicle, his face the color of a raspberry, waving a sheet of teletype paper. AP had beaten us on this story or that. Did we want to be second best? Were we wire-service men or not? Did we want to hang on to our jobs? (UPI was always on the verge of folding.) We listened, trying to keep a straight face, winked at Ansa, then, when the storm had passed, went on with our work. As Ansa said, cheerfully mixing her metaphors, we all knew that behind Hank's geyserlike eruptions was a heart like a Hershey's Chocolate Kiss.

Among my colleagues, I never found the equivalent of the "boys of the Via Panisperna." Our bureau stars were the two Hollywood reporters. One kept to himself and impressed me as grim and determined, like a police interrogator. He wore brown suits that matched the imitation wood of the rewrite desk, or gray suits that harmonized with the gray of the cement on the floor. When he was in the office, before he sat down to his desk, he carefully and neatly rolled up the sleeves of his white dress shirt, as if he were a police detective preparing to grill a suspect. I imagined him boring in during his interrogation of a rising starlet: Are you really having an affair with your leading man? How sick were you on the set, or were you faking it? Is it true that your glamorous screen name is really a front for a series of unpronounceable Polish syllables?

The other Hollywood reporter, Vernon Scott, was far more personable. He favored bow ties and plaid vests and dark-rimmed glasses. If anyone had made a movie about Vern, Cary Grant might have played the lead, except that Cary Grant was not the type to chew gum. From time to time, Vern threatened to give it all up—the Hollywood beat, the movie and TV column. He would jettison everything for his secret passion—archaeology, he said. As he often confided to me, he had visited Rome once, taken a tour of Hadrian's Villa. Like the King of Sweden at that time (who was also an amateur archaeologist)—perhaps *with* the King of Sweden—he would finally unearth the emperor's villa in all its glory, Vern said.

In the bureau manager's eyes, I should have been communing with Stan, a rosy-cheeked baby-face. With his blond pompadour falling over his forehead, he looked as if he were distantly related to Elvis. Stan's nasal twang reminded me of a loosely strung guitar. His chief virtue in my eyes was that he typed incredibly fast. If Stan was a future star with the organization, I concluded, I was in the wrong galaxy. So far as I could tell, the rest of my colleagues simply wanted to go home to their wives and children, or to the apartments they were fixing up, or to their bottles of bourbon or rum. Others went home to read novels—and to write them, or so I heard. They never invited me to find out.

I did find one soulmate, Alan Fitzgibbon. He was a moon-faced, owlish-looking Harvard graduate, brilliant, literate and savvy. He, too, was the son of an academic, but had his doubts about an academic career. Alan was serious about the craft of working for a wire service; he mastered procedures and routines; he knew how to develop a story so that it would come to the attention of the New York office. In patient, typewritten notes to me, he tried to teach me what he knew, including UPI style. I learned only grudgingly that "assistant" had to be abbreviated as "asst." and "more than" was to be used in place of "over." At times, especially when I worked the overnight shift and tended to doze off at three in the morning, Alan caught some of my gems from the police beat, for example: "Booked was John Smith whose body was found on the lawn at the home of his ex-girlfriend."

After hours, Alan and I had dinner together, discussed literature, commiserated about our condition at UPI and planned what we would do when we joined a serious newspaper, meaning, of course, *The New York Times*, *The Washington Post* or *The Wall Street Journal*. Unfortunately for both of us, Alan was abruptly recalled to active duty with the Army during a Cold War alert in 1961. Eventually he became a highly paid reporter with a medical news service. "Keep sane," he told me, as always, when we parted for the last time.

My job with UPI, which had always been temporary, ended in December 1961. Following six months of military service, I was fortunate enough to be hired as a reporter with *The Wall Street Journal* in San Francisco.

My father looked relieved. He had followed my career with UPI dubiously. I heard about it on the weekends when I flew home from Los Angeles to the Bay Area. How could a bathing-beauty contest or the conversion of an Amazonian Indian get me any closer to my goal of making pronouncements about the future of the American presidency or the latest current in the Cold War? I was a dilettante; my journalism was only a "flash in the pan," he declared, and my mother echoed his opinions.

It was hard for him to find fault with the *Journal*. The *Journal* was located in an airy loft, on the second floor of a building on upper Market Street. Hollywood reporters, drunks and Elvis look-alikes were nowhere to be found. Like me, all my colleagues wore ties and dress shirts to work. Their colleges and universities tended to be in the Princeton, Stanford, Harvard category. Like me, they were serious, driven, absorbed in their stories, in advancing their careers. I had had my doubts about inviting my parents into the UPI office, introducing them to my colleagues. The *Journal* presented no such problems. Nor did I have any hesitation about showing my father the stories that I published.

The atmosphere in the *Journal* office mirrored our sense of high purpose. Nobody grunted or snorted, "UPI, Segrè," his shoulder cradling the receiver, fingers still flying over the typewriter keyboard. Nobody shouted across the room, "Hey, Al, some flack wants you." At the *Journal*, we answered the telephones in subdued, mellifluous tones: *"Wall Street Journal*, Segrè speaking." With each other we were polite, subdued, almost absentminded at times. "George, when you've got a minute, could you call back the secretary of labor's office." "Pete, I hate to interrupt, but the chairman of Coca-Cola left you a message." Nobody yelled, "Faster, men, faster," even in jest, because we were all going as fast as we could. We were set up like a rowing crew, I thought, with our desks laid out in four rows facing our coxswain and manager, Charles N. Stabler. He wore pin-striped suits and striped ties and a hat, and his hair was a neatly styled executive gray. On Friday afternoons he often invited us to gather for a round of drinks at the Roosevelt, a little bar around the corner. Over beer or Scotch (always Cutty Sark) we discussed our craft, especially the progress of our current stories and projects for future ones. These colleagues, these impromptu seminars and social hours, resembled what my father had known on the Via Panisperna, I decided.

Like the companies we covered, we were at the *Journal* to produce. Instead of sewing machines or barrels of petroleum or gaskets for ice cream machines, our product was business news. We were each assigned half a dozen companies in the area. Our job was to follow each company, to keep up with its new products, new personnel, and especially its earnings reports. But the *Journal* has always interpreted business news broadly: not just earnings, but also trends in education or politics or society that would affect business. As reporters we were measured largely by our ability to generate front-page "leaders," the long, magazine-like stories on the far-right and far-left columns of the front page.

Though we were there to produce, we did not feel like automatons on an assembly line. This was, after all, *The Wall Street Journal*. It was like being at Harvard. We reporters, especially those just starting out, couldn't understand how we, out of hundreds of applicants, had been considered worthy. But now that we were there, we wondered how we could hang on and how we could uphold the *Journal*'s standards and traditions. As our editors often reminded us, what we wrote would be quoted in the boardrooms and breakfast nooks of America. The *Journal*'s reputation was not just mystique; it was real. We recognized that daily, in the ease with which we got through to senior vice presidents, in the way that sometimes even chairmen of the board returned our phone calls.

I quickly realized that my colleagues were serious journalists. Perhaps I might even be in the company of journalistic supermen, I thought. Two of my colleagues went on to win Pulitzers, and one eventually became chairman of the board of Dow Jones, the *Journal*'s publisher. I, too, felt like a serious journalist. I was freer to do research, to go out on articles of general interest. I was writing long and substantial stories about social trends or the direction education was taking. From time to time I also wrote lighter pieces, such as one on the corporate fad for hiring British secretaries for their accents. I enjoyed walking by newsstands in San Francisco on the way to work or to the grocery store, and glancing at the *Journal*. There was my name on the front page, and I knew that 700,000 other readers (at that time) from Des Moines to Miami Beach had seen it, too.

Outwardly, at least, I had a bright future ahead of me. In quieter moments, I had my doubts about who I was and where I belonged. In Los Angeles I had felt rootless. The city, I noted in my diary, was "one of those fast growing weeds that spring up in the desert, the roots shallow, the plant easy to eradicate." I experienced periodic waves of nostalgia for Rome, for my apartment there, for my friends, for the sounds of the church bells, and the distant buzz of the cabinetmaker's saw. "A travel poster of Piazza di Spagna tugged at me: there are things to love there, beautiful things, places with character." "Everything except the occupation would draw me back to Italy: friends, family, tradition, beauty," I wrote. I went through the patronymic ritual. I was the son of Emilio Segrè of Tivoli, the grandson of Giuseppe Segrè of Bozzolo. What was I doing in Los Angeles, California, working for a cheapskate outfit like UPI? What direction was my career taking? When I walked into the UPI office and contemplated the rewrites that faced me, I knew that I did not feel the "immense enthusiasm" that my father had for physics. Nor did I feel as if I were in love with my work. My schedule of alternating between the day shift and the overnight, from ten in the evening until six in the morning, had worn me down.

At the *Journal*, I felt no more assured. For a few months, I stayed with my parents in Lafayette and commuted to San Francisco. My parents lived in a world of hardwood floors and Persian rugs, of tailored suits and English bone china. At home we drank espresso, played Scrabble; my sisters played recorder duets. It

was a refined, Mandarin world divorced from the one I was en-
countering outside, I felt. I belonged with my colleagues, I
thought. That meant I should be living in some cold-water flat
or boxy bachelor condo in San Francisco or in an East Bay suburb. Yet I dreaded sinking into the standardized, mass-produced,
"store-bought" world of America, as I called it.

At the *Journal*, I was an "information shovel," I noted in my
diary, and the "continual handling of new things that you only
half grasp . . . the torrent of information that is forever running
through one ear and out the other" bothered me. I wanted to
know a few things well. Nor was my work wholly my own. The
stories were always edited—usually for the better. But the end
product struck me as "blocks of facts piled on each other."

Most of all, I sensed that at the *Journal* I was part of Corporate
America. I could be transferred at will. Already I had been invited
to move to Los Angeles and had declined. If I wanted to make
my way up the organizational ladder, next time I would have to
go. Furthermore, my future plans seemed shapeless. I didn't
know what my next move should be. Get transferred to Washington and cover politics, my father said. I asked my bureau manager, Charley Stabler. He was very kind and supportive, but he
said that after a year, it was a little soon to be transferred to one
of the plum jobs in the organization. I watched what my successful colleagues did: they got transferred to Detroit to cover
automobiles, or to New York to cover the food industry. (Eventually, they did get the call from Washington.)

My father had his own agenda for my future, I suspected. I
should go back to Italy, work for the new owners of the paper
mills. "I suddenly thought one day that he would die happy if
he had seen his grandchildren once again playing on the terrace
in Tivoli," I noted in my journal. Italy remained alluring, yet
Italy also seemed "an enormous hoax, a longing for an impossible
dream. Rome isn't Tivoli of 1914; the mills are a questionable
financial proposition." Nevertheless, I could not escape the feeling of an "accusing finger pointed at me." With my parents,

especially my father, "I feel on thin ice. Without [the accusing finger], I have confidence in myself. I'm reasonably intelligent. I can write. With the finger pointed at me, I feel like Sisyphus."

Briefly, I considered going to law school. The Law School Aptitude Test persuaded me otherwise. I still wanted to be a writer, but if I couldn't commit to a career in journalism, what was left? Was there a family trade or business other than the paper mills? There was, I realized, the higher-education business. I could be an academic. For years I'd revolted against it. Ever since my Los Alamos childhood, I'd hated being a "four-eyes," a "brain," a "teacher's pet." After college, I'd been in and out of graduate schools, tried other careers. Yet what I knew best were the rhythms and seasons of academic life. If there was a family trade, that was it. I had a father in it; I had uncles and great-uncles in it. I'd grown up with it as a child.

An image from my childhood often recurred to me. The Jewish tradition speaks of the languor of the Sabbath, the lassitude of the afternoon as the day of rest fades away. For me, Sunday evenings were like that. After a family outing climbing Mount Tamalpais or Mount Diablo or hiking along the beaches of Marin County, I'd come home physically tired but spiritually revived. I'd feel ready for Monday, eager to meet the challenge of the school week again.

After supper, my father often returned to his desk. Sometimes sitting, sometimes kneeling on a chair, he worked at his notes for Monday's lecture. Secretly I began to imagine myself at my own desk preparing my own notes for my own Monday class. I didn't really know what my notes would deal with—most likely, literature or history. The subject didn't seem to matter much. What mattered was being on campus, waving to colleagues, having lunch at the faculty club, chatting with students, having something to say in front of a class—maybe even something worthwhile. What mattered was reading some interesting books, discussing provocative ideas, satisfying one's curiosity by doing some research in the library.

I knew that life well. Perhaps it was more deeply ingrained in me than I realized, and I should really try it. Since I hadn't found English to my taste, I decided to switch to history. I would play to my strengths. With my background, European history appealed more than American. Modern European sounded as if it might even connect with the journalism I was familiar with. Since I knew the language and the country well, why not modern Italy? I wasn't sure that I felt any great passion for it, as my father had for physics, but I felt utterly safe. This was something I knew I could do; I would be competent at it—perhaps even do well. If I were an academic, a colleague, I mused, perhaps my father might even invite me to join the Club of the *gente colta*. I wasn't sure how much I cared about that. I worried more about what might happen to my career as a writer. On the other hand, perhaps the Club would bring my father and me closer together. I decided to quit the *Journal* and go back to graduate school, this time in modern European history, this time at UC–Berkeley. It was a big decision. I screwed up my courage and tried something that frightened me more than the decision itself: I risked confiding in my father.

"I'm thinking of going back to graduate school," I say to my father one evening during the spring of 1962. He and I are sitting in the living room of his big house on Crest Road. A huge picture window frames Mount Diablo. Down in the valley, the freeway glows with the endless chain of car headlights. I want my words to sound calm, decisive, like a professional football quarterback throwing a precise, businesslike pass. What I hear sounds wobbly, slightly out of true, the way I used to pass footballs when I was in junior high. For a couple of days I have been hinting to my father that I'd like to talk to him, that I'm not sure I want to stay with the *Journal*. Nevertheless my declaration appears to catch him by surprise.

"Stupid," he lashes out, and I hear the Basilisk. Like the fabled lizard-like monster, he looks at me as if his glance or his breath could kill. "I've never heard of anything so stupid."

I know that neither his glance nor his breath will do me in. Nevertheless, I'm furious at his outburst. I don't need this. Now, glancing at him, I see that his face is at once angry, solemn, frightened. A less grandiose metaphor than Basilisk comes to mind. He's more like one of those lizards or toads that puff themselves up to frighten away their enemies. It's his way of denying, dismissing, chasing away things that go bump in the night. But I'm not there to understand or explain him; I want him to help me. I want his support, his reassurance. He's my father.

What I get is rapid-fire questions, some real, some rhetorical, all scathing. I see that I'm not a son; I'm a defendant. Why history, when before I'd studied literature? Did I really want to become like one of those English or history professors? Did I realize how badly they were paid? Under his cross-examination, my replies sound erratic. I remember that night on Spruce Street a decade earlier, when I was in high school, defending my choice of going to Reed College.

This time I feel less tender, less vulnerable. My voice may be on the verge of cracking and whining like that of a sixteen-year-old, but I'm not a teenager anymore, I tell myself. I may be seething, but I lower my voice. I try to sound firm, smooth, confident, as if I were talking to my boss or going through a job interview. This time I have some answers—or I think I do.

My decision is the result of a process of elimination, I tell my father. I don't want to become a literary scholar or critic, so there's no point in continuing in English. I want to be a writer. History appears to encompass anything and everything, engages all my talents and capabilities: my desire to write, my intellectual curiosity, my languages, my love for Italy.

"You won't last six months in graduate school," my father assures me. When I venture that teaching sounds appealing, he snorts: "A university professor? In the humanities? Better to be a postman." Scholars in the humanities—"with notable exceptions, of course," my father declares—are thin, nervous, ascetic, furtive. Most of them tend to be divorced from the world, to know a great deal about not very much, he says. They look ridiculous, especially the ones who shuffle around with long hair and sandals. It's hard to tell them apart from their students.

He has other plans for me, I learn. To me, they appear to be fantasies. They're based on his own guilt, I suspect, over the fate of the paper mills and his feelings of inadequacy in financial affairs. I ought to go into the banking business, he tells me. I should get a job as a factotum to an important businessman—this last notion apparently lifted straight out of a biography he was reading at the time. He sounds as if he is striking out wildly, grabbing at any solution that seems plausible, that fits into his scheme of what would be a proper, safe, appropriate career for me. I see that he means well. I wonder if he ever thinks of his own example: the incredible plunge that he took with his own career when he switched from engineering to physics. I wonder if his own father bombarded him in the same way when he decided to take that decisive step. I vow that with my children it will be different.

Out of habit, out of deference, I listen to his thunderings and fulminations. I've been trained to listen, to wait until he has finished. I hunker down patiently, and I notice that I'm hunching my shoulders protectively, as if I were a soldier in the trenches during one of those First World War artillery bombardments.

Through the roaring and the explosions, I hear him faintly, as if he were reporting from some forward outpost. I strain to listen, and I become aware that he is relaying important information. Studying history, for me, he says, is a compromise. I'd hoped to join his Club of the well-educated, well-rounded, but he's right when he says that I don't really have the mentality and temperament of a real *erudito*. He uses the Italian word, with its overtones of the scholar who is truly learned in some exotic field. If I could find myself a hero, someone I truly admired, then I would pull through, he says. Perhaps he understands me better than I realize, I concede to myself, but I don't tell him that. Silence is my best weapon.

"Stupid. You won't last six months." Even now, in memory, that burst frightens, deafens, enrages me. I feel shell-shocked, numb. Those explosions drown out his other observations about my talents and interests. I also have a hard time recognizing a very different side to my father—one that is caring, supportive. It's indisputably there in old letters and postcards. "I'm very sorry that your affairs have gone so badly and I write more to encourage you and give you a moral 'eskimo kiss' than for anything else." So he wrote me in January 1961. I'd just quit Columbia University graduate school and was looking for a job. The important thing was to work at something that I really liked to do, he advised. He remembered clearly his student experiences at the University of Rome. He performed well the first two years, when he had to learn subjects that were more or less scientific, but did "much worse when I had to do engineering courses that didn't interest me." He studied "with great pleasure when I transferred to physics." If I wanted to be a writer, then I should write, he urged me: "Write, I say, not publish. I understand that the two things are quite different and I wouldn't, for awhile, at least, worry about rejection slips." If I wanted to find a job in journalism or the publishing world, "or in whatever other field satisfies you, that's fine with me; all I care about is that you should be satisfied," he added. A recurrent phrase in his letters was: "For your first best seller, you might think of writing"— and he would suggest something. He would also barrage me with "Well, how many stories, poems and plays have you written lately?" I know he means well; I also know the effect on me is numbing, paralyzing.

"Stupid." The word rings in my ears. But I'm not stupid. When I show him, I'm a little surprised at my capabilities—and then enraged that I have to keep on proving them to him. Some years later, as a graduate student, I take a Sunday-afternoon beach walk with my parents. My father asks me how my work is going. I've been reading Benedetto Croce for a seminar, I tell him, knowing full well that he is no fan of the Italian philosopher-historian's prolix, windy style and diaphanous concepts. "A real idiot," my father mutters. I reply with a clear, well-organized defense of Croce's ideas about history, a real mini-lecture. I do it in Italian.

My parents appear surprised, a little shell-shocked themselves. They compliment me, both on the content and on my fluency. I'm stunned as I listen to myself. For years I've heard my father and his friends hold forth on this level—the conversation of friends who are well educated, even learned, who deal with interesting ideas and alluring theories and concepts. This is the discourse of the *gente colta.* Without much thinking about it, I've learned to do it. Have I become one of them? Has the day arrived? Maybe, unconsciously, I've become a member of the Club. I'd like to feel the pride and joy of the newly initiated. Instead, I feel mostly rage. I've done it. Once again, I've proved myself, like Sisyphus: how soon before I'll have to do it all over again—and again?

For a few weeks, after my father's outburst about graduate school, I feel as if I were once again a child poised at the edge of the diving tower. I'm shivering. The wind whips in from the Golden Gate. Twenty feet down, the blue-green waters of the Men's Gym swimming pool beckon, warm and embracing. Some of my friends have shaken their heads and retreated down the ladder. All I need to do is to take that step into the void and point my toes. Gravity will do the rest.

I took the plunge. I went back to graduate school at Berkeley in the fall of 1962. The Vietnam War was heating up; so were the worldwide student protest movements. Berkeley was no longer the quiet, provincial town with orange streetcars and old-fashioned drugstore soda fountains where, when I was a boy, "big kids" from high school and Cal students hung out. Espresso coffeehouses were beginning to sprout along Telegraph Avenue and Bancroft Way. On the north side of campus, fresh-pasta places and chocolate specialty shops began to appear next to dime stores and hardware stores. The university was no longer the provincial Cal I knew as a child. The grassy fields below the President's House, where I'd played touch football, lay buried beneath huge multistory classroom or laboratory buildings. In the 1950s, under the leadership of Chancellor Clark Kerr, California pioneered the multicampus statewide higher-education system that served as a model for the rest of the country. The Berkeley campus, in particular, had blossomed into a world-class institution, and in the 1960s, revolution was in the air.

Almost daily, as I crossed Sproul Hall Plaza on my way to class or to the library, I pushed through chanting crowds, skirted thickets of placards. Usually I lingered for a while. The ripples of excitement pulsing through the crowds infected me. In my stomach I felt the knots of anger and frustration at the world's injustices as I listened to the harangues of speakers like Mario Savio or Art Goldberg, or, on occasion, to Joan Baez's sweet and plaintive songs. This is the way it is with crowds, perhaps the way it was in Paris during the French Revolution, I told myself. Perhaps, I mused, this was what my father might have seen in Piazza Venezia when Mussolini harangued his Blackshirts— though, so far as I know, he never went to those rallies. This was history being made.

But, I learned quickly, history—even revolution—takes a long time. My pulses of excitement turned into twinges of guilt. I had to think of the other way of making history. Reading assignments, book reviews, term papers, oral presentations beckoned. The revolution—if it was one—would pass in time, I told myself, and so would my life, my career, if I didn't bring it under control. I was in my mid-twenties. It was time I made something of myself. I trudged off to learn the other way of making history: in the library stacks, in seminar rooms, in professors' offices.

I still looked for the "immense enthusiasm" that my father brought to physics. I hungered for deep discussions about the meaning of history. From time to time, over dinner in the Bear's Lair or while drinking coffee on the Terrace with fellow students, I debated the meaning of the scenes we were witnessing. We argued the great issues: freedom versus authority, free speech versus the need for order, the morality of violence. According to our fields of interest, we made grand historical comparisons: Sproul Hall Plaza became Paris in 1789, Vienna or Berlin in 1848, Saint Petersburg in 1917, Rome in 1922.

Most of the time, however, my classmates appeared more comfortable in the library stacks than in the Plaza. They seemed less absorbed in what history is and how to write it than in the mechanics of getting through graduate school. What were the important books and articles to read to pass the examinations? What questions was Professor So-and-so likely to ask? And there were rumors that he wasn't getting along well with his wife. How would that color his exam? Through these conversations I learned something about how and why people did history, and yet these talks never seemed as brilliant, as fascinating, as insightful as I imagined my father's had been on his Sunday walks with his colleagues.

If I did not find the passion I was seeking in the subject, I did find some masters. For his flashes of brilliance, for his machine-gun responses, for his nimble mind and his ability to weave a complex theory out of what I saw as ordinary, sometimes disconnected facts, I admired Richard A. Webster, in my field of modern Italian history. In contrast to the air of hard-edged professionalism that was so prevalent at Berkeley, Carlo M. Cipolla personified the humane gentleman scholar. A handsome and elegant man with a slight Italian accent, he delighted undergraduates by interweaving his subject of medieval economic history with commentaries on California wine. For him, the story of clocks or the history of world demography was an amusing pastime, the sort of thing that gentlemen of leisure pursued. Like

Professor Webster, he didn't seem much concerned with what I took to be the "great events" in the Plaza.

This apparent indifference to the tumult on campus disturbed me. History was not merely knowledge. It was more than clever theories and amusing insights. History was about people and what they did. How could so many of my professors remain so detached from the history being made around them? What was the relationship between the Plaza and the stacks? I puzzled over these questions one day with a classmate. "Maybe you should go see the Old Man," he said.

"Who?" I said.

"The Old Man—you know, Sontag," he said. *The Old Man.* In that single epithet, I heard admiration, reverence mixed with respect for a patriarch, and not a little fear. As I discovered later, during his twenty-four years of teaching at Berkeley, Raymond James Sontag had become a quasi-mythic figure as a teacher and master.

I wondered why I hadn't come across him before—until I discovered that he was a man apart—quite literally. His office was not in Dwinelle Hall, where the History Department was located. His was hidden away in splendid isolation on the fourth floor of the Main Library. Graduate-student gossip hinted darkly at the reasons for the separation. After figuratively brawling with various colleagues, it was said, Mr. Sontag had retired to the Library in disgust. Just who was involved and why always provided lively—if highly speculative—discussions over coffee on the Terrace or dinner in the cafeteria.

Going to see the Old Man was an undertaking, a small pilgrimage. After ascending three floors by slow elevator, I went right down the linoleum-covered hallway that smelled of dust and books, then took a sharp left at the corner, and about halfway down the hall was his office. That first time, and ever afterward, I had the feeling that I was going up the mountain to receive the Mosaic tablets, and I liked the sensation. The Library was one of the older buildings on campus, one of the cornerstones of the university. I was back in touch with an older academic tradition, I felt, with the university before it had exploded into what the administrators often proudly referred to as the all-purpose, all-things-to-all-men "multiversity." As I made my way down that fourth-floor hallway, I knew I had returned to a world not simply of higher education but of learning, a world that sought wisdom as well as knowledge.

Behind a nondescript door with a frosted-glass window, I discovered a plain, functional office. Bookshelves covered three of the walls. A desk stood at an angle in a corner so that Mr. Sontag faced you when you entered. A large seminar table filled the center of the room. Light streamed in from a big French door that opened out on a little terrace and overlooked Wheeler Hall. To the left, up the gentle slope, loomed the Campanile, the university's landmark.

I found myself face-to-face with a big man, a substantial one. Without being overpowering, he seemed to overshadow even a six-footer like me. Arthritis and age had bent and curved his shoulders a bit. I found the effect reassuring. He appeared to have come down from Olympian heights to listen to me—to me, a mere graduate student. He looked as if he were sifting through my uncertain pronouncements and explanations to find out whether, from time to time, I might actually have something worth saying. His wiry gray hair was short and parted in the middle. He peered at me through severe, round wire-rimmed glasses that suggested discipline, seriousness, hard work. Yet, for the most part, his eyes twinkled with warmth, good humor, support and encouragement. I sensed right away that this man, too, pondered the connections between the Plaza and the stacks. He, too, understood that the two were linked in one confusing human process.

In his dark suit and striped dark tie, Mr. Sontag looked like a professor of the old school. His traditional garb, I found out, reflected both his generation and his long years of study and association with the world of diplomacy. His specialty was European diplomatic history, and one of his greatest scholarly achievements was acting as editor of the State Department's German War Documents Project. His former students included major American diplomats like George Kennan and Jacob Bream, who both served as ambassadors to Moscow.

I thought of my father's general disdain—with "notable exceptions"—for his long-haired colleagues in the humanities. Clearly Mr. Sontag was one of those "notable exceptions." That first time I met Mr. Sontag and ever afterward I felt at ease with him. He appeared whole and normal, an academic whose mental constructs were in proportion and in harmony with the real world. He was a devout Catholic who prayed for divine guidance to help him in his "unbelief." He was intelligent, and he had a good sense of humor, but he was not clever or brilliant. He had a normal family life, a wife and children. He was a sophisticated and worldly man, whose pleasures ran to nothing more exotic than bourbon and football. If I became anything like Mr. Sontag, if I had a career anything like his, I would not have to apologize to anyone for anything, I decided.

The Mr. Sontag I knew was expansive, reflective and ruminative. In the historiography seminar that I took with him, he asked the big questions that puzzled me. What was the connection between the historian's personal life and his work? Why had the historians we studied taken the approaches that they did? By asking these questions, he seemed to show us again and again the intimate connection between history and life, between the Plaza and the stacks. History was more than the way my father knew it, mostly facts, names, dates, genealogies. History was perhaps a profession, even a technical discipline that involved crunching numbers and developing elaborate tables and graphs. But history also had to mean something—and not just to other specialists in the field, Mr. Sontag insisted. The best history spoke across generations; the best history, he showed us, celebrated certain universal themes and values—power won and lost, human dignity gained and dissipated. He was not afraid, for example, to talk about Italian Fascism as a "tragedy" and Mussolini as a sinister and cynical charlatan—terms that suggested that history was art and literature as much as social science.

Through him, I came to understand what great teaching meant—not only scholarship, but also wisdom; not just next week's test or paper, but "what will you do with your life?" A lecture must be like a James Thurber cartoon, made up of huge and simple but telling lines, he said. His lectures, clear and well-organized, tended to be largely traditional—chronological narratives with interludes of analysis. Yet his commanding presence and his shrewd sense of show business transformed them into performances that usually packed the lecture hall.

One of his favorite tricks was to creep to the edge of the stage and teeter for a while—usually at a climactic moment in the story—say, the Munich crisis in 1938, when Europe was about to go to war. Just when the audience was sure he would fall over into the front row, he'd pull back—just as Europe did after the crisis.

I learned something else: that at critical moments, when Sproul Hall Plaza or its equivalent was seething, people often turned to historians as a source of wisdom, even comfort, as if they were secular prophets. At the time of the Cuban missile showdown in 1962, for example, when the world appeared on the brink of nuclear war, students flocked to Mr. Sontag's lectures. His air of authority, of dignity, of toughness and sober wisdom, shot through with flashes of humor, had a calming effect on his audience. He explained how the crisis had come about, how it compared to similar ones in the past, what some of the options might be. He couldn't promise a happy solution, but many listeners reacted like one woman student who sighed afterward: "I just feel better after I've heard him talk about it."

Those packed lecture halls at such moments were a supreme tribute to his reputation as a teacher and wise man, for, as I discovered more and more, Mr. Sontag was not in tune with the antiwar, antiestablishment spirit of the 1960s. For some years, he took an unabashedly hard line on Vietnam. The Communists had to be stopped, the Russians taught a lesson. But as American casualties mounted, and American planners waffled, Mr. Sontag came to understand that this was more a civil war than a test of American vital interests in Southeast Asia. He changed his mind. Nobody seemed to notice his about-face except those of us who followed him. We learned that even men like him were fallible and that their mistakes did not detract from their greatness.

Memories of the crowds in Sproul Hall Plaza, the conflict between Plaza and stacks, between history makers and making history troubled me as I began my own academic career; they still trouble me. When an unseemly number of doubts gnaw at me, I simply remember the Old Man. I forget that he slipped away peacefully in his sleep in 1972. Once again I imagine myself at his Cuban missile crisis lecture, watching him teeter reassuringly on the edge of the stage.

"You won't last six months," my father had predicted when I told him I planned to return to graduate school. I lasted seven years—as I had no doubt I would. In 1970 I, too, became "Dr. Segrè." In the meantime, I married. In 1957, a decade before my marriage, my father made one of his rare and typically cryptic pronouncements to me on women and marriage: "With regard to women, for many reasons I prefer them to be Jewish, at least, and especially if they come from a well-bred family." I followed his advice. At the time, my wife, Elisabeth, was studying for her doctorate in French literature at Berkeley. My sister Amelia invited her to a Thanksgiving dinner at my father's house in Lafayette. There, my future wife radiated all the bounce, charm and energy of her nickname, "Zaza." Dark-haired and vivacious, with gorgeous brown eyes that flashed with all the passion of her Russian-Jewish soul, she was irresistible. In 1967 we were married. Three years later, our first child, Gino, was born; Francesca followed in 1973, and Joel in 1980.

In the fall of 1967, I began teaching as an instructor in Stanford's Western Civilization program. On Sunday nights, in a tiny rose-framed apartment a few blocks south of the Berkeley campus—and not very far from the house on Piedmont Avenue where my parents had begun their American life—I sat at my desk, as I had seen my father do. I sat at my desk and prepared for my Monday classes. I was in the family trade. I had become like my father. That, I imagined, would bring us closer together.

CHAPTER 11

Loving Gunfighters

Now that we were both in the same trade, both professors, both teaching at large American state universities, I anticipated that my father and I would have lots to talk about at last. We would rejoice over promising students, grumble over the "donkeys"; we would plot strategies for getting tenure and grants, grouse at committee work and the bullheadedness of colleagues, cheer the occasional report or committee recommendation well done and adopted; we would curse the labyrinth of academic politics, moan about the obtuseness of university administrators and boards of regents, despair over the indifference and incomprehension of our ultimate employers, the citizenry. We would also marvel at the institutions that employed us, at the incredible educational opportunities they provided at bargain prices.

I thought we might even get beyond comparing our professional lives. During the first few weeks after Zaza and I arrived in Austin, I often imagined my parents in Berkeley at the end of the summer of 1938. Like them, we, too, with our firstborn son, were settling in a new land, exploring a new culture. In Austin in 1970, fresh-pasta places and *The New York Times* delivered daily to your door were unheard of. When I asked for espresso coffee in the grocery stores, clerks told me cheerfully, "We don't carry that brand." Just as my father had investigated the mysteries of peanut butter, and my mother had sniffed at hot dogs, Zaza and I explored the wonders of barbecue and chicken-fried steak, of "ahs tee" and Dr Pepper. We studied the intricacies of air-conditioning; we discovered that if our Texan neighbors spoke a peculiar variant of American English, with a little patience it was perfectly comprehensible.

Often I pictured my sisters, compared my immigrant's life with theirs. Amelia, settling into a California-style house in a suburb north of Tel Aviv, had to master the gutturals and glottals of a new language—and to do that, she had to begin with an entirely new alphabet. Hummus, pita and falafel became the staples of her dinner table. Fausta, living at first in the fog, the rain, the green of far North Wales, and then alongside the Bristol Channel, did not have to wrestle with a new language. Yet, as I noticed when I visited her, the image of "the American," like a faint halo, still followed her in her rounds to the grocery store in search of a "bit of mutton" or the right "straw-bry" jam.

Yet in my bones, I knew I was no immigrant. The Tower atop the University of Texas Main Administration Building reassured me. I preferred the Venetian lines of Berkeley's Campanile to the Stalinist grace of Austin's Tower, but I was confident about what lay ahead. I knew what faculty life was like at a large American state university. I'd grown up with it.

I knew, for example, how the university's weekly calendar of events would read, like the menu of an incredible intellectual and cultural cornucopia. It made my mouth water, just as it had my father's. Out of every day of the week poured lectures, concerts, conferences, art exhibits, symposia, distinguished speakers, movies. The university catalog was much the same. At the daily intellectual and cultural potluck, I could taste everything from astrophysics to zoology, from black holes to Yiddish literature, from paleontology to Swahili, from Chinese ceramics to Persian poetry. The menu also listed modern Italian history. For this last dish I was responsible. Modern Italian history on the fringes of the Texas Hill Country? Was that any more outlandish than nuclear physics by the shores of San Francisco Bay? I asked myself.

My father and I talked quite regularly by phone. That didn't mean that we had much to talk about. I never quite knew what to say. I always felt I had to be careful, cautious. I had to measure my words, weigh them carefully. "What's new?" he would usually begin, affably enough. Not "How are you? How are things?" To me, "What's new?" usually meant one thing. Like my department chairman, he wanted to know: How was my book coming? Had I had any articles accepted recently? What about invitations to conferences? Eventually, we touched on what I had imagined we might have in common: stories about students or recalcitrant regents or the drudgeries of committee work. More likely, we went on to personal matters: bits and pieces about my family, his grandchildren, our tax situation.

On the best days, we talked about a book he had just finished reading, or he asked my advice on what to read next. "I don't understand these Germans," he would say. "Do you know a good book about German history—but not too scholarly?" I would suggest a title. He would read it. "That was a good book, but there was too much detail on Frederick the Great," he would say. Sure enough, in the professional reviews, the author would be faulted for focusing too heavily on Frederick the Great. Or my father would say to my wife (who has a doctorate in French literature): "What do you think of Victor Hugo?" And they would launch into a heated discussion of whether *Les Misérables* was worth reading anymore. Discussion? With my father, it was usually like arguing with the Pope. We could discuss, perhaps disagree on specifics, but in the end, he pronounced: "You may not agree, but it is so," and there was nothing more to say.

His letters, too, arrived regularly enough. During his last years, he enjoyed appearing at meetings in the United States or abroad and giving public lectures, often nontechnical ones. "*Vado a fare la pianta ornamentale* [I'm going to play the decorative houseplant]," he would say. From these tours, he would return happily with another medal or silver dish or tray to add to his collection of honors.

Often his letters, encased in envelopes decorated with bright splashes of foreign stamps, amounted to notes jotted while in flight. In that lucid handwriting that to me reflected the clarity of his mind, he chronicled what conference or what meeting he'd attended, what part of the globe he'd seen, whom he'd had dinner with—usually people I didn't know. Sometimes he included shopping lists of things he needed, or telegraphic outbursts about the state of international relations, or a one-line pontifical pronouncement about a book he'd read. I hungered for other things. How did he feel about aging, or his grandchildren or his second marriage? What did he think about the joys and frustrations of doing science? What did he think about children, his children— me? I found nothing. I even tried reading between the lines. There was nothing there. For years, when the mail arrived, I dutifully opened his letters first. Then gradually, furtively, as if someone were looking over my shoulder, I turned to bills and solicitations first.

Nearly eighteen hundred miles of plains, mountains and deserts stood between my father and me. Though we exchanged visits during Thanksgiving, Christmas and spring breaks, and summer vacations, I needed that space. I sometimes forgot why. I was grown up, I told myself; I had a family, a career, a life of my own. I felt young, tough, flexible. Meanwhile, age had dampened the Basilisk's fires. If he fumed and flamed from time to time, I could take it, I told myself.

Then certain visits jolted me into remembering why those mountains, those deserts between us were a comfort. "A heavy day of death, taxes and property," I noted after a visit to my father's house, together with my sisters, during the summer of

1981. "This morning we were summoned for a meeting in Papà's study about his estate and how to dispose of it. We are made aware of all that needs to be done in taking care of the estate, of all the pitfalls." We hear about potentially valuable papers and books, book dealers who are "all thieves and bandits," legal and tax tangles that might arise with our remaining interests in Italy.

The forefinger points. The "shoulds" drop on us like a load of bricks from a dump truck. The tasks appear huge, insurmountable; those entrusted with them—my sisters and I—weak, stunted mortals, pygmies, Lilliputians, before the Herculean tasks which we—could anyone?—were not likely to complete satisfactorily.

On my sisters' faces I see "stubborn trudgers, patient, long suffering." Amelia leans on the steel filing cabinet for a while, hovering on the fringes. Then, ignoring the chair I offer her, she sits on the floor, back against the wall, her face heavy with gloom. Behind the severe little steel-rimmed glasses, Fausta's blue eyes look frightened, as if she were unsure of her footing, always afraid that along these slippery paths the ground will give way. My father rages on. For years he had been saying that this or that ought to be done, for example, files arranged, reprints sorted (and some had been). Then the *cacadubbi* pronounces: lists of crises and disasters that will follow if thus and such isn't done.

It's as if we were all sinners and there was no hope—or very little—of salvation. An Old Testament prophet couldn't have put it more clearly. No wonder at times I felt oppressed and gloomy when I grew up with him. No wonder the air in that house seems stifling.

I understand at last why one of his graduate students once told me—to my surprise—that he found my father's house at Crest Road "cold and distant."

When I thought of my father, I often pictured his houses. Unlike the two in Berkeley—the rented rose-covered cottage on Piedmont Avenue, though I barely remember it, and the cream-colored stucco on Spruce Street—these houses in Lafayette were no longer "home" for me. They were difficult to reach, as splendid in their isolation, as Olympian in their aloofness as Los Alamos had been. They were like him, I thought.

The first, on Crest Road, perched on a hillside. Just before the dead end of the steep and winding road, you made one last twist and lunged up the driveway, between two thickets of pyracanthus bushes. In February, laden with red-orange berries, the bushes looked almost obscene, like a baboon's behind. A brick walk marked the path across the lawn, past the rose bushes, the plane tree, to the front door. In the early morning, deer wandered down from the hillsides covered with eucalyptus, oaks and thickets of greasewood and manzanita to browse on my mother's roses. To her delight, rabbits nibbled on the margins of the lawn, ears twitching, ready to vanish back into the hedge and the safety of their burrows.

Inside, the ranch-style house rambled through three bedrooms, three baths. In the living room, through the picture window, I watched Mount Diablo change color with the seasons: in the spring, a brilliant green that reminded me of travel posters of Ireland; a white gold in the summer; browns and grays in the fall and winter. In my father's wood-paneled study, he still kneeled on a chair as he worked at his desk, then perhaps napped on the foldaway couch. He stuffed the little bar with fishing tackle, his colored slides, and his pipes. From the veranda, I often heard the *cluck, cluck* of the Ping-Pong ball and sporadic shouts of glee or frustration as my parents or my sisters squared off in ferocious matches. Or I heard my mother practicing Chopin preludes on the Steinway grand in the living room. Just off the breakfast room was a redwood picnic table so that we could eat outside when the weather was good. When I visited, I felt as if I were on vacation—as I usually was.

In many ways, the house was magnificent, a mini-estate, fit for a patrician. *Signorile* (genteel), my father might have called it—though he never did. For example, to my mind, the front lawn was made to hold a small wedding; in fact, on a bright sunny day in 1970, beneath a *chuppa*, the traditional Jewish wedding canopy, my sister Amelia married Joseph Terkel. It was a house worthy of someone who had arrived, a good place to dazzle guests, to impress newspaper reporters—a place to hide in stately surroundings. Admire me, admire my brilliance, admire my achievements, the house said. Also: We are too busy with ideas, with important tasks, with high ideals and standards to bother with mortal friendships, relationships. It was a wonderful house to be alone together as a family. Except for one of my father's colleagues, we knew scarcely any of the neighbors. To go any-where, you needed to get into a car. For company, you needed to invite friends. Grandeur, gentility, yes; fun, no. As the king's son, it was a relief for me to go forth among the commoners again, back to college, back to my job, back to the world.

The house on Quail Ridge was not very different. It, too, could be reached only after an even longer and steeper climb than that of Crest Road, this time to the top of a ridge, then almost to the end of it—and to the edge. This house, too, had picture windows. These framed huge oaks where robins chirped and jays jeered at the aerial circus of squirrels making death-defying leaps from branch to branch. Just below the deck, deer browsed confidently among the grasses and bushes. Across the valley, hawks circled lazily over the crests of the hills.

Like the house on Crest Road, this one, too, was filled with things: my father's papers, books, memorabilia from his many trips—and tax records. Even more than at Crest Road, neighbors who lived directly across the street or next door did not seem to exist. For company, my father frequently invited houseguests. Down in the valley, Lafayette sprawled, a jumble of shopping centers and service stations where you bought groceries by the cartful and filled up the tank on the way to the university. Like so many American suburbs, Lafayette was anywhere and nowhere. It was not an easy place to reach my father.

My mother's death did not make matters easier. In October 1970, during a trip to Italy with my father, quite suddenly she succumbed to a heart attack. Her demise was particularly stunning because so far as we knew she had been in good health. Had duty finally taken its toll? I wondered.

I was confident about my father. Of course he would mourn her, he would miss her, I thought, but I was certain that he was self-sufficient, that he would be able to care for himself. After all, he had taught us, she had taught us, toughness, self-reliance. Doing was more important than being. Work was life. Duty, discipline would carry him through, I told myself.

They didn't. For weeks, he was like a beetle on its back, thrashing, rolling, helpless. He couldn't seem to get organized. For me, this was a shock and a revelation. Even more stunning to me—and a measure of his anguish and desperation—was the way that he turned to me. How long would the pain last? he asked. How long would he miss her? he wondered—as if this were some kind of disease that would pass. I didn't know. Uncertain what else to suggest, I thought of a man as wise and humane as he was learned. So I advised my father to consult his colleague (and my old professor), Mr. Sontag. He, too, had recently lost his wife. It was a sign of my father's grief and misery that he actually went to see Mr. Sontag.

"What did he tell you?" I asked afterward. "He's very Catholic," my father parried, and then, "There's nothing to be done." He sounded disappointed. "He says the pain never goes away. He says I will always miss her."

I missed her, too. When I heard of her death, I felt a sudden void, a silence, but in my grief, I felt uneasy. This was not the

meditative stillness of remembrance that I sought; this was silence. I missed her now, but I wondered if I hadn't always missed
her. The day after I got the news of her death, I had to meet a
class. Out of respect for her, I didn't want to, but I couldn't think
of what else to do. I heard her voice: *Man muss. Il faut.* Carry
on. I paid her the ultimate tribute: I met the class.

At the end of the spring semester, 1972, my father retired. He
was sixty-seven. For more than three decades, with time out for
Los Alamos, he had been on the Physics Department faculty at
Berkeley. I balked; retirement was something that didn't happen
to him. At best, I could accept it as a bureaucratic formality that
governed regulations on teaching schedules, pensions and the
like. Anyway, I knew he would go on doing what he'd always
been doing—physics, writing, traveling, brooding over his finances.

I wondered about the department's plans to mark the occasion. What place would the organizers choose for the dinner?
Who would be there? What would people say in their speeches?
I knew what would happen. His colleagues would call him "Emilio"; they would tell little stories about him as if he were one of
them, as if they knew him. I would listen; I would feel slightly
embarrassed. Except perhaps as a scientist, he wasn't one of
them, I thought; he never had been. "They aren't Europeans,"
my mother used to say. "They'll never understand."

On a chilly evening in June, I attended the Physics Department dinner in a restaurant at the end of the Berkeley Pier. The
interior was dark and thickly carpeted; easy-listening music
boop-booped subliminally. The only redeeming feature of the
decor was the magnificent view of San Francisco and the Golden
Gate Bridge through a picture window. The food matched the
decor: sirloin tips with partially frozen vegetables, soggy ice
cream cake roll, cheap, slightly sweet red wine. Whoever had
chosen this restaurant, planned this menu, obviously knew noth-

ing of my father's tastes. My mother was right, I thought; they'll never understand.

Nor did the speeches seem right. His colleagues praised him as a great physicist. I couldn't really judge that. Here and there, I thought I recognized the man I knew. One colleague described the frugality of my father's experiments and his uncompromising stand in favor of merit when it came to deciding promotions. That sounded like him. Others praised him for his dedication to his work. That sounded right, too.

Other speakers tried to define his personality. They told anecdotes about him: how he was a fierce Ping-Pong and Scrabble player; how he made scrambled eggs with tomatoes and zucchini. All correct, yet to me the comments rang as true as those of political candidates at a whistle-stop. Enthusiastically they mouthed their lines without knowing firsthand what they were talking about.

As if to confirm my feelings, I was overhearing snatches of conversations around me. Mostly they had to do with my father's Italian roots. I listened to well-meaning quips about "Eata da spaghetti," Godfathers and red wine. Obviously the speakers understood nothing about Tivoli and my father's pride in his family. I also heard awed whispers about the great polymath who spoke several foreign languages and quoted Dante. Then I listened to my father. For more than three decades, he had worked with his colleagues, but even from the way he pronounced their names, "Bohb," "Beell," "Kahrl," they sounded as alien to his tongue as they had when I was a boy.

What could I expect? I wondered. What would have been appropriate? If the same ceremony had been staged in Italy, the orators would have spoken of *"la California"* as if it were some fabulous and distant wonderland, and confidently referred to the *"l'università di Berk-e-leh,"* as if the American university system were administratively no different from the Italian.

In his speech at the end of the dinner, my father seemed to corroborate my thoughts. He told an anecdote about the man who looked at a bird in a tree. When the bird said, "Good morn-ing," the man said in reply, "Good morning." Then, rather puz-zled, he replied, "Excuse me. I thought you were a bird." I understood: he was that strange bird that said "Good morning." I felt satisfied, even a little smug. The "strange bird" could not fool me.

A few weeks later we are driving along Highway 24 toward Walnut Creek, cruising through the darkest heart of California suburbia. In both directions, along eight lanes of concrete, the river of brightly colored plastic and steel corpuscles, the Cali-fornia bloodstream, flows ceaselessly. Along the edges of the highway, four lanes over, wood, steel, concrete and blinking neon have obliterated the gentle valleys of fruit orchards and rolling hills where cattle once grazed. Miraculously, before us Mount Diablo looms, pristine, defiant.

I listen, waiting for my father to mutter, as usual, "They've ruined everything!" Instead, he murmurs, "*Quant' è bella la Cal-ifornia!* [How beautiful California is!]." I'm shocked, momentar-ily disoriented. I flash on Copernicus proposing his heliocentric universe. After decades of declarations that nothing could com-pare with the beauties of Europe, now, suddenly, "How beautiful California is"—*this* California? I hear; I balk. This would mean rearranging my entire mental landscape, redoing all my myths. "These lupins are not as blue as the ones around Tivoli," "This hot dog is not as good as a real frankfurter," echo from distant memories. I think of the retirement dinner. Maybe my mother was wrong, and maybe I was the one who had understood nothing.

My father's retirement made little difference in our relationship. We talked, wrote, visited as usual. Everything was as it had al-ways been—an uneasy balance, or so I told myself. But in that steadiness, that continuity, there was comfort, solidity, something I could hang on to, count on. If, occasionally, while talking to

him, or after reading one of his letters, I felt subterranean trem-
ors, potential lava pools simmering inside me, why did he have
to know about them?

But he did know. "Why do you hang your head—so?" my
father sometimes said to me, and he would imitate the way I
dipped my chin. In his presence, friends said, I hunched my
shoulders and my head drooped. I cowered like a dog who had
been beaten too many times. Why did I respond that way to
such a charming, sophisticated, worldly man? they wanted to
know. So did I, and in 1979, I decided to find out.

For me, that year was a dream turned nightmare. My wife and
our two children, Gino and Francesca, eight and six, had returned to California with dreams flying high. I had a year off in
the Golden State, in—for Zaza and for me—Paradise Lost, the
San Francisco Bay Area. My mother-in-law had put at our dis-
posal a lovely little brown shingled house that she owned near
Stanford. The backyard blossomed with pink "naked ladies" and
the apricot trees promised a splendid summer harvest. Smoke-
colored squirrels chattered and skittered among the branches of
the huge, towering pine at the edge of the sidewalk.

I had great plans. I was working on a biography of the Italian
Fascist aviator and politician Italo Balbo (1896–1940). I would
finish my book; I would also write other pieces, journalism, crit-
icism, fiction.

The high didn't last. Zaza went back to work. Although I had
always shared in the housework and parenting, I had never really
experienced being a houschusband. The role reversal strained my
marriage. Uprooted from my job, my colleagues, my friends, I
began to feel alone, isolated. I brooded about having reached
forty-one. I read a lot of books about midlife crises. Soon I found
myself drifting, thrashing and bobbing about in an ocean of time.
I began to suffer bouts of depression, severe enough that I sought
the help of a psychologist—and even of my father.

His response was true to form. "Depressions," he wrote me
as a follow-up to a telephone conversation, "are fairly common

and more or less everyone I know has had them, including me. Fermi and Amaldi are the exceptions, but they are exceptional people." The best cure, my father assured me, was his old standby, getting away to the mountains. "Physical tiredness, beautiful natural surroundings, distractions from one's thoughts are all very effective cures and certainly CAN'T DO ANY HARM," he wrote. Antidepressants were a second line of defense, "to be done only under the direction of an intelligent doctor who has the time to take care of you." For the sake of my children, especially, I should "put good will" into taking care of myself. If that meant looking after myself first, in the long run that would be best for my family, too. "This is a complicated bit of reasoning, but a correct one," he wrote. "Finally, depressions pass," he assured me. "Even if they're unpleasant, they don't last forever."

The letter infuriated me. What I wanted from him was a friendly, reassuring face, a pair of encircling and encouraging arms, a soothing voice saying perhaps nothing more than "Oh, poor thing." As I read it, what I got was a doctor's prescription, a health professional's policy statement. I remembered my father visiting me in the hospital at Los Alamos when I'd sliced open my arm. I was the little monkey; he was the zoologist, the primate specialist, the medical researcher, observing me. But I was not a little monkey; I was his son. The more I grappled with my dark moods, the more I thrashed and drifted, the more my father's figure loomed. Of course, I could not trace all my troubles to him, but he was a beginning. In the past, silences, distances had protected me, served me well. They had preserved the relationship. Maybe now was the time to break the pattern. I decided to face him, to tell him how I felt about our relationship. Why now? I asked myself. And yet, why not? If not now, when? I called him and arranged for a visit.

During the days before our meeting, moments of dread mixed with rushes of exhilaration. This was like the edge of the diving tower. This was the plunge down the steep hill on my bicycle when the wind roared in my ears; this was diving down the ski slope that dropped off so suddenly that it took my breath away; this was the moment in the marathon after twenty miles when legs wouldn't churn anymore and I had to will myself through the last six miles; this was the shootout. This would be a verbal *High Noon*. The shootout? That made me a gunfighter—a loving one, I concluded wryly. My father would see my courage, my mettle. He would admire me, recognize me for what I was. We would be together at last.

After a shootout? At the time, I didn't see the contradictions of the metaphor. Nor did I see how it appeared to vindicate Freud. Was I trying to kill my father? Of course I wasn't; of course I was. Either way, how could this manly face-off bring us together, as I hoped so fervently?

Nevertheless, on a foggy morning in late February 1979, I drove to my date with destiny. This shootout would take place around noon, I noted, but not in the regulation dusty street of some small Western town. The blacktopped road of an expensive ridgetop California housing development would have to do. On the ridge, except for the buzz of power mowers or the shrieks of blowers, a well-bred and well-heeled hush reigned. I worried about shattering the peace with the sounds of something so mortal, so domestic and intimate, as a father-son showdown. Anyway, this was not likely to be a public one. We would be inside my father's standard-looking, cream-colored stucco house, with its standard two-car garage.

As always, when he first opened the door, my father looked genuinely glad to see me. In his gray eyes, I saw a flicker of joy, like a puppy's when someone has come to play. I don't recall what he was wearing. Probably he was shuffling around in his old slippers, dark and liver-colored now, baggy corduroys and an old sweater, or perhaps his plaid house jacket. His white hair, still surprisingly thick, was combed straight back. He smelled faintly of lavender, the familiar scent of the brilliantine that he sometimes used on his hair.

His initial joy at seeing me gave way almost immediately to

his solemn, owlish expression, the one from the Nobel awards ceremony. We must never forget that the world is a serious and frightening place, those bushy eyebrows, that furrowed forehead said. How were my depressions? Was I getting any better?

He led the way into the breakfast room, just off the kitchen. We sat at the Formica-topped table, drinking tea. Through the sliding glass doors, the late-winter sun was breaking through the fog that shrouded the peaks across the valley. The greens of spring grass were barely visible. A hawk soared lazily, disdainfully, over patient little trails of cars weaving in and out among the houses below in the valley. My father dropped a couple of saccharine tablets into his cup. His tongue flicked unconsciously. Like a child, he seemed absorbed in the task of stirring his tea. As he aged, the contours of his body had rounded, softened enough to suggest a life-size teddy bear—but not so his mind, I thought.

I don't remember all that I said or that he said that morning, though I made extensive notes afterward. I am sure of the gist of our conversation. He wanted to help me, my father said. Yet when he saw me, as my friends noted, I usually looked like a "beaten dog." When he called, I barked or growled. What had he ever done to me to provoke these reactions?

I took a deep breath. I would try to explain, I told him. Already, I could feel my shoulders sagging, my chin drooping. I spoke slowly, as if I were a Himalayan sherpa bearing a great load. I had to watch my footing. I began gingerly, obliquely. I owed him a great deal, I said. He had given me a love of learning, a sense of standards. He had provided for my financial security and for that of my children, I said.

"*Ma* [But]?" he said sharply.

I had been a little slow and uncertain in finding my way, in working out a profession, in settling down, I continued. But I had done so at last. I had found a respectable career. I was a tenured professor at a good university. I had a good marriage, two children (at the time). I was garnering my share of awards, fellowships. My father nodded, as if, from some mental list, he were checking off the elements of a well-ordered life.

I had done these things—to what end? I said. Why did I not feel satisfied or fulfilled? Why did I feel so empty, except for a burning, corrosive drive that pushed me harder and harder? Why did that drive leave my spirit forever shrouded in feelings of unworthiness?

My father glanced at me, puzzled, as if he didn't understand what I wanted, or why, as I confronted him, my face contorted with rage. Naturally that rage and frustration brought me exactly the opposite of what I craved. The friendly, reassuring face, the pair of encircling, encouraging arms were nowhere to be seen; the soothing voice saying nothing more than *"Poverino"* was nowhere to be heard. At the least I had been hoping for the equivalent of a manly, paternal shout from the far end of the dusty street at high noon: "Son, what you've done makes a man proud. I'm sorry it has to come to this." Nothing of the sort. We were in the wrong movie.

I decided to be blunt. "Are you satisfied with my position?" I said.

"Well, you're no Mommsen," my father retorted, referring to the eminent nineteenth-century German historian of ancient Rome. "But you're at a good place and you have the esteem of your colleagues. What else do you want?"

I could feel the lava simmering inside me.

This wasn't *High Noon*— not even close; this wasn't even a good movie; this was talking to a fence post. How would I ever get through to him, clear away the emotional fog in that wonderful paternal brain? I thought of Mussolini and his reputed recipe for dealing with recalcitrant opponents who didn't see things his way: *"Picchiando sui crani snebbieremo i cervelli* [Bash their skulls a bit—that'll defog their brains]."

"Are you at least proud of your grandchildren—my children?" I thundered, exasperated.

"Yes—though I don't see them that often." He looked utterly

bewildered, as if I were speaking Chinese to him. That caught me off guard. Defogging his brain was going to be harder than I thought.

He also had his own agenda. I should assert myself, he said. That was the only thing he wanted to see me do. Take off for the mountains when I felt depressed or whenever I felt like it. Damn the family and the responsibilities, he said. If my wife didn't like it, then just yell at her. She'd get the message. That's what he'd always done. "At the expense of the rest of us," I shrieked, thinking of me and my sisters, but also of my mother.

For some reason, I asked him about his honeymoon with my mother. They went skiing, he said. Did she get cold? I remembered dimly that once she had complained about it. Maybe she did, he said, but she followed him anyway. That was the important thing. "But what about *her*? How *she* felt?" I yelled.

"Your screaming doesn't make me hot or cold, doesn't bother me one way or the other," he said in Italian.

By this time, we had drained our teacups and wandered from the breakfast room to his study. Outside, jays and sparrows harangued each other in the live oaks as I harangued my father about his eternal high standards. From their frames on the wall, the bookcase, the desk, Fermi, my mother, my sisters and me with our spouses and children, my father's Dutch mentor, Pieter Zeeman, all looked on, while I blustered and scolded. My father, apparently calm and indifferent, shuffled papers on his desk, but I knew that he was listening. I'd tried to meet his high standards, to please him, I said; it never seemed enough.

He sighed and shook his head. "Children will rebel against their parents, will blame them for all their troubles," he muttered a number of times. What could he do about it? Such behavior was one of the facts of life, a law of nature, as predictable as a chemical reaction, he suggested. Like blacks and machinery? I snorted to myself.

The more he sighed, the more he appeared to detach himself, the more I was determined not to let him slip away. This time he wouldn't escape, I told myself. This time he would give me what I so desperately craved—some sign of his approval. I was going to get it if I had to tear it or bang it out of him. Would a change of scene help? We left the house, wandered out into the street, climbed between the houses on Quail Ridge.

The neighborhood was silent except for the chatter of the squirrels, the cooing of the doves, the distant sighing of the freeway. My father was grumbling to himself. "Poor Claudio, so badly treated, so abused." Out he came with a long list of verbs about what he had done to me: "tyrannized," "trampled on," "oppressed," "neglected." He invited me to add others.

His little sarcasms cut and pricked; yet I sensed that perhaps something was happening at last. His thoughts seemed to ramble, as if all our sparring had made him a little groggy. He'd taken me fishing many times, he said abruptly. Had I forgotten? He had the pictures to prove it. How could I say he'd neglected me?

Maybe I *was* getting through, I thought. Maybe Mussolini had been right, after all.

Yet my father appeared more baffled than ever. All this "poison" that I was spitting—he made it sound as if I were a coiled snake—where had it come from, anyway? he wanted to know. If it helped me, I should come back and "spit" some more; he would offer me tea and biscuits, he said. He sounded as if he were baiting me again, as if he didn't quite believe in my pain.

This was too much. Exasperated, enraged, frustrated, I decided that the time for talk, for grand declarations and gestures, was over. Out here at noon on the blacktop, it was time to let him have it. So I did. To my father, to the squirrels, to the jays, to the passing traffic—and perhaps to the silent neighbors behind their standardized doors and two-car garages, I screamed: "My feelings are real. My pain is real."

My father winced, perhaps even shuddered a bit, as if some of my verbal bullets had found their mark at last.

"I know," he said suddenly. At least I had shot away his lofty detachment. He spoke softly, he looked disoriented, as if perhaps he were bleeding a bit emotionally. "I know. But what can I do about it? Tell me."

I glanced at him. Figuratively, I stood over him. I glanced down, expecting to stare triumphantly into the face of a grizzled, manly gunfighter. The face that met mine was that of a bewildered child.

I felt utter dismay. I should tell *him?* But he was supposed to know. He knew everything. He was the father. He was the model. He was the superman.

My dismay gave way to fright. Raging at him had been easy. I had been so sure: his detachment, his aloofness, his sarcasm were merely screens. When I tore them away, when I reached him, I would find the empathetic father who would take me on his knee. And now? Like Dorothy and her friends in *The Wizard of Oz*, I had peeked behind the curtain and discovered the mortal fumbling reality behind the Great Oz.

Now what? Would I proclaim my discovery to the rest of the world? What right did I have to do that? Anyway, who would listen to me? For the first time, I thought, I understood the passage in the Bible when the sons of Noah, discovering him drunk and naked, turned away and "saw not their father's nakedness" (Genesis 9:23). To the world, my father was—he would always be—the great scientist, the man of culture, the walking encyclopedia, the dazzling mind. I wasn't going to change that. Even if I managed to, what good would it do me in my relationship with him?

We walked back to the house. I decided to leave. What else was to be done? Furious, humiliated, I marched out to the car, buckled up my safety harness, started the engine. This wasn't what I'd intended at all. Where was the manly showdown, the flash of recognition, the embrace of reconciliation? Our scene together had all the dignity of two nursery school brats screaming at each other, all the epic qualities of two lobsters stalking each other in a dark tank.

I didn't want our scene to end that way. I turned off the motor and marched back to the house and knocked at the door. My father, getting ready to go to a dinner party at the university chancellor's house, looked startled at my return.

What had brought me back? he wanted to know. I apologized for my behavior. I didn't answer his question; I couldn't. How could I explain to him my shame, my embarrassment, my frustration? What courage did it take on my part to scream, with the accumulated rage of four decades, at a seventy-four-year-old man? The thought merely stirred the rage inside me. Why should I have an emotional lobster for a father?

"What can I do about it? Tell me," my father had pleaded, bewildered. Maybe it was up to me to show him, at least to change the ending of the scene. For a moment, my mind was blank. Then I flashed on that old familiar anxious and electric moment from my childhood. "*Nasacocchia,*" I declared tentatively. In my voice was that odd mix of commanding and coaxing that I remembered in his voice. Then, more decisively, I said, "*Nasacocchia.*" "He was delighted and I think I expressed my feelings," I noted afterward. "I don't hate him. How can I hate an intractable moody child?"

"I'm proud of myself," I wrote later. I had faced him down, I told myself, but this was bravado to lift my spirits. What had I faced down? How could I be proud of such a fiasco? Most of all, why hadn't we done better? I thought of his own father; I thought of Fermi's coldness; I thought of him. High standards for me, high standards for you, I had challenged him. We both had failed.

CHAPTER 12

Fathers and Sons

The shootout doesn't lessen the gap between my father and me. We steal back to where we were. My common sense—and probably *his* common sense, too—prevails. Be reasonable, he was always pleading with my mother—or even with me when I lost my temper with him. Be reasonable. Is it reasonable to resent him for what he isn't? I ask myself. It's as if he were tone-deaf. Would I shout at him at a concert because he couldn't really hear the music? Anyway, by feuding with him, wouldn't I only be punishing myself? Much easier to close that gap, to span it as best I can. Do I really want to? Or am I merely once again the dutiful son, doing what any son from a good family, as my father might say, does?

If I'm ambivalent, my father is not. His letters, I notice, become less self-absorbed. He suggests interesting books; he mails me clippings; he talks to people about me, sends me greetings from them. He even praises my university to his friends. "I feel as if I've become a fund raiser or a promoter for Austin," he notes in December 1982. My birthdays now become dates to be carefully observed. He knows that I'm a runner, so one year he simply wishes me "two hours for a marathon, 27 minutes for a

266

10 km. run, and 13 min. for a 5 km. run" (all world-class times).
Another year he remembers with the opening line from Dante's
Divine Comedy: "I hope that you're 'in the middle of the path
of your life'—and not beyond." He also delights in his grandchildren—and gives the parents credit: "Your excellent products
[are] very cute and well educated" and "The compliments also
extend to the parents."

Rereading his old letters now, I discover lines of support and
concern. Slender, fragile, though they appeared to me, they are
unmistakably there. "For whatever I can do to help you morally
or in other ways, you can count on me," he wrote when I complained about UPI. The lines were there; perhaps I'm the one
who was too timid to test them.

His old fantasy about having his children living around him
creeps into his conversation more and more. In his dream, my
sisters and I, with our respective families, build homes on lots
next to his on Crest Road. In his vision, I imagine, bulldozers
terrace the steep hill behind his house among the live oaks and
the poison oak, where deer graze and blue jays jeer. In their
place, Fausta and her husband, Tony, Amelia and her husband,
Joseph, Zaza and I overlook his garden from our California-
style houses. Our various offspring gallop down the driveways,
whooping and screaming to visit Nonno and Nonna. It's a trans-
position of the Italian family of his generation, one that my Uncle Marco realized in Rome. In the fashionable Parioli district,
in the same big, blockish apartment house, with large sunny ter-
races and ivy dripping over the wall, my cousin Renata and her
family lived below my aunt and uncle; my cousin Gallo and his
family lived across the hall. My cousin Claudio lived in Paris or
Geneva, but kept an apartment in the building for occasions
when he came to visit.

But we aren't living in Rome. My father's home is in Lafayette, California; Suburbia, USA. At night through the picture
windows the endless glowing belt of automobile lights girds the
lumpy California landscape; outside, on the porch, we strain our

voices to be heard over the sounds of traffic. This is not the land of togetherness and family bonds; this is the land of spaces, of sprawling over the landscape, a paradise where each can enjoy his isolation. In any case, my sisters and I all scattered: Amelia and Joseph (who is Israeli) to a suburb of Tel Aviv; Fausta and Tony (who is English) to Wales, and then to Bristol; Zaza and I to Texas.

My father's letters, his wistful fantasies aren't enough to bridge the gap between us. Far more powerful is the bond of a grandchild, I discover. My son, Gino, my firstborn, named in part after my father, becomes a major link between my father and me. When Gino was small, my father, as he usually did, showed a mild curiosity about the creeping, crawling creature who happened to be his grandson. Dutifully, because he didn't know what else to do, he took pictures and began providing for Gino's college education. When Gino reached high school, an age when it was "possible to reason with him," the two developed a warm relationship, just as my father did with his other grandson, my sister Amelia's son, Amir, when he reached the same age. "Nice boys," my father often said about them. With them he appeared more at ease, knew better what to do with them than with his granddaughters, my daughter, Francesca, and my niece, Vivian.

Gino generally enjoyed my father's company. They could compare stamp collections, talk about photography, go hiking together. Gino's mind, I noticed, seemed to resonate and empathize with my father's. In a way that they never came to me, solutions to my father's mathematical problems and puzzles came naturally to Gino. Moreover, from electric pencil sharpeners to computers, Gino has a passion for gadgets and sophisticated machinery. So when, in his early eighties, my father took on the challenge of mastering his first personal computer, Gino naturally became his teacher.

In the fall of 1988, Gino entered Berkeley as a freshman. In my father's office, on the third floor of LeConte Hall, in the shadow of the Campanile, grandfather and grandson met from time to time to work on the grandson's calculus problems. On my father's last day, before his last walk, grandfather and grandson puzzled together over the computer in my father's study in Lafayette. What I never was with my father, what I could not be, what, in the end, I did not want to be, Gino, to my great pride and satisfaction, was.

The written word, too, became something of a link, a bridge between my father and me. Yet when we got on it, that bridge also tended to swing and sway like one of those shaky rope affairs that span jungle chasms.

What my father had to say to me about being a writer was usually nothing I wanted to hear, especially when I was young. Art is long, life is short, and anyway, how was I going to make a living at it? he wanted to know. He read my editorials doubtfully when I edited the student newspaper, the Reed College *Quest*. He glanced at the occasional freelance pieces I published while in college, and the articles I wrote during a summer job on the Oregon small-town weekly, the Canby *Herald*. He leafed through the college literary magazine that I edited. One issue included a parody I had done of Hemingway. I thought the piece was delightful. "It stinks," my father assured me.

As the years went by, he appeared relieved that I had a stable profession as an academic. He noticed that I was getting published, not only in academic journals but in major newspapers and magazines. When I freelanced editorial pieces to *The Wall Street Journal*, essays and book reviews, he approved—and raised the ante. "You really ought to be on their editorial board," he suggested casually, as if I should have no problem insinuating myself among many of the biggest names in American cultural life. But his letters also contained encouraging notes. "I've always thought that you write well . . . and that you would do well to develop this ability, which can also, with luck, bring money," he wrote. Another time, he commented, "It occurred to me that for your first best seller, you might write the story of ——" And he cited a bizarre item culled from a newspaper.

He urged me to be entertaining—and to make money. "There's no reason for scholarship to be boring and if that's the way professors want it to be it's because they don't know how to be entertaining," he groused. Barbara Tuchman, who wrote the best-selling histories *The Guns of August* and *The Proud Tower*, and Garrett Mattingly, the Columbia University historian who produced the classic *The Spanish Armada*, were his models for me. Another favorite was Laura Fermi's family memoir, *Atoms in the Family*. At times, my father's generic encouragement turned to directive. I really should do a series of portraits of Italian Fascist leaders, he urged me repeatedly. "The idea is to make money Mattingly style, and thus [it's] risky, but more certain than scholarly material."

When he retired, my father turned to his own writing projects. He produced a two-volume popular history of modern physics, *From X-Rays to Quarks* and *From Falling Bodies to Radio Waves*. He also did journalistic pieces for Italian newspapers and magazines on subjects ranging from science education in the United States to the future of nuclear physics. Finally, he wrote his autobiography, *A Mind Always in Motion*. About these works he grumbled, "Compliments and nice reviews, yes, but not money," though over the years, his popular histories of physics have been steady sellers.

From time to time, he asked me for help with these projects, especially with editing, correcting his English and translating. That was when the bridge began to swing and sway. He did not take my corrections and suggestions easily. Yet, to my surprise, I also noticed during his last years that he asked for more than editorial help. "I'd like your opinion when it will be finished," he wrote about a fantasy chapter at the beginning of *From Falling Bodies to Radio Waves* in which he imagined himself visiting great physicists like Galileo, Huygens and Faraday. We began to exchange comments about writers—a fantasy of my own that I never dared believe in. My father and I writing to each other about literature? Yet there it was: "According to your orders, I read Conrad. Aside from the material I'll never be able to write like that. I can't compete with him." Another time, I received a note that surpassed my wildest fantasies: "I'm frustrated that I don't know how to write English as you do," my father wrote. "*From X-Rays to Quarks* in English is interesting for its content, but much inferior in form to your . . . article."

In 1987 I published *Italo Balbo: A Fascist Life*, a biography of the Italian aviator and Fascist politician. The book won prizes both in the United States and in Italy. "Too Fascist," my father complained about the book. Perhaps I was trying to be fair and balanced, but he didn't like the way I made critical comments of Balbo and then I "took them back." "You write as if you were driving an automobile which you have to straighten out after every turn." I should have stressed the "backwardness and provinciality" of Fascist Italy and the "rottenness" of the regime "for which Balbo, too, had his responsibilities," my father remarked. Anyway, he assured me, Balbo was not such a significant figure. "What the physicists were doing was infinitely more important than any of the [Fascist] regime's works," he announced. "There have been plenty of truly great Italians, in recent times, too, and they were serious, hard working, not full of rhetoric. I wouldn't count Balbo among them." Nevertheless, his critique was not intended to detract from his "generally positive evaluation" of the book, he wrote. "Bravo. I read it with care and I even had a good time with it. It's a good book."

I read the last words over and over, as I had read and reread his comment that he was frustrated at not knowing "how to write English as you do." I knew what the words meant; I even mouthed them. It was as if I couldn't hear him. I'm like the pioneering pilots of Balbo's generation, I thought. Too many hours in an open cockpit, exposed to the roar of the engines, often deafened them.

By the spring of 1989, I sense that my father is fading away. I find it hard to believe. A world-famous physicist, a Nobel Prize winner, an architect of the atomic age—he's granite, he's a monument, I tell myself. People like him don't fade away. If he does eventually, it will be several geological eras down the road, I reassure myself.

In fact, at eighty-four, my father remains clearheaded, active, vigorous. Time hasn't mellowed his vision of the world. He's always the *cacadubbi*; he still fixes on the cloud and grumbles that the silver lining will tarnish, anyway. So when I call him, he pronounces gloomily on Gorbachev's prospects for reforming the Soviet Union, the dangers of German unification, the flaws in the University of Utah experiments on "fusion in a bottle." He rails against bureaucrats and taxes. In funereal tones he announces the passing of old friends.

In quite another voice, as if he were once again ten years old and proving that he was the smartest kid in his grade, the "first in the class," he informs me which rival colleagues he has outlived. With raucous glee, savoring the English slang, he turns away from the phone and I can hear him shouting to my stepmother, "Rosa! What do you think? He croh-ked, didn't he? Rosa? What do you think?"

For nearly seventeen years now, as my mother did, Rosa Mines Segrè, my father's second wife, has been caring for him. Rosa, too, shares his honors and his tantrums. She is a striking woman: tall, with a mass of white hair. She has an air about her that sometimes impresses people as imperious. Her eyes, somewhere between gray and hazel, startle me; in them, I often glimpse my mother. Nevertheless, physically and temperamentally, Rosa is very different. She towers over my father. Together, they look like the odd couple, but they are well matched. She admires his brilliance, his encyclopedic mind, his sense of humor. He enjoys her stories and the piquant Spanish aphorisms she learned growing up in Uruguay. He relishes the odd moments when she cuts loose with her tongue and flays a pompous politician or self-important host or colleague. Most of all, as he did with my mother, my father depends on Rosa to help him cope with worries about his health, crank mail, nuisance lawsuits, tax headaches, visiting dignitaries, plans for his many trips abroad. At times, Rosa draws the line. She retreats to what she calls her "sulking room." On the door, a yellow-and-red sign (borrowed from a military reservation) warns: "Danger! Mines."

Rosa's tenacious care can do nothing to slow the processes of time. When I visit my father, I'm startled at the way his body is giving out. He appears to be shrinking beneath the official five feet eight on his driver's license; his shoulders stoop, so that his back and his head form one long curve, as if he were gradually reverting to that primal position from whence he came. His hair, once dark brown, almost black, is now entirely white and thinning; though, like the wild patch of his bushy eyebrows, the hair is indisputably there. He does not complain about his eyes, yet I notice that they are clouding, like those of an old dog. I feel that he is glad to see me or to hear from me, but also that he is withdrawing, becoming more and more self-absorbed. Far more than in the past, he appears content to sit around in his old baggy clothes and watch television from his big leather easy chair. I can't shake the uneasy feeling that he is fading away. Or is it fading out, like some distant space probe whose signal gradually weakens as it journeys ever farther from my world? The letters from him, the phone calls, always compressed and cryptic, appear even more abbreviated, abridged. I sense that these may be last messages. Beyond the grumbling, the complaints, the dire predictions, he appears satisfied. As a scientist, his reputation is secure. So is his family. His personal affairs are in order. His life is complete. I'm relieved.

Complete? In order? Perhaps for him, but not for me, his

firstborn, his son. There are all those jagged edges of our relationship. What will he do about them? I wonder. What will I do? Old-fashioned deathbed rituals in which fathers bless sons, and each asks forgiveness of the other, are no longer in fashion. Every time I visit my father, I wonder what the contemporary equivalent will be. Walking around the Lafayette reservoir in the shade of the oaks, with joggers puffing by? Or sitting in the fortress of his study, with the desk littered with papers, and the squirrels chattering nervously through the picture window? What will we say? He will fulminate about taxes, I imagine. He will make dire pronouncements about the present, and the future of the world. And then? Will he have some grand declaration to make about Life, offer me some last bit of memorable wisdom based literally on a lifetime of experience? Will he quote—as he often did—from Dante or perhaps Petrarch, or Alessandro Manzoni's novel *The Betrothed*, or some other classic of Italian literature? Something new might be nice. If he's in a dark mood, perhaps, like Kurtz, in Joseph Conrad's *Heart of Darkness*, he might conclude savagely, "The horror" or "Exterminate the brutes." Or might my father allude to death as a beautiful veiled woman in traveling dress, as the Prince does in Giuseppe di Lampedusa's epic novel of Italian unification, *The Leopard*? Might he cite some Torah passage, or at least refer to one? Not likely. That's me, not him. But then, aren't we father and son? Anyway, I'm likely to have a long wait, I decide. At the rate he's fading, the finale won't come for years.

"Lunch in Lafayette. Climbed on the roof to clear drains, other little chores," my journal for April 16, 1989, reads. I have no recollection of what we said over morsels of cold roast beef, bits of cheese, stalks of fennel, a bottle of California wine. *Other little chores* is etched in my memory.

Ever since my childhood, I have loathed handyman projects. *Opere del regime* (public works projects), my father used to call them. With his usual sarcasm, he was recalling his student days in Rome when Mussolini celebrated every road extension or bridge repair with a brass band and a fancy speech. My public works rarely merited celebration. When I did them, my father's critical eye was usually on me: "That's the wrong screwdriver." "You need metal screws for a job like that." "You didn't drive the nail straight." "Don't you see? That piece isn't level." In the past, I had always found ways to put off such projects.

Not this time. Fortunately, the task is simple. He wants me to set up some metal brackets in the basement for a shelf to support some of his papers. I have to do it and he'll be watching me. Three decades have passed since I last felt such twitches of fear and trepidation. To compound my anxieties, I have very little time. I have to catch a plane. This time there's no hiding place, nothing to do but plunge. Down my father and I go into the damp basement, with its half-finished walls and its smells of mold and dust.

With his eyes on me, with that old familiar barking in my ears, I go to work. "Make the marks here." I mark. "Now put in the screws there." I place the screws where he indicates. "Set the shelf on the brackets." I do so. "Arrange the papers so they don't slide over." I arrange the papers as he orders. I sweat; I glance at the digital numbers on my runner's watch as they creep up to the moment when I must leave.

Miraculously, we finish. My father wanders off upstairs while I put away the tools. I survey my work and I notice something: the screws *are* flush; the shelf *is* level; the papers *are* straight. Of those things, I'm sure. Could this be an *opera del regime* at last? I can't tell. I know only that I feel an odd sense of exhilaration bubbling up. I go upstairs, wash my hands and face, wink at myself in the mirror and give a thumbs-up sign. In the kitchen, my father is having a cup of tea.

"Well, we did it," I say tentatively.

"*Sì,*" he grumbles. But he does offer a grudging little smile over his teacup.

"Really?" I say.

"*Sì.*" Then he says it. "A true *opera del regime.* Have some tea."

I don't have time to savor the moment. I gulp some tea and I'm on my way. "Be well." I bend over him to shake hands. That feels too formal, too distant. Then, almost as an afterthought, I bend over him again. Gently, as I often did as a child, I rub his nose in a kiss, Eskimo-style, and I'm gone.

A level shelf, some screws flush with the wall, some papers set straight? An Eskimo kiss? A little flat as a finale, I ruminate as I race to the airport. I hunger for more ritual, more grand gestures, more theater. But the shelf *is* level, and the screws *are* flush. For him, the physicist, the scientist, the perpetual seeker after order and neatness, what could be more satisfying as our finale? And that Eskimo kiss, that quick, almost playful rubbing of noses, that tentative sign of nuclear affection? That, too, feels right. That's him, that's me, that's us, I realize. I shake my head. The deep pronouncements, the meditations, the blessings, the Torah quote, the valedictory messages from father to son will have to come later, maybe next time.

There is no next time. Six days later, in the little valley below the Lafayette reservoir, my father's heart gives out; finally, irrevocably, he is gone.

Memorial services are seldom happy events. Yet the one we held for my father a week after his death feels that way. Not that the service is joyous. There is mourning, there is grieving, but no despair or pessimism. The only moment that brings tears to my eyes is the sweet melancholy of the Bach violin partita.

My father left strict instructions about rites and observances after his death. If there was to be a memorial service, it must be on the University of California campus. He even designated the speakers—or, rather, he designated the ones he did *not* want. As Rosa and I work frantically to make the arrangements, we feel

"the ghost"—as he used to refer to himself in his last years—
shaking his head, predicting disaster. I can hear the *cacadubbi*'s
voice: on such short notice, we won't be able to find a room; the
speakers won't appear, or they will mumble so that no one can
understand them; no one will attend. At moments, I wonder if
he is right. We find a room at the Law School, but how can we
ever fill up such a cavernous auditorium? We need to have music.
On such short notice, who will play? What is appropriate? We
need food for a reception afterward. There is no time to mail
invitations. Will the papers publish a notice of the service soon
enough?

At moments our resolve sputters. Perhaps we should put the
whole thing off until the fall. Then we will have time to plan, to
arrange. For most people, the deepest need for mourning, for
remembrance, is now, I remind Rosa. The service is for us, not
for him. We must do the best we can. We plunge ahead with
our preparations.

On that April Saturday morning, when I first enter the auditorium, I feel tears of joy. Old family friends, Carl and Betty
Helmholz, have arranged to decorate the stage with boxed redwood seedlings and loose branches. From time to time, I smell
the fragrance of the redwood forests and the Sierras that my
father so loved. Just in front of the speaker's podium, Rosa has
set my father's academic mortarboard, the one with the green
pompom, the one from the days in Rome when he was one of
the "boys of the Via Panisperna." Somehow the notice about the
service made the papers after all, and the auditorium is comfortably full. My sisters, still a bit jet-lagged from their transat-
lantic flights, are there, and so is my Aunt Lilli. I recognize many
familiar faces, some dating from my childhood. There are also
many I don't know, including a strikingly handsome young man
in a navy blazer who sits in the front row. With a start, I recognize my son Gino.

The speakers, all old friends and colleagues, pay tribute to my
father's scientific achievements. As they did at his retirement,

they also evoke the man—including some of his warts. "Physicists' families have to compete with physics for their father's love—but that is an occupational disease that comes with the territory," his fellow Nobel laureate and colleague Owen Chamberlain remarks. I know that, I mutter to myself. "He insisted on excellence. This was probably one of his greatest strengths. Of course he had to know what excellence is and how to recognize it. . . . He did not suffer fools, but he knew there were fools and he did the best with them that he could," Carl Helmholz observes, after more than half a century of experience as my father's colleague and close friend. I know that, too. I also know my father's talents for napping during seminars and then "waking up at the end to ask the most pertinent question," as Eugene Commins, a colleague, puts it.

I know what I know, I thought smugly. Others knew other things, no less true or valid, I realized with a start. As a lecturer, he wasn't afraid to make a mistake—which he corrected easily—now and then; his style was an "exciting" one because his reasoning suggested "what real physics is like," recalls Chamberlain, remembering his student days. Though I had never considered my father a bridge between scientific generations, "our link to the past golden era of physics," as Commins, a generation younger than my father, points out, I had often thought of my father as at least a competent handyman around the house. Yet as a physicist "he was not a 'machine man,'" Carl Helmholz recalls. My father never liked getting down in the two-and-a-half-foot-high basement of the old cyclotron to check electrical circuits and small vacuum pumps. My father generally did not care for faculty parties, I know. Yet at one in particular, Carl recalls, wives were complaining that their husbands never noticed the clothes they were wearing. The men agreed—except for my father. "Give me ten minutes and I'll tell you the material of each lady's dress here," he declared to the thirty women present. Ten minutes later, he delivered.

I'm the last to speak. I ought to be nervous, I ought to be too grief-stricken to do this, I'm thinking. But I'm not nervous, and I feel little sadness. When my turn comes, I step confidently, almost eagerly, to the podium. I feel myself standing straight and tall. I hear my voice boom, clear and assured, at ease. Is this rush of energy a sign of relief that he is gone? After so many years of living in his shadow, is this outpouring of energy a celebration that I'm free, that I'm visible, at last? I wonder if that's what my audience is thinking; I wonder if that's what I'm feeling. I notice my sisters' eyes on me. I feel like the Coach again. I see Gino watching me. *This* brother, *this* father, I say to myself, is going to show them how it's done, how in public a son can pay a loving and humane tribute to an often difficult father.

"Family Sayings" is the theme of my eulogy. Through the phrases that were family sayings, I sketch out what it had been like to live with my father, what values and ideals he taught us, what the bridges were between generations, the bonds between my father and me. The first two sayings are in Italian. "*S'alza alle dieci* [He gets up at ten o'clock]" is a dismissal of slugabeds, an exhortation to get up early and work hard. It's no guarantee of bright ideas or of success, but it's a good start. "*Press'a pochismo* [more-or-lessness]" is a condemnation of sloppiness, an appeal to be precise in all aspects of our lives. Finally, there's the German "*gewust wo* [knowing where]," the punch line in a story that my father liked to tell. "*Gewust wo*" was his cry of triumph when he had resolved a difficult problem. To me the saying had always been emblematic of him. According to the story, a motorist was trying to start his stalled car. A little boy who was passing by offered to help. He peered under the hood, turned a little screw and the engine roared to life. Astonished and amused, the motorist asked, "How much do I owe you, my little man?" "A hundred marks," the boy replied coolly. "How so?" demanded the outraged motorist. The reply came back: "One mark for turning the screw, ninety-nine for '*gewust wo*.' "

The more I speak, the more I understand my rush of energy. The gap between my father and me, life and death, seems to narrow. There is death in life, but in death there is also life. I feel it pulsing in me. This is not Kurtz's "Exterminate the brutes" in Conrad, nor, in Lampedusa, the Prince's fatalistic and welcome embrace of everyone's ultimate fate. This is Molly Bloom's passionate, life-affirming "Yes" at the end of James Joyce's *Ulysses*.

I also know that though my father is gone, I haven't heard the last of him. Sure enough, I can hear him now. "Too literary," he protests about my Joycean image. Anyway, Joyce is not a great writer; he's an industry for English professors, my father carps. I grumble and protest. He grumbles and protests in turn, and has what he thinks is the last word: "You may not agree, but it is so." But I shake my head. I will have the last word—or at least I'll have my word: "It is not so." I'm laughing. I can hear myself, loudly and clearly, at last.

I seldom visit my father's grave. As he requested, he lies in a cemetery in Lafayette, in a plain pine casket with a star of David on it. The rugged granite tombstone says merely: "Emilio Segrè, Physicist, 1905–1989."

The site has a magnificent view of Mount Diablo, a view that reminds me of the one through the picture window of his house on Crest Road. The great mountain peak looms so huge that it seems to enfold and overwhelm, like the images on a giant movie screen. The oaks are old and stately and give the grassy slopes a sense of peace and continuity. In the spring, the rolling hills outside the cemetery are lush with tall green grasses, with golden poppies and blue splashes of lupins.

Yet even when I concentrate on Mount Diablo and the flowers; even when I block out the clusters of television antennas on the roofs and the distant glitter of neon signs; even when I listen for the wind over the freeway's hum, I feel uncomfortable here. This is his final resting place. He chose it. Is it where he belongs? Here, in this California cemetery, this carefully, perpetually manicured green spot of American suburbia? For so many years, he had thundered against places like this as blights on the land-scape, fulminated at the way "They've ruined everything." Yet where else? At the municipal cemetery in Tivoli? In the Jewish section of the Campo Verano, on the outskirts of Rome, where his parents are buried? But my father never asked to be returned to Italy. Or does he belong among the mesas and canyons of northern New Mexico, not far from Los Alamos? Where should a man who aspired to be—and in many ways became—a citizen of the world be buried? Where should a superman be finally laid to rest? Not here, I'm sure; yet this was the place he chose. I remember his exclamation shortly after his retirement, when we were speeding down the freeway: "How beautiful California is!"

As the condolence letters pour in from around the world, my image of who he was and where he belongs wavers. The writers remember him as a staunch and generous friend, a comfort at moments of crisis in their own lives, a link between generations. "He was almost like a second father for me in monitoring my career," the son of a family friend remarks. A distant cousin of my father's writes from Florence, "You're lucky to have had a parent who was not only illustrious but was also full of common sense in dealing with everyday life." A friend of mine who lost his father young writes me, "I am glad you had as many years with yours as you did."

Did I know the man? Which man did I know? I ask myself. And where does he finally belong, if not literally, then at least figuratively? One place I'm sure of is a redwood memorial grove in Hendy Woods State Park, near the community of Philo, about two hours north of San Francisco. For some time, my father had thought of honoring his parents with a memorial grove; now the huge stands in the Giuseppe, Amelia and Emilio Segrè Memorial Grove honor both him and his parents. Another place my father belongs is in these pages. For so many years, for me, we were never so alone as when together. Now I really am alone, without him. Yet perhaps these pages have bridged the silences and we have been together at last.

NOTES

In addition to my memories and the published works cited below, I have based this work on my journals and my father's letters to me.

Chapter 1: *Son of Superman*

Page

8 "Segrè . . . soul of a professor": Giancarlo Masini, "Honoring Nobel Laureate Emilio Segrè," *Il Caffè*, 6:4 (September 1986): 7.

Chapter 2: *The Beautiful Place*

29 "In science . . . not people": Emilio Segrè, *Enrico Fermi, Physicist* (Chicago: University of Chicago Press, 1970), p. x.

29 "With science": Ibid., p. 176.

33 "like being in love": See, for example, Emilio Segrè, *A Mind Always in Motion* (Berkeley: University of California Press, 1993), p. 48.

34 For Lawrence as promoter: Ibid., pp. 134–35.

34 "the fastest thinker I ever met": Segrè, *Enrico Fermi, Physicist*, p. 134; see also Segrè, *A Mind Always in Motion*, pp. 138–39.

38 "We were too many of a kind": Richard Rhodes, *The Making of the Atomic Bomb* (New York: Simon & Schuster, 1986), p. 564.

38 "We didn't have telephones": Ibid., p. 567.

Chapter 3: *War Heroes*

54 For my father's work at Los Alamos: Rhodes, *The Making of the Atomic Bomb*, pp. 540–41; Segrè, *A Mind Always in Motion*, pp. 185–86.

Chapter 4: *All-American Boy*

75 "She was kind, intelligent": Silvia Treves Levi Vidale, *All'ombra degli avi* (Florence: privately printed, 1990), p. 38.

77 *"Mia figlia non ha volontà"*: Ibid., p. 36.

79 "with an obstinacy": Segrè, *Enrico Fermi, Physicist*, p. 140.

85 It had been hot in the desert: For my father's reaction to the Trinity test, see Segrè, *A Mind Always in Motion*, pp. 201–2; *Enrico Fermi, Physicist*, p. 147.

87 "I did not jot them down": Segrè, *A Mind Always in Motion*, p. 204.

88 "It seems to me . . . Politicians do not come out well . . . Many scientists nurtured illusions": Ibid.

Chapter 5: *American Primitives*

96 "the layers of almost a century of culture . . . how complex the education of a European is . . . Claudio and sisters . . . barbarians": Segrè, *A Mind Always in Motion*, p. 224.

97 "pergolas . . . wines from the Castelli": Ibid., p. 223.

98 "impossible to send a telegram": Ibid., p. 225.

Chapter 6: *People of the Book*

116 ". . . never had a religious crisis": Segrè, *A Mind Always in Motion*, p. 34.

116 Some he found "sublime and rich": Ibid., p. 35.

116 The varying images of "Adonai": Ibid.

116 "they remind me of people I once loved": Ibid.

116 And yet in doing scientific research, Einstein: Helen Dukas and Banesh Hoffmann, eds., *Albert Einstein, the Human Side: New Glimpses from His Archives* (Princeton: Princeton University Press, 1979), p. 32.

118 "my children shall be brought up in their father's religion":

Quoted in Robert Byrne, *1,911 Best Things Anybody Ever Said* (New York: Fawcett Columbine, 1988), p. 300.

119 "It was worth it just to see": *Journals*, 12, Christmas, 1957, p. 60.

119 "they don't provide a very good outlet": *Journals*, 8, July 30, 1954.

119 "Plain on the outside, plain on the inside": *Journals*, 8, June 27, 1954.

119 "Very unattractive": *Journals*, 8, July 4, 1954.

120 "Service long and not very interesting": *Journals*, 8, October 6, 1954.

121 "I kept thinking that": *Journals*, 9, December 1954, p. 56.

123 "On that ridiculous": *Journals*, 17, August 12, 1960.

123 "just a plain old healthy child": Ibid.

123 "but better that": Ibid.

Chapter 7: *Civil Warriors*

129 "I believe parents should educate their children": Segrè, *A Mind Always in Motion*, pp. 284–85.

130 "Some of their decisions left me perplexed": Ibid.

Chapter 8: *European Conflicts*

151 "As you know, your mother is German": *Letters*, April 12, 1955.

154 "All in all you're American": *Letters*, February 12, 1962.

158 "People could settle down": *Journals*, 14, September 8, 1959, p. 164.

158 "rustic" . . . "countrified": Treves Levi Vidale, *All'ombra degli avi*, p. 39.

162 "warmth and passion" in his voice: Ibid., p. 38.

164 "Incomparable teacher, disinterested friend": L. Maddalena, "Claudio Segrè," *Bollettino società geologica italiana*, 47 (1928).

171 "a member of the Comintern": Segrè, *A Mind Always in Motion*, p. 215.

Chapter 9: *Royalty*

190 "with a hurried sidelong glance": *Journals*, 15, October 29, 1959, p. 43.

190 "His last great wish": *Journals*, 15, October 23, 1959, p. 35.
190 "a man apart": Ibid., October 26, p. 40.
191 For my father's hopes on winning the Prize for transuranic elements: Segrè, *A Mind Always in Motion*, pp. 259–60.
191 "spasms of self pity": *Journals*, 12, May 18, 1958, pp. 1–2.
193 "He said to keep it under my hat": Ibid., p. 2.
200 chief among his thoughts were regrets: Segrè, *A Mind Always in Motion*, pp. 271–72.
204 The other, "perhaps a little less intelligent": Ibid., p. 271.
206 From Fermi, my father concluded: *Les Prix Nobel 1959*.
210 "Agreed, but you could trade your work for one of Einstein's": *A Mind Always in Motion*, p. 273.
211 "sees the resemblance and is pleased": *Journals*, 12, July 11, 1959, pp. 3–4.

Chapter 10: *Family Trades*

213 "A remarkable series of circumstances": *Journals*, 18, August 4–6, pp. 122–23.
214 My father came to physics: *A Mind Always in Motion*, pp. 19–20.
216 "How many cerebral cells work": Laura Fermi, *Atoms in the Family* (Chicago: University of Chicago Press, 1954), pp. 66–67.
218 "above the transient noise": Segrè, *Enrico Fermi, Physicist*, p. 102.
218 "natural reserve . . . he seldom commented": *Ibid.*
219 "completely absorbed in physics": Ibid., p. 56.
223 "like building a brick wall": *Journals*, 18, March 8, 1961.
231 "continual handling of new things that you only half grasp": *Journals*, 20, March 2, 1963, p. 44.
233 "I'm thinking of going back to graduate school": *Journals*, 20, May 12, 1963, p. 12.
244 "With regard to women": *Letters*, October 1958.

Chapter 11: *Loving Gunfighters*

250 "The forefinger points": *Journals*, August 19, 1981.
250 "It's as if we were all sinners": Ibid.

257 "Depressions are fairly common": *Letters*, September 21, 1979.
265 "He was delighted and I think I expressed my feelings": *Journals*, February 27, 1979, p. 29.

Chapter 12: *Fathers and Sons*

270 "There's no reason for scholarship": *Letters*, March 11, 1980.
271 "I'm frustrated": *Letters*, April 4, 1978.
271 "Too Fascist," my father complained: *Letters*, February 12, 1988.